CHINA
An Introduction

Compiled by Qi Wen
Translated by Zhou Yicheng

FOREIGN LANGUAGES PRESS
BEIJING

First Edition 1984

ISBN 0-8351-1360-4

Published by Foreign Languages Press
24 Baiwanzhuang Road, Beijing, China

Printed by Foreign Languages Printing House
19 West Chegongzhuang Road, Beijing, China

Distributed by China International Book Trading Corporation
(Guoji Shudian)
P.O. Box 399, Beijing, China

Printed in the People's Republic of China

The national flag of the People's Republic of China

The national emblem of the People's Republic of China

中华人民共和国国歌

田　汉作词

聂　耳作曲

The national anthem of the People's Republic of China

NATIONAL ANTHEM

(March of the Volunteers)

Words by Tian Han   *Music by Nie Er*

Arise, those who do not want to be slaves!
We will use our flesh'n blood to build another Great Wall.
China has reached the brink of national collapse.
All the people have been making their last outcry.
Arise! Arise! Arise!
All our hearts become one.
Let us face the angry guns. March on!
Let us face the   angry guns. March on! March on !March
on! On!

Contents

Dawn over the world's highest
mountain — Qomolangma.

Agriculture is an important part of the Chinese economy; the total acreage of sown land is 100 million hectares.

Pasture in northwest China.

Bo, a large musical hanging bell, dating back to the Spring and Autumn Period (770 B.C.-476 B.C.)

The painted twin-eared pottery jar, more than 3,000 years old.

The Great Hall of the People, where sessions of the National People's Congress and other important meetings are held.

Tiananmen Square, in the heart of Beijing, is the site of mass meetings. It is the largest square in the world.

A view of the Dai people's area in Yunnan.

Kazak herdsmen.

Bull-fight, a festive activity of the Hui people.

The irrigation labyrinth of the Uygur area, Xinjiang.

Monks gathering to perform a Buddhist rite
at Tar Monastery, Qinghai.

Muslims at prayer in the Niujie Street Mosque, Beijing.

The Catholic church in Harbin is now open to visitors.

The National Flag, the National Emblem and the National Anthem

The National Flag and the National Emblem

The national flag of China was adopted at the First Plenary Session of the Chinese People's Political Consultative Conference held in September 1949, shortly before the founding of New China.

The flag of the People's Republic of China is red in colour and it has five yellow stars. The colour red symbolizes the spirit of the revolution, and the five stars signify the unity of the people of China under the leadership of the Chinese Communist Party. The flag first went up in Tiananmen Square on October 1, 1949, upon the formal announcement that New China was founded.

The design of the national emblem of the People's Republic of China, published by the Central People's Government on September 20, 1950, shows Tiananmen under the light of five stars, and it is framed with ears of grain and a cogwheel. Tiananmen is the symbol of modern China because the May 4th Movement of 1919, which marked the beginning of the new-democratic revolution in China, was launched there. It is also the place where the inauguration of the People's Republic of China was held. The cogwheel and the ears of grain represent the working class and the peasantry respectively, and the five stars symbolize the solidarity of the various nationalities of China. The emblem clearly indicates that New China is a socialist state led by the working class and based on the alliance of the workers and the peasants.

The National Anthem

The words for the national anthem were written by Tian Han, and the music was set by Nie Er in 1935. Originally known as the *March of the Volunteers*, it was the theme song of *The Sons and Daughters in Times of Turmoil*, a film that depicted how Chinese intellectuals marched bravely to the front in the War of Resistance Against Japan.

Sonorous, militant and inspiring, the song describes the wrath of the Chinese people against imperialist aggression and their determination to protect their motherland against foreign invaders. During the 2nd World War it was also sung by people of other countries who sympathized with the Chinese people in their anti-Japanese struggle. In 1949 it was appropriately chosen to be the national anthem of the People's Republic of China.

Geography

Territory

China is situated in eastern Asia, bounded by the Pacific in the east. The third largest country in the world, next to the Soviet Union and Canada, it has an area of 9.6 million square kilometres, or one-fifteenth of the world's land mass.

The coastline of the mainland of China extends well over 18,000 kilometres, washed by the waters of the Bohai, the Huanghai, the East China and the South China seas. The Bohai Sea is the inland sea of China.

China has more than 5,000 offshore islands. Of these, the largest is Taiwan, with a total area of about 36,000 square kilometres, and the second, Hainan. The South China Sea Islands are the southernmost island group of China.

Topography

China has a varied topography and diverse physical features. With all the mountains and hills, basins and plains, the whole topographical appearance is like that of a gradient staircase, high in the west and low in the east.

In the west of the country lies the Qinghai-Tibet Plateau, the highest and the largest plateau on earth. Known as "the roof of the world", it measures 2.3 million square kilometres and is about 4,500 metres above sea level. Here is the world's highest peak Mount Qomolangma, 8,848 metres above sea level, on the Sino-Nepalese border.

The terrain in the central part, with its basins and plateaus, drops to between 2,000 and 1,000 metres above sea level. The Inner Mongolia Plateau with its vast grasslands is an important stock-breeding centre of China. But in the east there is a comparatively low terrain, less than 1,000 metres above sea level. Here to be found are plains and the country's farming centres.

Rivers and Lakes

The rivers in China have a total flow of more than 2,600,000 million cubic metres, an equivalent of that in the whole of Europe. With a reserve of 680 million kilowatts, it leads the world in hydro-electric power potential.

The Changjiang River, also known as the Yangtze, is China's longest river. It is the third largest in the world, after the Nile and the Amazon. Its original source is in the Qinghai-Tibet Plateau in the western part of China, and it flows 6,300 kilometres before reaching the East China Sea. With a total catchment area of 1.8 million square kilometres, it is the major water transport artery of China. The delta in the lower reaches of the Changjiang River, because of its fertile soil and abundant natural resources, is known as the "country of rice and fish".

The Huanghe or Yellow River is the second longest river in China. Draining an area of 750,000 square kilometres, it flows 5,464 kilometres before emptying into the Bohai Sea. The Huanghe River valley is the cradle of ancient Chinese civilization.

There are also many man-made rivers. The Grand Canal, for example, has a length of 1,794 kilometres and it was cut 2,400 years ago. It was then extended first in the 7th and finally in the 13th century, and eventually it provided the link between Beijing in the north and Hangzhou in the south. It is the longest man-made river in the world.

There are numerous lakes in China. Most of them are freshwater lakes; a few are salt lakes.

Climate

Most regions of China lie in the temperate zone, although geographically the country stretches from the tropical and subtropical zones in the south to the frigid zone in the north. Pronounced dissimilarities in climate are found in various parts of the country. For example, the average January temperature difference is 33 degrees Centigrade between Harbin in the northeast and Guangzhou in the south.

Mean Temperature Comparison Between China's Major Cities

Cities	January	July
Beijing	-4.8°C	25.8°C
Shanghai	3.5°C	28°C
Guangzhou	13.7°C	28.3°C
Wuhan	2.7°C	29.1°C
Urumqi	-15.8°C	23.9°C
Harbin	-19.7°C	22.5°C

The coastal regions in the southeast have a humid climate and a large precipitation, and the temperature difference there is very small. The far-flung northwest regions have an arid climate and a scanty precipitation, and the temperature difference there is great. The coastal regions in the east, for instance, have an annual rainfall of 1,600 mm. By contrast, the inland region in the northwest has little rainfall. The outlying districts of the Tarim Basin have an annual precipitation of less than 10 mm. and sometimes there is no precipitation at all for the whole year.

Fauna and Flora

China has a great variety of wildlife. There are 1,100 species of birds, comprising 13.5 per cent of the world's total; about 420 species of mammals, amounting to 11 per cent of the known species of the world; more than 200 species of amphibians; and 300 species of reptiles. Of the wild animals, the giant panda, snub-nosed monkey, takin, white-lipped deer, Chinese river dolphins and Chinese alligators are rare species in the world.

The giant panda, well loved by people all over the world, has its habitat on the high mountains in the areas extending from Sichuan and Gansu to Shaanxi. Living mainly on bamboo leaves though a carnivore thousands of years ago, it has some of the special features of the ancient mammals and is of special interest to scientists in their zoological analysis.

China also has a great variety of plants. It has 32,000 species of higher plants, including nearly all the major kinds of vegetation found in the frigid and temperate zones of the northern hemisphere. Of its 7,000 species of woody plants, 2,800 are arbors. The species, rare in the world but found in China, include the golden larch, Taiwan pine, metasequoia, China cypress and Chinese red juniper (*Chamaecyparis formosensis*).

The metasequoia, a stately species, grew widely in East Asia, North America and Europe in the early Cretaceous Period of the Mesozoic Era 100 million years ago. Scientists believe that it became extinct during the glacial period of the Quaternary. The discovery of more than 1,000 metasequoias on the Sichuan-Hubei border in 1941, therefore, was immediately regarded as an important event. Since 1949, it has had an extensive transplanting and growth in other parts of the world outside China.

Mineral Resources

China possesses great mineral wealth. More than 140 kinds of minerals are to be found in the country, making China one of the few countries in the world endowed with a fairly complete range of minerals. Preliminary survey indicates that it has a coal reserve of 640,000 million tons and an iron reserve of 44,000 million tons. Petroleum resources are fairly widely distributed, and the country's continental shelves are also rich in oil. It leads the world in the deposits of many nonferrous metals including tungsten, antimony, zinc, lithium, rare earth, titanium, vanadium, molybdenum and tin. Oil shale, phosphorus, sulphur, magnesite, salt and gypsum are in sizable reserves.

Administrative Division

China is divided into 22 provinces, 5 autonomous regions and 3 central-administered municipalities.

The administrative units under a province or autonomous region are cities, autonomous prefectures, counties and autonomous counties while those under a county or autonomous county are townships and towns.

In the country there are more than 2,900 cities and

towns. Among these 7 have over 2 million people each, 13 between 1 million and 2 million each, and 28 between 0.5 million and 1 million each.

Beijing is the capital of the People's Republic of China. It has a population of 9,190,000, and is the country's political, economic and cultural centre. With a history of more than 800 years as the nation's capital, Beijing has many scenic spots and places of historical interest.

Shanghai is the largest city, and it is also one of the major cities of the world. With a population of more than 11 million, it is an important industrial base of China.

History

Ancient and Modern

Primitive men lived in China about 1.7 million years ago. Historical research has produced evidence that approximately 400,000 to 500,000 years ago the famous Peking Man could make and use simple tools and knew how to use and control fire.

The Xia Dynasty (21st-16th centuries B.C.) saw the first introduction in Chinese history of the slave system. In the dynasties after the Xia, that is the Shang (c. 16th-11th centuries B.C.) and the Western Zhou (c. 11th century to 770 B.C.), a slave society was firmly established. Then came the transitional phase from slave to feudal society in the Spring and Autumn Period (770-476 B.C.), when the princely rival states were fighting for supremacy. In 221 B.C., Qin Shi Huang, the First Emperor of the Qin Dynasty (221-207 B.C.), unified the country and established the first centralized feudal state in Chinese history. This was followed by the Han, Wei, Jin, the Southern and Northern Dynasties, Sui, Tang, the Five Dynasties, Song, Liao, Kin, Yuan, Ming and Qing dynasties. In short, up to the Opium War in 1840, for more than 2,000 years China remained a feudal society.

China was one of the first countries in world history which practised economic development. As early as 5,000-6,000 years ago, agriculture was seen as the main production activity by the settlers on the middle and lower reaches of the Huanghe River while at the same time they went in for livestock breeding. Gradual advances were made in science and technology. By the time of the Shang Dynasty, bronze smelting had begun and iron come into use. Silk weaving also reached a fairly high level, and led to the invention of the earliest devices for figured fabrics weaving. The technique of steel making began to develop in the Spring and Autumn Period. With the progress made in agriculture during the Warring States Period, water conservancy projects were launched on a colossal scale, including the building of the world-famous Dujiangyan Dam in Sichuan.

In the Han Dynasty (206 B.C.-A.D. 220) great advances were made in handicrafts, commerce and agriculture. Zhang Qian's mission to the Western Regions inaugurated the route from Chang'an (now Xi'an in Shaanxi Province), through Xinjiang, to the eastern coast of the Mediterranean. This was the famous "Silk Road" on which ancient China sent its silk goods to the West.

Economic prosperity and cultural achievement continued in the Tang Dynasty (618-907). Commercial cities sprang up. Economic and cultural contacts were extensively developed between China and Japan, Korea, India, Persia and Arabia. In the Song (960-1279) and Yuan (1271-1368) dynasties, there were further developments in commerce and foreign trade. The four famous ancient inventions of paper making, printing, the campass and gunpowder along with new inventions were introduced into Korea, Japan, Arabia and Europe. The Ming Dynasty (1368-1644) saw increased friendly exchanges between China and other Asian and African countries. Early in Ming, Zheng He made seven voyages to more than 30 countries, and on the longest one he and his fellow voyagers reached Somali on the east coast of Africa.

In the long history of Chinese culture, the list of distinguished intellectuals is also long. Among the great thinkers of the past are Lao Zi, Confucius, Mo Zi, Shang Yang, Han Fei, Wang Chong, Fan Zhen, Li Zhi and Wang Fuzhi; as to be expected, there is a host of poets, dramatists, men of letters and historians: Qu Yuan, Sima Qian, Li Bai, Du Fu, Han Yu, Liu Zongyuan, Su Shi, Xin Qiji, Lu You, Guan Hanqing, and Cao Xueqin, to name a few. In military history, the best-known strategists are Sun Wu and Sun Bin.

The achievements in science and technology in ancient China also deserve to be mentioned. In the work *Shi's Classic on Stars*, of the Warring States Period, is to be found the first star map with 800 stars. Recorded in the same work are the specific locations of no fewer than 120 stars. Zhang Heng of the Han Dynasty invented the world's first seismograph and armillary sphere which have since contributed much to the studies of astronomical phenomena and the detection of earthquakes. Zu Chongzhi, the outstanding scientist of the Southern and Northern Dynasties (420-589), was the world's first scientist who worked out the precise ratio between the circumference and diameter of a circle, that is between 3.1415926 and 3.1415927. In the Tang Dynasty, Monk Yi Xing observed the movement of the stars, and his discovery was 1,000 years before that of the British scientist Edmund Halley in 1712. Shen Kuo of the Song Dynasty did a lot of valuable exploratory work in many scientific fields. His best-known work, *Notes Written in Dream Brook Garden*, for example, contains an extremely useful introduction to the scientific and technological achievements of ancient China. Traditional Chinese medicine and acupuncture have proved to be a great asset to the history of world medical science. *The Yellow Emperor's Canon of Medicine,* China's earliest book on medicine, came out in the 5th century B.C. Among the significant pharmacological works is *Compendium of Materia Medica,* which was written by Li Shizhen in the 16th century. Today, the book has been translated into many foreign languages.

The history of modern China began with the Opium War in 1840. Subsequent invasions by the imperialist powers gradually reduced China to the status of a semi-colonial and semi-feudal country. The double yoke of imperialism and feudalism held back the development of China's economy, science and culture. Their country crippled and their lot at its worst, the Chinese people began a long and courageous struggle against the oppression of feudalism and foreign aggression. The Revolution of 1911 led by Dr. Sun Yat-sen overthrew the Qing government and the Republic of China was founded.

Then came a period of chaos and division under the rule of feudal warlords in semi-colonial and semi-feudal China. In 1917, the October Revolution broke out in Russia and it made a great impact on China, as people in the country were introduced to the ideas of Marxism-Leninism. Numerous Chinese intellectuals, as represented by Li Dazhao, Chen Duxiu, Mao Zedong and Zhou Enlai, pledged their faith in communism. Two years later, in 1919, the May 4th Movement was launched, as the Chinese people were determined to fight against imperialism and feudalism. For the first time, the Chinese proletariat showed their great strength in the movement, and this led to further dissemination of Marxism-Leninism, which soon became the guiding spirit behind the working class movement in China. In Shanghai the First National Congress of the Communist Party of China was called by China's first group of Marxists on July 1, 1921, and the founding of the Chinese Communist Party was announced. From then on, the Chinese revolution took on a completely new look.

Under the leadership of the Chinese Communist Party and Mao Zedong, for 28 years the people carried out an arduous struggle against imperialism, feudalism and bureaucrat-capitalism. First came the Northern Expeditionary War (1924-27), then the Agrarian Revolutionary War (1927-37), the War of Resistance Against Japan (1937-45), and the War of Liberation (1946-49), which finally led to the fall of the reactionary rule of the Kuomintang government headed by Chiang Kai-shek. On October 1, 1949, the People's Republic of China was founded, marking the victory of the new-democratic revolution and the beginning of socialism in China.

The People's Republic of China

The People's Republic spent its first three years (1950-52) rehabilitating the economy. It took over all bureaucrat-capitalist enterprises, turning them into socialist ones owned by the state. In addition, it abolished feudal land ownership; land was taken from the landlords and distributed among the landless or poor peasants. Meanwhile, monumental efforts were made to improve the war-ravaged economy left over from old China.

In June 1950, instigated by American imperialism, the Syngman Rhee clique of South Korea launched an attack on the Democratic People's Republic of Korea. Immediately after, the American Government despatched its 7th Fleet to Taiwan and carried the flames of the Korean war to the northeast border of China. The Chinese people had to fight yet another war, this time to resist U.S. aggression and aid Korea. In spite of all this, the Chinese Government

13

took only three years to accomplish the task of economic rehabilitation. By the end of 1952, it had achieved a record in agricultural and industrial production in the country's history. On this basis, it began its economic construction in a planned way.

Steps were taken to establish public ownership of the means of production under socialism. Starting from 1951, agricultural producers' cooperatives were organized on a voluntary basis by the peasants. Likewise, handicraftsmen's cooperatives were formed by handicrafts people, and a changeover of capitalist-run industrial and commercial enterprises were transformed to become joint state-private enterprises. The socialist transformation of private ownership of the means of production was basically completed in 1956 in most parts of the country, and the supremacy of socialist public ownership of the means of production established in the national economy.

In 1956, the planned targets of the First Five-Year Plan to develop the national economy were met, one year ahead of schedule. Many basic industries essential for China's industrialization had been built in spite of the very weak basis of old when these projects began. Between 1953 and 1957, the gross industrial output value grew by an annual average of 19.6 per cent, while an average of 4.8 per cent was registered in agriculture. The market prospered, and prices remained stable. There was a marked improvement in the people's living standard. The average yearly wage of workers in units under public ownership rose from 446 yuan in 1952 to 637 yuan in 1957.

The period of 1957-66 was one marked by great successes in China's full-scale socialist construction. Compared with 1956, fixed assets in industry in 1966 grew 4 times in terms of value. Considerable increases were reported in the output of coal, crude oil, electricity, steel and other major industrial products. Capital agricultural construction and technical transformation were also carried out on a large scale. There was a 7-times increase in the number of tractors and chemical fertilizer consumption, and in rural areas the use of electricity increased 71 times. Developments in sciences and technology were highlighted by fulfilment of the 12-year Programme for Scientific and Technological Development (1956-67) in 1962, five years ahead of schedule; and a rapid development in atomic energy, jet technology, computer science, semiconductor technology and the technology of automatic control, etc.

However, during these ten years there were also some serious errors made such as the broadening of the scope of the anti-Rightist movement in 1957, and impetuosity for successes in economic development disregarding economic laws. These brought great setbacks to the national economy in the period 1959-61. In 1961, a policy of "readjustment, consolidation, filling out and raising standards" was adopted in order to put the economy back on its feet, and socialist construction flourished again with a concerted effort made by the whole people.

Then, unfortunately, in May 1966 came the "cultural revolution", as the result of a gross blunder perpetrated in guideline. It continued till October 1976. The undermining activities of the two counter-revolutionary cliques headed by Lin Biao and Jiang Qing respectively brought the biggest setbacks and losses to the country since the founding of the People's Republic.

In October 1976, with the overthrow of the counter-revolutionary clique headed by Jiang Qing, China entered upon a new historical period. In December 1978, the Third Plenary Session of the Eleventh Central Committee of the

Chinese Communist Party was held. It made a strategic decision to shift the focus of the Party's work to socialist modernization in line with the policy of "emancipating the mind, using the brain, seeking truth from facts and unity to look forward". The result was the emergence of an excellent political and economic situation after a tremendous amount of construction and followed-up reform had been done.

Population and Nationalities

Distribution and Density

China is the most populous country in the world. According to the census taken in July 1982, it has a population of 1031.88 million, which is 22 per cent of the world's total. The distribution of population in the country, however, is most uneven. The national density is 107 persons per square kilometre, but in the 11 coastal provinces, autonomous region and municipalities, the average figure is 320.6. By contrast, the vast areas of the 18 provinces and autonomous regions in the interior are thinly populated and the density is 71.4 persons per square kilometre. Of these interior provinces and autonomous regions Tibet, Xinjiang, Qinghai, Gansu, Ningxia and Inner Mongolia have the lowest density, averaging 11.8 persons per square kilometre.

Population Growth and Population Control

In 1949, the Chinese population was 540 million. In the first 20 years after the founding of New China, the figure went up rapidly to over 820 million, as a result of vastly improved medical care and insufficient understanding of the importance of limiting population growth. During the 70s, China began to carry out policies of birth control and the growth rate had since dropped year by year from 26 per thousand in 1970 to 11.5 per thousand in 1983.

At present, the Chinese population is characterized by a large proportion of young people, with an estimated annual total number of more than 20 million who will come of marriage age, and a baby boom is therefore not unlikely. In order to effectively control population growth, the Constitution of the People's Republic of China specifically stipulates that "the state promotes family planning so that population growth may fit the plan for economic and social development". Late marriage and late birth are therefore encouraged and the goal is to keep the population under 1.2 billion by the end of this century. The government has adopted many effective measures of population planning, including explaining to the masses the need for population control, giving technical guidance, giving awards to those who do well in family planning and adopting economic sanctions against those who violate government policies in this respect.

Ethnic Groups

There are 56 ethnic groups in China. The Han people form the largest, numbering 930 million and making up 93.3 per cent of the country's population. The other ethnic groups, that is the minority nationalities, total 67 million, only 6.7 per cent of the Chinese nation.

Of the minority nationalities, 15 have over a million people each; 13 over 100,000 each; 7 over 50,000 each; and 20 have fewer than 50,000 people each.

The population size of various minority nationalities is shown in the table on the next page.

The Han people live all over the country but their compact communities are in the Huanghe, Changjiang and Zhujiang valleys and the Songhua-Liaohe Plain of the northeast. The minority nationalities inhabit 60 per cent of

Number	Nationalities
Over a million	Zhuang, Hui, Uygur, Yi, Miao, Manchu, Tibetan, Mongolian, Tujia, Bouyei, Korean, Dong, Yao, Bai, Hani
Between 100,000 and a million	Kazak, Dai, Li, Lisu, She, Lahu, Va, Shui, Dongxiang, Naxi, Tu, Kirgiz, Qiang
Between 50,000 and 100,000	Daur, Jingpo, Mulam, Xibo, Salar, Blang, Gelo
Under 50,000	Maonan, Tajik, Pumi, Nu, Achang, Ewenki, Jino, Ozbek, Jing, Benglong, Yugur, Bonan, Moinba, Drung, Oroqen, Tatar, Russian, Lhoba, Gaoshan, Hezhen

the country's total area, and they live mainly in the border regions.

Spoken and Written Languages

Of the 55 minority nationalities in China, the Hui, Manchu and She use the same Han languages while the other 52 each have their own spoken languages. Before Liberation, only 21 of the minority nationalities had their own written languages, including the Hui, Manchu and She which used the Chinese script. After Liberation, the Chinese government set up relevant departments to help create and standardize written languages for 10 minority nationalities including the Zhuang, Bouyei, Miao, Dong, Hani and Li. The Uygur, Kazak, Jingpo, Lahu and Dai have also been given help to have their written languages reformed.

National Regional Autonomy

All nationalities in China are equal, as stipulated by the Constitution of the People's Republic of China. They take part in the administration of state affairs as equals, irrespective of their numbers or the size of areas they inhabit. Every minority nationality is represented in the National People's Congress, which is the highest organ of state power of the People's Republic of China.

National regional autonomy is practised in areas where the minority nationalities live in compact communities. There are 5 national autonomous regions equivalent to provinces, 30 autonomous prefectures and 75 autonomous counties (or banners in Inner Mongolia). Local autonomous governments are established and local affairs are administered by the minorities themselves. All national autonomous regions are inalienable parts of the People's Republic of China.

At present, because of various historical factors the minority nationality areas are less developed than Han areas economically and culturally. Over the last three decades, the Chinese Government has adopted many policies and measures, including the provision of manpower, financial and technical support, to help develop these minority nationality areas. Such help, of course, is a two-way street, for minority nationality areas have also contributed to the economic development of the areas inhabited by the Han people.

Structure of the State

The System of People's Congresses

People's congresses at various levels are all organs of state power. The National People's Congress, as the highest organ, has the sole power to amend the Constitution, enact laws and decide on major issues related to the nation's political life. Local people's congresses at different levels have the power to decide on major issues in their own administrative areas. Local people's congresses at provincial, autonomous region and municipality levels have the power to enact local laws. The administrative, judicial and procuratorial organs at various levels are elected by the people's congresses at corresponding levels, to which they are responsible for their work, and under whose supervision they operate.

The term of office of the National People's Congress is five years; it meets once in a year. Its permanent organ is its Standing Committee. The National People's Congress has under its jurisdiction several working committees, such as the Nationalities Committee, Law Committee, Financial and Economic Committee, Education, Science, Culture and Public Health Committee, Foreign Affairs Committee and Overseas Chinese Committee. They are entrusted with the task to discuss, examine and draft relevant proposals and motions.

21

The President of the People's Republic of China

The President and Vice-President of the People's Republic of China are elected by the National People's Congress. Their term of office is five years.

The President, in pursuance of the decisions of the National People's Congress and its Standing Committee, promulgates statutes, appoints or removes the Premier and other members of the State Council, confers state medals and titles of honour, issues orders of special pardons, proclaims martial law, proclaims a state of war, issues mobilization orders, receives foreign diplomatic representatives on behalf of the People's Republic of China, appoints or recalls plenipotentiary representatives abroad, and ratifies or abrogates treaties and important agreements concluded with foreign states.

The Vice-President assists in the work of the President and may perform the functions and exercise the powers of the President as may be deputed by the President. In case the office of the President falls vacant, the Vice-President will succeed to the office of the President.

The State Council and Local Governments

The State Council of the People's Republic of China, that is, the Central People's Government, is the highest state administrative organ. It enforces the laws and decisions formulated and approved by the National People's Congress and its Standing Committee, to which it is responsible and accountable. Within the limits of its power and functions, it has the power to adopt necessary administrative measures and regulations, and issue orders.

The Premier takes overall responsibility for and directs the work of the State Council. He calls and presides over executive and plenary meetings of the State Council. Members of the executive meetings are the Premier, Vice-Premiers, State Councillors and the Secretary-General. Plenary meetings are attended by the Premier, Vice-Premiers, State Councillors, the Secretary-General, ministers in charge of ministries and commissions and the Auditor-General. Decisions on major issues concerning the work of the State Council must be discussed and approved either at the executive meetings or the plenary meetings of the State Council.

The State Council exercises unified leadership over the work of the ministries and commissions and the local governments at different levels. It directs and administers affairs of economy, finance, banking, commerce, education, science, culture, public health, physical culture, family planning, public security, urban and rural development, judicial administration and supervision. In addition, it is responsible for the strengthening of national defence, and conducts foreign and civil affairs as well as affairs concerning the nationalities and overseas Chinese.

At the local level China's state administrative bodies are local people's governments. Under the leadership of the governments at the next higher level and the State Council, they implement the decisions of the people's congresses at corresponding levels, and direct the administrative work in their respective areas.

The Central Military Commission

The Central Military Commission is instituted by the state to direct the armed forces of the country. The Chairman of the Commission is elected by the National People's Congress and is responsible to the Congress and its Standing Committee.

At present, China's armed forces consist of field armies, regional armed forces and the people's militia. The field armies are the backbone of the armed forces and their responsibility is to carry out mobile operations in the country. The duty of the regional armed forces is the protection of local areas. The militia is an armed force formed of people not disengaged from production.

People's Courts and People's Procuratorates

The people's courts are state judicial organs. There are different kinds of people's courts in China. The Supreme People's Court is the highest state judicial organ. Higher people's courts are established in the provinces, autonomous regions and centrally administered municipalities. Intermediate people's courts are established in prefectures, autonomous prefectures, centrally administered municipalities, and cities under the direct administration of provinces and autonomous regions, while basic people's courts can be found in counties, cities, autonomous counties and municipal districts. All cases in the courts are heard in public except those involving state secrets, personal shameful secrets and juvenile delinquencies. The accused has the right to defence. Besides personally defending his case, he may be defended by a lawyer, a near relative or guardian.

The people's procuratorates are state organs for legal supervision, established largely in correspondence with the people's courts. They exercise procuratorial authority over the activities of state organs, functionaries and citizens, and bring suits in the criminal courts against those who have violated the law and committed crimes.

The people's courts and the people's procuratorates exercise judicial and procuratorial authority independently in accordance with law, and are not subject to interference by administrative organs, public organizations or individuals. In the exercise of their judicial and procuratorial authority, the law is applied equally to all citizens, and no favouritism is allowed.

Political System

People's Democratic Dictatorship

The People's Republic of China is a socialist state under the people's democratic dictatorship led by the working class, and based on the alliance of workers and peasants. People in the country enjoy democracy while the state adopts strict measures to protect them from subversive elements. Hence the term "people's democratic dictatorship".

Workers, peasants, intellectuals, and all patriots who support socialism and also those who work for the unity of the motherland belong to the category of the people. As citizens of the People's Republic they enjoy extensive rights of freedom and democracy including the following: the right to vote and to stand for election, the right to exercise supervision over state organizations and their personnel; freedom of speech, of the press, of assembly, of association, of procession and of demonstration; freedom of religious belief; freedom of person; freedom from violation of personal dignity and infringement of residence; the right to work and rest and the right to receive financial assistance from the state and society when they are disabled; the right to education; and the freedom to engage in scientific research, literary and artistic creation and other cultural pursuits.

Besides protecting the people and suppressing the enemy, the state provides leadership and organization in economic and cultural development with the aim of building

China into a strong socialist country with its own special features of culture and concept of democracy.

The Leadership of the Communist Party of China

In China, the working class exercises its leadership through the Communist Party.

The Chinese Communist Party devotes itself whole-heartedly to the service of the people. It exercises its leadership by formulating and implementing correct lines, principles and policies, making sure that Party members fulfil their exemplary role in every sphere of work and every aspect of social life. The Party conducts its activities within the limits stipulated by the Constitution and laws of the state. Every Party member is expected to be a model leader in observing the Constitution and laws of the state. The legislative, judicial and administrative departments of the state and the economic, cultural and people's organizations work independently and with their own initiative.

The System of People's Congress

In China, all power belongs to the people. The organs through which the people exercise state power are the National People's Congress and local people's congresses at different levels. Deputies to the people's congresses are elected by the people. They come from different social circles, nationalities, and classes.

In accordance with the stipulations of the electoral law, deputies to the National People's Congress and people's congresses of provinces, autonomous regions and centrally administered municipalities, cities divided into districts, and autonomous prefectures are elected by the people's congresses at the next lower level. Deputies to people's congresses of cities not divided into districts, municipal districts, counties, autonomous counties, townships, nationality townships and towns are elected directly by their constituencies. All elections are by secret ballot. The electoral units and electorates have the power to remove and replace the deputies they have elected.

The Capital Iron and Steel Company in Beijing is one of the largest in China.

Gas pipes being installed at the giant Baoshan Iron and Steel Plant, now under construction in the suburbs of Shanghai.

Oil industry is developing rapidly in China. Picture shows an offshore drilling platform built by China.

An endless stream of oil being shipped out.

Shanghai wharf.

The Silk Printing and Dyeing Mill of Hangzhou, famous for its silk.

T.V. set assembly line at the Tianjin Radio Factory. Sophisticated assembly lines have been introduced from abroad to meet the increased demand of the people for colour T.V. sets.

Paddy-fields. Rice is a main crop of China.

Spring ploughing.

Herd raising by the Mongolians.

A tea exporter. China has a long history in tea production.

Indoor fishpond in a production brigade.

Chickens raised by a peasant woman. Individual household side lines are now encouraged in China.

Trade negotiations with foreign businessmen.

Political Parties and Social Organizations

The Chinese Communist Party

Founded in July 1921, the Party now has a membership of more than 40 million.

Over the years, the Chinese Communist Party has provided the people with strong leadership and the list of achievements is long. It led them in the long and hard struggle against imperialism, feudalism and bureaucrat-capitalism. Final victory came in 1949 with the founding of the People's Republic. After that, as the party in power, once again it led the people in their successful attempts to maintain the country's national independence and security. The concerted efforts of the Party and the people have made it possible to complete the socialist transformation of the private ownership of the means of production. Large-scale planned socialist economic construction is now moving rapidly. Under the leadership of the Communist Party, China has achieved great economic progress, unprecedented in its history.

The highest leading body of the Party is the National Congress (held every five years) and the Central Committee elected by it. The Party Central Committee, at its plenary session (held at least once a year), elects the Political Bureau and its Standing Committee, the Secretariat and the General Secretary of the Party Central Committee. When the Central

Committee is not in session, the Political Bureau and its Standing Committee exercise the functions and powers of the Central Committee. The Secretariat attends to the day-to-day work of the Central Committee under the direction of the Political Bureau and its Standing Committee.

Democratic Parties

There are eight of them in China:

China Revolutionary Committee of the Kuomintang Formed in January 1948, it consists mainly of the patriots and democrats of the former Kuomintang.

China Democratic League Set up in October 1941, it is composed mostly of intellectuals working in the fields of culture and education.

China Democratic National Construction Association Founded in December 1945, it consists mainly of former national industrialists and businessmen and associated intellectuals.

China Association for Promoting Democracy Established in December 1945, it is composed mainly of primary and middle school teachers and people engaged in cultural and publishing work.

Chinese Peasants' and Workers' Democratic Party Its predecessor was the Provisional Action Committee of the Kuomintang, founded in 1930. Most of its members are intellectuals doing public health and medical work as well as those working in the fields of culture and education.

China Zhi Gong Dang It was formed in 1925 by some members of the Hong Men Zhi Gong Tang in America. Most of its members are returned overseas Chinese.

Jiu San Society This society grew out of the Democracy and Science Forum, founded in 1944 by a group of intellectuals from cultural, educational and scientific circles engaged in the movement for democracy. It adopted its present name on September 3, 1945, in commemoration of the victory of the worldwide anti-fascist war ("Jiu San" means "September the Third" in Chinese).

Taiwan Democratic Self-Government League Founded in November 1947, it consists mainly of patriots and democrats from Taiwan now residing on the mainland.

Relations of cooperation with the Communist Party were established when these democratic parties were founded. In September 1949, together with the Chinese Communist Party and other democrats they attended the Chinese People's Political Consultative Conference (CPPCC), held in Beijing. It was at this conference that the Common Programme of the CPPCC was adopted, the Central People's Government elected and the People's Republic of China inaugurated. The CPPCC holds meetings periodically in order to discuss matters related to the country's political life, economic construction and the united front.

In recent years, the democratic parties have expanded their membership and set up local and grass-root organizations in most of the country's provinces, autonomous regions, municipalities directly under the jurisdiction of the Central Government, and many large and medium-sized cities.

Trade Unions The leading class in China is the working class and the trade unions are the broadest mass organizations in the country. They are formed by the workers of their own accord.

The All-China Federation of Trade Unions is the supreme leading body of all local federations of trade unions throughout the country. It has a membership of 73 million belonging to more than 430,000 trade union organizations at the grass-root level.

As a pillar of the people's regime, the trade unions

speak on behalf of the workers and look after their interests in ways which are different from those in capitalist countries. Under the leadership of the Chinese Communist Party, they work on their own and play an active part in the formulation of all government policies and laws related to labour, wage commendation and reward, culture and education, welfare and labour insurance.

The fundamental tasks of the trade unions in China are: 1. to protect the democratic rights of the workers and staff members in enterprise management and to implement and continually improve the system of the workers' representative conference; 2. to speak on behalf of and work for the interests and well-being of the workers and staff; 3. to enhance literacy of the workers and encourage them in their pursuit of political studies, to help them acquire scientific knowledge and technological skills, to find ways which will enable them to understand better the state laws and policies as well as labour discipline; 4. to mobilize and organize the workers and staff members so that through socialist labour emulation they can achieve, well ahead of time, the goals as envisaged in the state plans.

The Communist Youth League of China The League is a mass organization of progressive youths of China. Its basic tasks are: to imbue youths with the communist spirit, to help them appreciate the truths of Marxism, Leninism, and Mao Zedong Thought, to help them acquire the knowledge of modern science and culture, and prepare them, through their participation in various modernization programmes, to become people with lofty ideals, moral integrity, high educational level and a high sense of discipline.

The Communist Youth League of China has a membership of 48 million and there are more than two million branches of the League in the country. Its highest leading body is the National Congress and the Central Committee elected by it.

All-China Women's Federation The aim of the Federation, also a mass organization, is the protection of the rights and interests of women and children, and the complete emancipation of women.

Women in China enjoy the same rights as men do. Post-Liberation China has witnessed the freeing of large numbers of women from household chores because of equal job opportunities. In recent years, there has been an increasing number of women who are involved in social work.

At present, there are more than 40 million women workers and this accounts for 36.3 per cent of the national work force. The state practises the principle of "equal pay for equal work" for men and women. It sees to it that women be properly represented in people's congresses at all levels. At the first session of the 6th National People's Congress held in June 1983, for example, 632 deputies were women, accounting for 21.2 per cent of the total number of deputies. Many women have also proved their worth and accordingly they have been given leading positions in governments at various levels.

In China today, women are no longer subjugated to men as in the past. They have been legally guaranteed not only equal opportunity to work and study but also the same right to family property. They share the responsibility of supporting their parents, rearing and educating their children. In general, husband and wife in China today assists each other in coping with the household chores. They show respect for the aged, and love for the young as they follow the tradition of Chinese family life.

Foreign Policy

An Independent Foreign Policy and Peaceful Coexistence

The People's Republic of China has been pursuing an independent foreign policy. It firmly believes in the peaceful coexistence of countries even though they may have different political and social systems. In foreign affairs, therefore, China has been making every effort to develop friendly relations with other countries, on the basis of equality and mutual benefit, to strengthen solidarity and cooperation with the Third World Countries and to oppose hegemonism and safeguard world peace.

Over the years, Chinese foreign policy has been guided by the Five Principles stated in the agreement signed with India in April 1954. These are: mutual respect for sovereignty and territorial integrity, mutual non-aggression, non-interference in each other's internal affairs, equality and mutual benefit, and peaceful coexistence. These Five Principles of Peaceful Coexistence were officially announced in the joint declarations made by Premier Zhou Enlai with Prime Minister Nehru of India and with Prime Minister U Nu of Burma, respectively, during the Chinese Premier's visits to the two countries in June of the same year. Since then these Five Principles have won worldwide support in the development of relations with countries which have different political and social systems. Consequently, China has established and developed relations of friendship and co-operation with many countries, including socialist ones.

The Chinese government and the Chinese people firmly oppose hegemonism. Both historical experience and present reality have convinced the Chinese people that preservation of world peace is inseparable from opposition to hegemonism. In striving for world peace, it is imperative to fight against the hegemonist aggression and expansion that threaten world peace. Only by waging an anti-hegemonist struggle can world peace be preserved.

Drawing upon its own intimate experience as a developing socialist country, China fully sympathizes with and supports the people of other Third World countries in their struggle for the preservation of independence and sovereignty and the development of national economies as well as their demand for the establishment of a new international order. Whenever possible China has provided friendly countries with economic and technical assistance and helped them develop their independent national economies. On his visits to 11 African countries at the end of 1982 and in early 1983, Premier Zhao Ziyang put forward the four principles for developing economic and technical cooperation with other Third World countries, namely, "equality and mutual benefit, stress on practical results, diversity in form and common progress".

Principles Governing the Establishment of Diplomatic Relations with Other Countries

On the inauguration of the People's Republic of China on October 1, 1949, the Chinese government solemnly declared: "This government is the sole legal government representing the people throughout the People's Republic of China. It is willing to establish diplomatic relations with

35

all foreign governments which are willing to observe the principles of equality, mutual benefit and respect for each other's territorial integrity and sovereignty."

The Chinese government has always maintained that Taiwan Province is an integral part of the country's territory. Any foreign country which wishes to establish diplomatic relations with China must make known its readiness to sever all diplomatic relations with the Taiwan authorities and recognize the government of the People's Republic as the sole legal government of China. The Chinese Government will never tolerate any country which seeks to create "two Chinas" or "one China, one Taiwan". Nor will it tolerate any move by the countries with which it has formal diplomatic relations to establish any form of official relations with the Taiwan authorities.

Acting in accordance with the above-mentioned principles, China has established diplomatic relations with 129 countries.

Foreign Trade

Development

Guided by the principle of "independence, self-reliance, equality, mutual benefit and supplying each other's needs", China has been active in pursuing the goals of doing more trade with the rest of the world. The policy of opening to the outside world, followed in the last few years, has enabled the country to maintain a steady growth in its annual total volume of import and export trade. In 1983, the volume reached a record $40.73 billion.

In the early 1950's, China had trade relations only with the Soviet Union and the socialist countries in East Europe. By 1983, however, it had established trade relations with 170 countries and regions. Of these, more than 80 had signed trade agreements or protocols with China.

In recent years, trade with Japan, Western Europe and the United States has been growing fairly fast. So far, China's main exports to Japan have been mainly crude oil, coal, textile goods, cereals and oil. Japan's major exports to China have been machinery and other equipment, iron and steel, and chemical fertilizers. In 1982, China's volume of import and export trade with Japan was $8.76 billion; that with the European Economic Community (EEC), $5.54 billion; and that with the United States, $5.34 billion. These figures accounted for 22.3 per cent, 14.1 per cent and 13.6

per cent of China's total import-export trade volume, respectively.

China lays great stress on developing trade relations with other Third World countries. It exports machinery, chemicals, light industrial products, minerals, hardware and textile goods. The imported items are mainly copper, cobalt, diamond, chemical fertilizer, rubber, timber, cocoa and coffee. In 1982, China's volume of trade with other Third World countries came to $6.06 billion, accounting for 15.7 per cent of the country's import-export total.

Since 1977, trade between China and the Soviet Union and East European countries has also shown continuous growth.

China's pursuit of international trade takes many different forms. For example, it imports raw materials for the manufacture of export goods, but also engages in processing and assembling imported parts and components. It also engages in processing with supplied samples while taking part at the same time in cooperative production and compensation trade.

Lineup of Imports and Exports

Compared with the early 1950's, recent years have witnessed substantial changes in the lineup of China's imports and exports.

In 1952, for example, 59.3 per cent of China's export commodities were agricultural and sideline products, while mineral and industrial products made up 17.9 per cent. By 1982, the situation had completely changed. Available figures for that year show that the former dropped to 14.9 per cent and the latter rose to 60.5 per cent.

There has also been a big increase in the variety of export goods. In the past China could not produce many of the items such as machine tools, complete sets of equipment and generators and it had to depend completely on imports from other countries. Now, these items are mass-produced for use at home and abroad. China today exports not only the special products of various localities, animal products and medicinal materials, but also crude oil, coal, machinery, instruments and meters, hardware and tools. In addition, China has provided some countries with complete sets of equipment.

Eighty per cent of China's imports or more are producer goods, since the government's policy is to give priority to the development of the means of production. The import commodities are mostly rolled steel, nonferrous metals, machinery, proprietary technology, automobiles, aircrafts, ships, and equipment, needed for the development of industry and agriculture. Other imports include wheat, maize, sugar, edible oil and medicine, and some consumer goods like wrist watches and tape recorders.

Joint Ventures with Foreign Countries

In 1979, the Law of the People's Republic of China on Chinese-Foreign Joint Ventures was promulgated. The new economic policy has since aroused great interest among foreign investors. By the end of 1983, for example, 188 joint ventures had been established in China with a total of $0.34 billion of investment from foreign investors, and 1,000 Chinese-foreign cooperative projects with a total of $3 billion of investment from foreign businesses. Twenty-three agreements for joint exploration of the country's offshore oil resources have been signed, for which purpose a total of $2 billion come from foreign investors. The number of investor countries and regions has come to a dozen including

Lineup of China's Import and Export Goods over the Years

Year	Lineup of export volume (total export = 100)			Lineup of import volume (total import = 100)	
	Industrial and mineral products	Agricultural and sideline products (processed)	Agricultural and sideline products (raw)	Means of production	Means of livelihood
1950	9.3	33.2	57.5	83.4	16.6
1957	28.4	31.5	40.1	92.0	8.0
1978	37.4	35.0	27.6	81.4	18.6
1982	60.5	24.6	14.9	70.8	29.2

Hongkong and Macao, and countries in Europe, America and Oceania.

To encourage the development of Chinese-foreign joint ventures, the Chinese Government decided in 1982 to further relax the policy in this regard.

Economy

Establishment of the Economy of Public Ownership

Socialist public ownership of the means of production is the basic characteristic of China's economic system of the means of production. Established immediately after the founding of the People's Republic, it consists of two forms. One is the state economy owned by the whole people, covering the state-owned factories, farms, shops, banks and enterprises for communications and transport. The other is the collective economy of the working people, including the rural people's communes and enterprises managed by them, producers' cooperatives and cooperative stores in the towns and cities.

Since the completion of socialist transformation of private into public ownership of the means of production, both the state and collective economies have been greatly developed. In 1952, the output of state-owned industry in the gross industrial output value accounted for 41.5 per cent, but in 1983 it rose to 77 per cent. Of the total retail sales, state-owned commerce in 1952 was 16.2 per cent and it went up to 72.1 per cent in 1983. There has been a slight drop in the proportion of state-owned commerce, because of the expansion of collective and individual commerce in the last two years. However, the state-sector still plays the predominant role in the national economy. At present, the taxes and profits turned in by the state-owned sector provide 85 per cent of the state income.

In recent years, there has been a rapid development in the collective economy. The industrial output value has consequently risen, now accounting for 20 per cent of the national total. Large quantities of export products are manufactured by the industrial enterprises of the collective sector. The people's communes have made valuable contribution to the state because of increased agricultural production. They provide the state with most of the sales and purchases of grain, cotton, oil-bearing material and other agricultural and sideline produce. There has been a sharp increase in commodity production since the introduction of the responsibility system on an extensive scale in agricultural production. In 1982, for example, state purchase of agricultural and sideline produce grew by 11.9 per cent as compared with the previous year. In 1983 it increased 14.6 per cent over 1982.

Although China's economy is characterized by public ownership, the state also allows individual economy to exist and develop as a necessary supplement to the socialist public ownership.

An Independent National Economic System

China's economy was extremely backward before Liberation, and industry and agriculture developed very slowly. But in New China, the economic rehabilitation and planned construction work have made it possible for the country to build up an independent and fairly comprehensive industrial as well as economic system.

In 1949, fixed assets of the country in industry were only about 12 billion yuan. By 1981, however, those under ownership by the whole people had risen to 374.8 billion yuan. The number of industrial enterprises grew from

170,000 in 1957 to 388,000 in 1982. That was a miraculous advance in the history of the country's industry.

The modernization programmes so far have yielded good results. China is now the third leading country in the world, after the United States and the Soviet Union, in the production of metal-cutting machine tools. It has as many hydraulic presses of 1,000 tons or more as the European Economic Community. Computer science, automatic control technology, atomic energy, laser technology and the related sophisticated sciences and technologies have played their respective, significant roles in many areas of production. Much progress has been made in agricultural mechanization and modernization because of the extensive use of electricity, chemical fertilizer and farm machines. There has also been a rapid development of transport and communications. At present, with the exception of Tibet, the capitals of all the provinces, municipalities and autonomous regions are accessible by railway, and a railway network radiating from Beijing has taken shape. Most of the rural areas are within reach as a result of the improvement in bus and automobile services.

The gross output value of industry and agriculture rose from 81 billion yuan in 1952 to 920.9 billion in 1983 (calculated on the basis of prices in the respective years). In 1983, the national income (covering the net output value of industry, commerce, agriculture, building, communications and transport) went up to 467.3 billion yuan, that is 6.4 times the 1952 figure. The value of industrial production in the gross output value of industry and agriculture rose from 30 per cent in 1949 to 66.1 per cent in 1983.

Economic Readjustments

In the early years of New China, national economic

planning was going well and it produced many good results. The healthy development of the national economy, however, was arrested from time to time: for example, the "big leap forward" movement in 1958 and the "cultural revolution" from 1966 to 1976.

In 1979, the Chinese Government decided on a policy of "readjusting, restructuring, consolidating and improving" the national economy in carrying out the modernization programmes. Over the last four years, China has achieved much success in economic readjustment. Readjustments have been made to the ratio between accumulation and consumption in the national income, and the income of both urban and rural population has increased. There has been a faster growth of agriculture and light industry, resulting in a rational change in the ratio between agriculture, light and heavy industries. The ratio between the various branches of heavy industry has been readjusted, and there has been a faster growth of the raw and semi-finished materials and power industries. Accordingly, an initial change has been made in the economic system. For instance, the system of responsibility, in various forms, has been adopted in agricultural production. In industry, the power of decision of enterprises has been enhanced, and income taxes have been instituted instead of profits turned in by the enterprises.

As a result, the country now enjoys a stable economy and its co-ordinated development. The consumption level of urban and rural people rose from 175 yuan in 1978 to 288 yuan in 1983.

The Sixth Five-Year Plan (1981-85)

The Sixth Five-Year Plan began in 1981 and the Chinese Government has been pursuing the policy of readjusting, restructuring, consolidating and improving the national

44

economy, in an effort to reorient its economic work with the view of increasing economic results. According to plan, the gross output value of industry and agriculture is to increase by 4 per cent annually; the per capita consumption of urban and rural people is to rise by an annual average of 4.1 per cent. With advances made in economy in this period, a faster rate of growth is expected to be attained during the forthcoming Seventh Five-Year Plan, so that a new era of economic renewal will be ushered in in the last decade of this century. By the end of this century, it is hoped, China will quadruple its gross industrial and agricultural output value and bring the consumption level to that of a well-off nation.

Growth of National Income

	Unit	1952	1965	1975	1982
Total income	100 million yuan	589	1,387	2,503	4,247
Growth index (1952 = 100)	%	100	197.5	384.7	579.1
Per capita income	yuan	104	194	274	421

Note: The figures for the national income are calculated on the basis of the price of the year; the growth index, constant price.

Agriculture

Development

China has favourable conditions for agricultural development and the tradition of intensive cultivation. With the adoption of the collective ownership of the means of production, the way has been paved for advanced agricultural production.

From 1949 to 1982, the annual average rise was 4.7 per cent in its gross agricultural output value, a fairly high growth rate even compared with those of economically highly developed countries. For instance, the total grain output in 1983 was 387,280,000 tons as against 163,920,000 tons in 1952, and cotton output was 4,637,000 tons in 1983, as against 1,304,000 tons in 1952.

In the rural areas today conditions for agricultural production have been greatly improved. With the completion of large-scale water conservation projects, by 1983 the national irrigated area had been extended to 44,640,000 hectares, 2.2 times as much as 1952. In 1983, total mechanical motive force came to 245.03 million horsepower and the number of tractors reached well over 3.5 million. The year 1982 also saw several-fold increase in the national consumption of chemical fertilizer, pesticide and power compared with that 30 years before. Thanks to the availability of technical knowledge and improved material, the capability to combat natural calamities in the country has been enhanced. This has been shown, over the last few years, by good crops yielded in many areas despite droughts, excessive rainfall or waterlogging. Advances made in agriculture have enabled China to feed and clothe its population of 1,000 million even though the per capita cultivated area is only 0.1 hectare. In recent years, China has imported large quantities to enrich the variety of food grain. In proportion to the national total grain output, however, the percentage is small, about 3-4 per cent.

The People's Communes and State Farms

The people's communes and state farms make up China's two major agricultural units. The people's communes were formed in 1958 by merging the agricultural cooperatives. Since then, they have been the biggest supplier of grain, cotton and oil-bearing material. The people's communes were originally administrative and managerial organizations. In 1982, township governments began to be instituted in China's rural areas, and the people's communes have since become purely economic units.

The state farms each specialize in a main line of production such as agriculture, animal husbandry, fishery and forestry. They are run under two main categories: those which undertake the task of producing farm and sideline commodity products, and the others which carry out scientific experiments and cultivate fine strains of seeds. In 1982, there were more than 2,000 state farms in the country with a total sown acreage of 4,555,000 hectares, about 4.5 per cent of the nation's total cropland. Though small in number compared with that of the people's communes, they provide a higher commodity production rate.

Peasant household sidelines are fairly important in China's agricultural production. According to the statistics collected in 1980, household sidelines accounted for 18.9 per cent of the gross agricultural output value. Pigs, poultry, and eggs purchased by the state and the farm and sideline produce available on rural markets are mostly from peasant households.

A Change in Managerial System

Since 1979, a number of important guidelines have been adopted for the promotion of China's agricultural production. These have led to the introduction of the responsibility system in production, confirmation of the power of decision of production brigades, increases in prices for farm and sideline produce purchased by the state, restoration and extension of the commune members' private plots, the reopening of free markets and eventually the development of a diversified economy. The result is a rapid expansion of agricultural activities and an unprecedented increase in productivity.

In Chinese terms, the system of responsibility in agricultural production is a socialist managerial system, which involves a series of specific ways and forms in its implementation. A common current practice is that part of the farmland is contracted to a particular peasant household, based on the principle of collective ownership and unified management by the production team. Extra yields will go to the peasant household, and the contracted amount of agricultural output is delivered to the state and the commune. The responsibility system has been working well throughout the country and has brought good economic results, for it has given the peasants the motivation to increase their yields. Consequently, there has been a sharp rise in the income of the state, collectives and contracting peasant parties, particularly that of the latter.

48

Carrier rocket launched in October 1982.

Chinese scientists with their foreign colleagues on a field trip observing an iceberg.

Chinese scientists took part in 1981 in exploratory work in the South Pole at the invitation of the South Pole Bureau of Australia.

A foreign student learning
Chinese acupuncture.

Radiation therapy in a recently open tumour hospital.

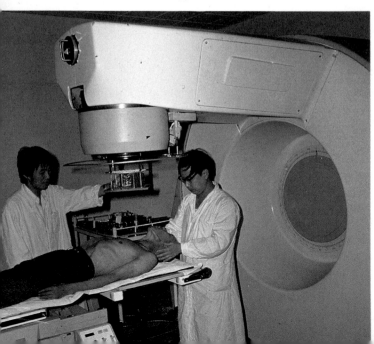

Western Languages Department students of Beijing University in an audio-visual class.

Beijing University students practising martial arts in after-class hours

Students of the Shanghai Workers' Sparetime College attending class.

Zhu Jianhua setting a world record in high jump.

Star gymnast W
Jiani shows her form
on the uneven bars
The Chinese gymnas
tic team has enjoye
much success in inter
national competitions

Han Jian of the Chinese badminton team, which has many world-class players.

The peasants in China today are much better off than before. Statistics from selected localities in 1982 showed that the per capita net income of the peasants for that year averaged 270 yuan, an increase of 136 yuan over the year 1978. In addition, many new houses have been built for the peasants in the countryside.

Total Output of Major Farm Products

	Unit	1952	1978	1982	1983
Grain	10,000 tons	16,392	30,477	35,343	38,728
Cotton	"	130.4	216.7	359.8	463.7
Peanuts	"	231.6	237.7	391.6	395.1
Tea	"	8.2	26.8	39.7	40.1
Aquatic Products	"	167	466	516	546
Big Livestock	10,000 head	7,646	9,389	10,113	10,350
Pigs	"	8,977	30,129	30,078	29,854

Note: The figure for big livestock and pigs refer to those on hand at the years' end.

Crop Farming

Grain figures predominantly in China's crop farming. In 1983, China had 114 million hectares sown to grain, accounting for 79.2 per cent of the total cropland, and 17.76 million hectares for industrial crops, accounting for 12.3 per cent of the total cropland. The major grain crops are rice, wheat, maize, sorghum, millet, tubers and soyabean.

China is the world's biggest producer of rice, which makes up 40 per cent of the nation's grain output. The next largest is the production of wheat and maize, which is second only to that of the United States. Industrial crops are mainly cotton, peanuts, oil-bearing crops, sugar crops, tobacco and bast fibres, and medicinal herbs. These form the bulk of the raw material for light industry for the country's export. China leads the world in its production of rapeseed and is second and third respectively in that of peanuts and cotton.

Industry

Development

Industry was almost non-existent in old China, and it had to depend heavily on imports for finished products. Today, the People's Republic manufactures a wide range of consumer goods including daily-use electric appliances. In addition, it also makes planes, ships, automobiles, electric locomotives and modern industrial equipment.

Before 1949, the country's industry concentrated in a few cities along the coast. Since the founding of New China, however, efforts have been made to install industrial plants throughout the country. About half of the country's capital construction investments have been used in the interior, thereby bringing about an increase in the industrial output value of the interior by 40 times or more. Many factories can now be found in the formerly out-of-the-way places.

For a period of time heavy industry was given top priority. From 1949 to 1981, the output value of heavy industry increased at an annual average rate of 15.3 per cent while that of light industry only 11.3 per cent. Over the last few years, however, light industry has gained a faster growth, and there has been a change in the ratio between light and heavy industries and the proportion between the various branches of the two industries.

Metallurgical Industry

Since the founding of New China, much effort has been

Output of Major Industrial Products

	Unit	1952	1978	1982	1983
Coal	100 million tons	0.66	6.18	6.66	7.15
Crude oil	10,000 tons	44	10,405	10,212	10,607
Electricity	100 million kwh	73	2,566	3,277	3,514
Steel	10,000 tons	135	3,178	3,716	4,002
Machine tools	10,000	1.37	18.32	10	12.10
T.V. sets	10,000	—	51.73	592	684
Bicycles	10,000	8	854	2,420	2,758
Wrist watches	10,000	—	1,351	3,301	3,469

made by the Chinese Government to develop metallurgical industry. Apart from renovating and expanding the old enterprises, it has built a number of new ones. The major iron and steel producing centres are found in Anshan, Baotou,

Wuhan, Chongqing, Panzhihua, Taiyuan and Shanghai. China is the 5th leading country in the world in the production of steel. Even so, the metallurgical industry still cannot meet the needs of the growing national economy. Every year large quantities of steel and rolled steel are imported. To increase the production of steel, in the last few years sophisticated technologies and equipment have been imported from West Germany and Japan.

Machine-Building Industry

In machine building, China has developed many key branches such as automobile, tractor, ship, precision machine tool, aviation and space industries.

A marked improvement has been made in the manufacture of complete sets of equipment. China is now capable of providing complete plants for integrated iron and steel works with an annual output of 1,500,000 tons of steel and oil refineries with an annual capacity of processing 2,500,000 tons of crude oil, as well as large-size hydro- and thermal-power generating units and large-calibre petroleum pipelines.

Chinese-made machine tools, forging presses, ships, electric motors, bearings, meters and instruments are sold to more than 100 countries and regions.

Power Industry

In 1983, 351.4 billion kwh of electricity were produced in China, ranking 6th in the world. In the country there are 2,800 power plants each with a generating capacity of 500 kilowatts and more, and 68 large power plants each with an installed capacity of 250,000 kilowatts and more. The total installed capacity of these large power plants accounts for over half of the national total. The major thermal-power plants include the Shijingshan Power Plant in Beijing, the Qinghe Power Plant in Liaoning, the Wangting Power Plant in Jiangsu and the Tangshan Power Plant in Hebei.

China's major hydro-power plants include the Liujiaxia Hydro-power Plant, the Danjiangkou Hydro-power Plant in Hubei, the Gongzui Hydro-power Plant in Sichuan, and the Zhexi Hydro-power Plant in Hunan. Besides, there are locally-run small hydro-power stations in the rural areas. The achievement and experience gained by China in this respect have attracted worldwide attention.

At present, there is still a grave shortage of power supply in China. To solve the problem, the government has been carrying out projects in the development of thermal-power in combination with hydro-power. A number of thermo-power and hydro-power plants are now being built. These include the Gezhouba Key Hydro-power Station, the largest of China, located at the outlet of the Changjiang Gorges.

Oil Industry

The completion of the Daqing Oilfield in the early sixties ushered in a new period for China's oil production. In 1963, China was basically self-sufficient in oil as its crude oil output shot up to 6.48 million tons, and this put an end to the country's dependence on foreign oil. After 1963, oil was discovered in other parts of the country and several other large oilfields were put into operation, including the Shengli Oilfield in Shandong, the Dagang Oilfield in Tianjin, the Liaohe Oilfield in Liaoning, the Jizhong Oilfield in Hebei, and the Zhongyuan Oilfield in Henan. In 1983, the country's total production of crude oil rose to 106.07 million tons, ranking 6th in the world; and natural gas, 12.21 billion cubic metres, ranking 12th in the world.

Great advances have been made by China in oil refining. Because of the increase in crude oil production, refineries have been built in 21 provinces, municipalities and autonomous regions, turning out 700 kinds of petroleum products every year. In 1973, China began to export both crude oil and oil products, including high-grade gasoline, lubricants, medical vaseline and paraffin wax.

In recent years, an intensive effort has been made by China in search of oil on its land or in the sea. It is particularly interested in offshore oil on the continental shelf.

In February 1982, the Chinese Government promulgated the Regulations on Joint Chinese-Foreign Exploitation of Offshore Oil. The document provides guidelines for oil exploitation in cooperation with foreign countries. Since then, a number of contracts have been signed between China and foreign oil companies for the exploration of oil in the Bohai Sea, the Beibu Bay in the South China Sea, the Yinggehai Basin and the sea area outside the mouth of the Zhujiang River.

Coal Industry

Rich coal reserves are a great wealth of China. Preliminary survey indicates that China has a coal reserve of 740 billion tons, 60 per cent of which are found in the north. Shanxi Province, for example, alone accounts for one-third of the country's total reserves. The next is Inner Mongolia.

Coal provides China with the principal source of energy, and it accounts for 70 per cent of the country's primary energy consumption. Large investments have therefore been made by China in the coal industry. In 1983, coal production reached 715 million tons, ranking third, after the Soviet Union and the United States. Most of China's coal is produced for home consumption, and only a small amount is exported. The largest open-cast coal mine in the country, the Helinhe Colliery of Inner Mongolia, is now under construction. A number of mining districts have been designated by China for cooperative exploitation with other countries.

Textile and Light Industries

In recent years the textile and light industries have witnessed a fast growth. Textile industry began only in the 1880's. There are now more than 5,600 textile industrial enterprises, with their production of cotton yarn, cotton-chemical fibre yarn and cotton cloth ranking first in the world.

Silk deserves special mention because it was first produced in China. As long as 2,000 years ago, Chinese silk was brought to Central Asia and Europe through the famous "Silk Road". Even today, silk is still an important export item, and textile industry accounts for 15 per cent in the gross industrial output value, and the retail sales of textiles account for about 25 per cent of the total volumes of retail sales of consumer goods in the country.

Light industry is also important in the country's domestic and foreign trade. There are more than 700 export items, sold to more than 150 countries and regions. A fairly comprehensive light industrial system has been built in order to increase productivity. Apart from paper, crude salt, table salt, cigarettes, ceramics, leather goods, arts and crafts, the list of products has now been extended to include wrist-watches, bicycles, sewing machines, photosensitive materials, household electric appliances and synthetic detergents. Many factories have been built in the interior and border regions including Xinjiang, which originally had little light industry.

Labour Insurance and People's Livelihood

Labour Insurance System

There are two systems of labour insurance in China. The first benefits the workers and staff members of state-owned enterprises while the second protects those who work for state organizations and institutions. On the whole, both systems provide equal benefits, although the specific details may differ.

All workers and staff members in state enterprises, as well as those who work in state institutions and organizations, are entitled to the same benefits of labour insurance, which covers items such as childbirth, sickness, injury, disability, retirement and death. Pregnant woman workers, for example, enjoy free medical care, including pre-natal examination, hospitalization and child delivery. In addition, they are entitled to a 56-day maternity leave with full pay. During this period, they receive allowance in accordance with the country's one-child policy for each family.

Male staff members in state organizations and institutions retire at the age of 60, and female staff members at 55 (55 and 50 respectively in the case of male and female factory workers). Their pension is paid in proportion to the length of their working years, varying from 60 to 75 per cent of the wages they receive before they retire.

Other Welfare Benefits for Workers and Staff Members

One of the main items of welfare benefits is housing. Over the past three decades and more, houses and flats with a total floor space of 927 million square metres have been built for workers and staff members working in state enterprises, organizations and institutions. The average floor space is now 5.9 square metres for each city dweller. In the countryside the figure is higher, 11.6 square metres, owing to the improvement of the peasants' livelihood in recent years. Throughout the country rent is low, only about 6 per cent of the income of an ordinary Chinese wage earner.

Most state enterprises, organizations and institutions have dining rooms, kindergartens, and nurseries. Both the prices and the fees are low. Take nurseries for example, the parents pay only three yuan a month for their child's day care. Other welfare benefits include various allowances such as those for heating in winter, transport in the cities, and travels on family visits.

Personal Income

In 1983, the average annual cash wage of workers in units under ownership by the whole people was 865 yuan, an increase of 35.7 per cent over the 1957 figure of 637 yuan. Though workers in China do not receive a high pay, their living standards are higher than their real wage income may suggest. This is because they are exempted from income tax, and vàrious welfare benefits and allowances are provided by the state.

Before 1978, the peasants' income growth was slow. However, since 1979, when the responsibility system in agricultural production was introduced and the state greatly raised purchasing prices of farm and sideline products, there has been a marked increase in the income of the peasants. According to statistics collected in selected localities, the average net income of a peasant family in 1983 was 310 yuan per member, that is, an increase of 4.2 times over the figure of 73 yuan in 1957. In recent years there has been a higher growth in the income of peasants than that of the workers, thus narrowing the gap of living standards.

As a result of higher incomes of residents in the cities and the countryside, their bank deposits have grown visibly. In 1983, the total savings deposits were 89.25 billion yuan, or 104 times as much as the 860 million yuan of 1952; the average savings deposits per person rose from 1.5 yuan to 74.3 yuan.

Consumption Level of Residents in the Cities and the Countryside

| | Consumption level per head (on the year's price in yuan) | | |
	For the whole country	Peasants	Others
1952	76	62	148
1978	175	132	383
1983	288	233	523

Consumption

In recent years, consumption level has also gone up considerably. In 1983 it increased 3.8 times as compared with 1952. Allowing for price rises, the net increase was 2.5 times, averaging a 3 per cent increase yearly. From 1978 to 1983, consumption level grew by 41 per cent, a yearly average increase of 7.2 per cent.

The Change in Consumption Pattern

The pattern of consumption has changed significantly. According to investigation into the income and expenditure of rural and urban families, the proportion of income spent on food has dropped since 1957 while that spent on clothing and articles for use has risen markedly. The amount of meat, poultry and eggs consumed has been increasing fast, and there has also been a rising consumption of wheat flour and rice instead of coarse grain. Cotton has gradually been replaced by chemical fibres, wool, silks and satins, and there is an increasing demand for sophisticated electric appliances. At present, for residents in the cities, there is an adequate supply of high-grade consumer goods, such as washing machines, refrigerators, electric fans, recorders, cameras, and modern furniture.

Medical and Health Work

Medical Service

Medical service has been vastly improved since the founding of the People's Republic. Before 1949, hospitals were found only in major cities and because of poor facilities they could not provide proper service. After Liberation, many of the old hospitals have been rebuilt with extensions added. New hospitals have also been built and medical institutions established in all parts of the country. Now, all the counties in China have general hospitals, health and anti-epidemic stations, pharmaceutical inspection institutions, as well as maternity and child-care clinics. The number of medical and health institutions in the country has grown to 190,000, staffed by four million medical and technical personnel including one million working in the countryside. The total of the hospital beds is well over two million. Because of the existence of a nationwide medical network, mortality rate has dropped drastically.

Much stress has been laid on medical and health work in the rural areas, where over 80 per cent of the country's people live. There are now hospitals in people's communes and medical centres or clinics in production brigades. Most patients in the countryside can obtain local medical treatment in the people's communes or the counties. If it is a serious case, the patient will be transferred to a regional or other hospital for special care.

Medical Institutions and Medical Technical Personnel

	Medical institutions		Medical technical personnel (in ten thousand)		Total number of hospital beds (in ten thousand)
	Total number	Including: hospitals	Total number	Including: doctors	
1949	3,670	2,600	50.5	36.3	8.0
1957	122,954	4,179	103.9	54 7	29.5
1975	151,733	62,425	205.7	87.8	159.8
1982	193,438	66,149	314.3	130.7	205.4
1983	196,017	66,662	325.3	135.3	211.0

Prevention and Treatment of Infectious and Endemic Diseases

There has been large-scale work of prevention and treatment of infectious and endemic diseases. The result is that formerly widespread diseases such as plague, smallpox, cholera, venereal disease, kalaazar and typhus have been eliminated or almost completely eliminated. The incidence of other infectious, parasitic, endemic and occupational diseases has fallen sharply. Schistosomiasis (snail fever), for

example, was once a common disease in south China, caus-
ing the loss of countless lives in the old days. After the
founding of New China, the schistosomiasis prevention and
treatment committees and research committees have been set
up in places where the incidence of the disease is known
to be high. Altogether, a total of 10,000 professional medical personnel are now working in this field. Now two-thirds
of the patients have been cured, and the disease has been
virtually eliminated in five provinces.

Maternity and Child Care

China pays great attention to the work of maternity and
child care. Besides gynecological, obstetric and paediatric
departments in general hospitals, there are 180 maternity
hospitals, over 20 children's hospitals and 2,000 maternity
and child health centres and stations, and over 50,000 doctors of gynecology, obstetrics and paediatrics in the country.

Intensive efforts have been made in many places to provide health protection for working women, and much work
has also been done in the prevention and treatment of
diseases which occur frequently among women. Early in
the 1950s, for example, the medical departments carried out
in the cities extensive checkups and treatment against cancer
of uterine cervix and achieved satisfactory results in the
treatment and prevention of the disease. Children in both
rural and urban areas were given, free of charge, BCG vac-
cines, and inoculated against smallpox, diphtheria, whooping
cough, measles and infantile paralysis. In many places,
children are given regular checkups.

As a result of all the work done in maternity and child
care, there has been a remarkable fall in the mortality rate
for both infants and women during childbirth. The infant

mortality rate in cities, for example, has dropped from 200 per thousand in 1949 to 12-15 per thousand.

Traditional Chinese Medicine

The Chinese people relied on their traditional medicine for centuries before Western medicine was introduced in the 1840's. Throughout Chinese history are found many famous medical scientists, and a wealth of medical texts. Incomplete statistics show that there are more than 8,000 such works, most of which deal with clinical medicine.

Oral medicines are mainly used in treating diseases. However, there are other therapies such as acupuncture and moxibustion, and treatment by massage and *qigong* (breathing exercises). Traditional Chinese acupuncture has proved remarkably effective in the treatment of many kinds of ailments with little or no side-effects.

Treating diseases by acupuncture and moxibustion involves pricking with a needle and, in the latter, cauterizing, with a burning moxa stick, selected points of the human body based on the Chinese medical theory of main and collateral "channels". This method was introduced into Korea in the 6th century and, later, into Japan and countries in Southeast and Central Asia. It became known to Europe in the 17th century and is now more generally used in many countries. After a world conference on acupuncture and moxibustion was founded an international organization for research on acupuncture and moxibustion and other relevant technologies.

The medical workers have, over the years, done a good deal of research on Chinese medicine and pharmacology in combination with Western medicine. Many good results have been achieved. Clinical instances have proved, for example, that acupuncture has the pain-killing effect, and

64

Some of the Chinese classics translated and published by the
Foreign Languages Press in Beijing.

Beijing Opera.

The site of the Gugi Kingdom (9th-17th centuries) on the Ali Plateau of Tibet.

The noted Chinese dancer Zhang Jun performing the Indian classical *Warram* dance.

The Yao *Drum Dance*.

Riverside Scene at the Q
Northern So

Festival, dated back to the
...sty (960-1127).

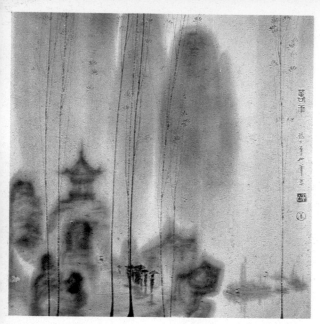

Spring Rain, an ink-wash painting by Zhu Junshan.

A traditional block-printed New Year picture.

Tightrope stunt.

A panda's entertaining performance.

Embroideress Huang Zu'an of Suzhou, a city known for its embroideries.

Homeward with Her Catch, a Nantong brocade painting.

it is now used as an anaesthetic in surgical operations. The patient under acupuncture anaesthesia remains conscious. He is able to cooperate with the doctor during the operation, suffers less post-operation pains and recovers faster. Acupuncture anaesthesia is now extensively used in operation on the head, neck and chest, and other surgical operations.

Clinical experience over the years has led to many new medical achievements. In acupuncture and moxibustion, for example, a number of new acupuncture "points" have been discovered. More than 300 types of ailments can now be treated with good results, including acute bacillary dysentery, gallstone, and neuroparalysis. Acupuncture can be used in the correction of the abnormal position of fetus. Bone-setting has seen new advances, too. Satisfactory results have been achieved in treating cervical vertebral diseases, prolapse of lumbar intervertebral disk, shoulderache, and other traumas of soft tissues. In treating fractures, small and light splints, instead of a plaster cast, are used. This is supplemented with oral Chinese medicines, the application of a poultice and light exercises at an early stage in order to hasten healing. Such methods reduce pain and limit local inflammation while stimulating blood circulation and bone growth.

The Chinese Government attaches great importance to traditional medicine and has established many academies, over 800 hospitals and some 20 colleges of Chinese medicine. There are more than 300,000 doctors and 140,000 pharmacists of Chinese medicine throughout the country. In 1979, the All-China Society of Traditional Chinese Medicine was founded at the First National Symposium of Traditional Chinese Medicine held in Beijing.

Education

The reorganization of education immediately began after the founding of the People's Republic of China. There were numerous problems, however, because the country was economically backward and educationally underdeveloped. Before Liberation, for example, over 80 per cent of the population were illiterate, and the percentage was higher than 95 in the rural areas. At present, primary education has been popularized in economically more developed rural areas, and junior middle school education in the cities.

The aim of educational planning in China is the development of a person morally, intellectually and physically. It is hoped that the student will have acquired, before graduation, socialist consciousness and culture so that he will be fully prepared for the role he is going to play in working for the country. From 1949 to 1983, higher educational institutions and secondary technical schools have respectively provided the state with over 4,110,000 and 7,220,000 specialized personnel. In particular, the university and secondary technical school graduates of the fifties and sixties have now become the backbone of the country in its socialist construction.

At present, in China there are over 800 universities and colleges with a total student body of one million. There are well over 100,000 secondary schools and 860,000 primary schools which offer courses to 40 million secondary school students and 136 million primary school pupils.

Pre-school Education

Women in China go to work without any worry about their children because they are well looked after in the nurseries and kindergartens. At present, there are more than 130,000 kindergartens and nurseries tending over 11 million children.

Nurseries and kindergartens in China are administered either by the state or the collectives. Those which are under the aegis of the state are run by various educational organizations, government departments, institutions or enterprises. The others, depending on location, are administered by neighbourhood committees in the cities, and the communes, or production brigades and teams in rural areas. The nurseries and kindergartens in the cities provide either day care or boarding. The parents have to pay for their children's food, but otherwise the fees are low, varying from 3 to 6 yuan a month, which is about 5 to 10 per cent of a worker's monthly salary.

Primary and Secondary Education

Primary and secondary schools in China are run mainly by the state. Tuition fees are very low; so, too, the incidental expenses. A change is now being made to extend primary and secondary school education from five years to six. Most of the full-time secondary school students live at home, but residence is provided in some of the schools. Government employment departments are in charge of arranging jobs for the secondary school graduates in the cities. Some factories and mines enrol secondary school graduates on their own through examination.

Higher Education

Of the country's 800 higher educational institutions, there are some key universities which have a long history of development and have attained a high level in teaching. These include Beijing University, Qinghua University, Fudan University, Tongji University, Nankai University and Nanjing University.

Beijing University, located in the scenic spot in the northwestern surburb of Beijing, is a well-known comprehensive university which offers a wide range of courses in the humanities and sciences, Formerly known as the Metropolitan College, founded in 1898, it acquired its present name in 1912.

At present, Beijing University has 25 academic departments, 73 special programmes and 19 research institutes, with a student body of about 12,000.

The university has attained a high level of excellence particularly in the fields of theoretical physics, mathematics and mechanics. Outstanding achievement has also been made by the Biology Department in the research on synthetic crystalline bovine insulin.

Qinghua University, founded in 1911, is a well-equipped polytechnic university. Having a highly qualified faculty, it is one of the best universities in the country, well known for teaching and research. The university has 19 academic departments and 49 special programmes, and a student body of more than 9,000.

All universities and colleges in China are state-run. The admission of students is handled by the enrolment committees of the central and local educational departments which admit candidates according to the needs of the state and the students' preference. Upon completion of their education, students are assigned jobs by the government.

In Chinese universities, tuition, lodging and medical care are free of charge. Students have to pay only for their food and textbooks. There are government grants for students with financial difficulties and these grants are also available to those studying in teacher training, physical education and ethnic minorities institutes.

There are two kinds of payment for postgraduates. Those who are already on the government payroll receive the same pay as they did before admission. The others receive state grants equivalent to 90 per cent of a university graduate's wage.

In 1981, higher educational institutions in China began to grant bachelor, master and doctoral degrees. There are now 18 doctorate, 15,000 master-degree and 320,000 bachelor-degree holders. In 1983, the honorary doctoral degree was introduced. So far, Amadou Mahtar, General Secretary of the UNESCO, the famous Japanese scientist Kaya Seishi, and the British scientist Joseph Needham have received the honorary doctoral degree from Beijing University, Fudan University and the Chinese Academy of Social Sciences respectively.

Adult Education

The students of adult education come from all walks of life. There are spare-time primary and secondary schools run by factories, government institutions, social organizations, state farms, rural people's communes, production brigades and teams. High-level adult education is also provided by open universities on television, correspondence colleges, night universities and factory-run universities for workers and staff. At present, more than a million students are studying in these higher adult educational institutions,

9 million in spare-time secondary schools and 8 million in spare-time elementary schools.

Workers and staff members, after graduation from spare-time universities and TV universities, will return to their former work units. The record of their attendance and accomplishment will be recognized. When necessary, changes will be made in their work so that they can make good use of what they have learnt.

Future Plans

Though much has been achieved in the training of personnel for the state, there are still many problems. There is a shortage of college graduates, and China needs more students majoring in the liberal arts, commerce and law. Not enough emphasis has been put on technical and vocational education. There is a crying need for qualified teachers in schools of all levels and types.

At the first session of the Sixth National People's Congress in 1983, Premier Zhao Ziyang presented his report on government work and emphasized that "we should make the development of intellectual resources an important item on our agenda". It is expected that education at all levels will undergo great changes in the next five years. The plan at the moment is that by 1987, enrolment in regular institutions of higher learning should have risen from 315,000 in 1982 to 550,000, in other words an increase of 75 per cent. More forms of conducting higher learning should be encouraged, such as radio, TV, and correspondence university classes. There should also be more evening colleges and colleges for training managerial personnel. The target is to raise the enrolment from 290,000 in 1982 to 1,100,000 in 1987, a 280 per cent rise.

Secondary school education will also be restructured. There will be greater emphasis put on the development of senior vocational middle schools, and it is hoped that their students will make up 40 per cent of the total number of senior middle school students in the next five years. Great efforts, too, will be made by the state to train primary and secondary school teachers and to ensure elementary education can be provided for all who need it.

Number of Schools and Students

	1949	1976	1979	1982	1983
Institutions of higher learning Students	205 117,000	392 565,000	633 1,020,000	715 1,154,000	805 1,207,000
Secondary schools Students	5,216 1,268,000	194,595 59,055,000	147,266 60,249,000	107,829 47,028,000	105,071 40,340,000
Primary schools Pupils	346,800 24,391,000	1,044,300 150,055,000	923,500 146,629,000	880,516 139,720,000	862,165 135,780,000

Note: Secondary schools include secondary technical schools, ordinary middle schools and secondary agricultural schools.

72

Science and Technology

In the socialist modernization of China, priority is given to science and technology. In 1980, a new policy for scientific and technological development was formulated on the basis of the experience gained in this field after the founding of the People's Republic of China. The central point of this policy is: the national economy depends on the progress in science and technology, which must therefore be developed to serve the national economy. Under the guidance of this policy, scientific research is playing an increasingly important role in economic construction.

Research Organizations

China has established a scientific and technological research system composed of the Chinese Academy of Sciences and the research centres and institutions operating in colleges and universities, industrial departments, national defence departments and the localities. With rational division of responsibilities and coordination among these scientific groups, each plays its part in the specific research work to be done. Advanced research, however, is concentrated mainly in the Chinese Academy of Sciences and a number of key universities and industrial departments.

Apart from government research organizations, there are more than 100 national academic societies under the jurisdiction of the Chinese Science and Technology Association. They have more than 2,000 branches in large and medium-sized cities, thus forming an extensive network for exchange of scientific and technological information.

The Chinese Academy of Sciences, founded in November 1949, is the largest comprehensive research centre of natural science. Since then, it has been playing an important role in socialist construction and in developing the country's science and technology. In particular, it has played a pace-setter role in basic natural science research and the development of new technologies.

When it was founded the Chinese Academy of Sciences had only 20 research units with about 200 research personnel. But today, the Academy has under its jurisdiction over 100 research institutes with close to 30,000 researchers. In 1954 it established a number of academic departments composed of outstanding scientists from various fields. It now has as many as 400 academicians.

Plans for the Development of Science and Technology

To meet the needs arising from economic development, the state in 1956 worked out the first long-term plan for developing science and technology: the 12-year Programme for Scientific and Technological Development (1956-67). This programme listed atomic energy, jet propulsion technology, computer science, semiconductor technology, electronics, automatic control and other advanced technology as the main areas for development. The main projects in this programme were completed in 1962, five years ahead of schedule.

In 1962, a 10-year programme (1963-72) was worked out, which gave priority to the development of agriculture and new materials, and the manufacture of machinery equipment. But the projects were not completed because of the unfortunate occurrence of the "cultural revolution".

The year 1977 ushered in a new historical period in China. A National Science Conference was called in order to formulate an eight-year plan (1978-85). The plan singled out eight main areas of development: agriculture, energy, materials, computer science, laser technology, space technology, high-energy physics and genetic engineering.

Today, work on a 15-year plan (1986-2000) for scientific and technological development is under way.

Major Achievements

In more than 30 years, China has built up its own scientific and technological research system and trained a considerable number of scientific and technological personnel with considerable knowledge and skill. It has made advances in a number of major scientific and technological fields. The gap in science and technology between China and the advanced countries in the world has been gradually narrowed.

New achievements of Chinese science and technology can be seen in the successful experiment with atomic and hydrogen bombs and also with missiles, the launching of artificial earth satellites and their recovery, the launching of a carrier rocket into a designated area in the South Pacific, the launching of a group of three satellites for spacephysics experiment with a single carrier rocket, the artificial synthesis of bovine insulin and the artificial synthesis yeast alanine transfer RNA.

Similarly, great progress has been made in scientific research on agriculture, textile, light and heavy industries, medical and health work, and in basic natural science re-

75

search. In 1980 there were good results in 2,600 scientific and technological items, and more than 4,000 in 1982. Moreover, 50 per cent of these have been put to good use in production. The popularization, over wide areas, of hybrid rice, the No. 1 Shandong Cotton and other improved strains has helped increase the output of grain and cotton.

Some Information About the 15 Man-Made Satellite Launched by China

	Item	Date	Remarks
1.	Man-made earth satellite	April 24, 1970	
2.	Scientific experiment satellite	March 3, 1971	
3.	Man-made earth satellite	July 26, 1975	
4.	"	November 26, 1975	Returned to earth according to plan
5.	"	December 16, 1975	
6.	"	August 30, 1976	
7.	"	December 7, 1976	Returned to earth according to plan

8. ˝	January 26, 1978	Returned to earth, having completed the planned experiments
9. Spacephysics experiment satellite		
10. Spacephysics experiment satellite	September 20, 1981	A group of three satellites launched with a single carrier rocket
11. Spacephysics experiment satellite		
12. Scientific experiment satellite	September 9, 1982	Returned to designated spot according to plan
13. ˝	August 19, 1983	
14. Experiment satellite	January 29, 1984	
15. Experimental communications satellite	April 8, 1984	

Literature and Art

Classical Chinese Literature

Classical Chinese literature can be traced back to very ancient times. *The Book of Odes*, the earliest collection of Chinese poetry, was compiled in the 6th century B.C. It contains 305 poems, and they had considerable influence on later development of poetic form and style.

In Chinese literary history, the first great poet is Qu Yuan (c. 340-278 B.C.). His best-known work is the long poem *Li Sao* or *Lament*, in which he expresses his undying love for his country and his unwavering devotion to the pursuit of truth. Qu Yuan has always been dearly loved by the Chinese people. In 1953, he was commemorated as one of the four cultural giants named by the World Peace Council. Together with the *Book of Odes*, *Li Sao* took classical Chinese literature to its first peak.

The golden age of classical Chinese literature is the Tang Dynasty (618-907) which produced a galaxy of distinguished poets and men of letters, including Li Bai (701-762), Du Fu (712-770), Han Yu (768-824) and Liu Zongyuan (773-819). *The Complete Collection of Tang Poems*, as it is presented today, contains 50,000 poems by more than 2,200 poets. The Tang poems, together with *ci* (poems written to music) of the Song Dynasty and *qu* (free-song) of the Yuan Dynasty, form the bulk of classical Chinese poetry.

The best-known dramatist in the history of Chinese

drama is Guan Hanqing (c. 1213-c. 1297) of the Yuan Dynasty. He wrote 67 plays, many of which are put on stage today. Appropriately in 1958, he was named by the World Peace Council as one of the cultural giants for commemoration throughout the globe.

In Chinese literary history, the Ming and Qing dynasties are best known for their novels, particularly the four classical masterpieces, namely *Romance of the Three Kingdoms, Outlaws of the Marsh, Journey to the West* and *A Dream of Red Mansions*. Of the four, the last-named has been acclaimed as the greatest Chinese classical novel. It has been the subject of intensive academic study by a host of scholars in China and abroad. There are also special research institutes which devote themselves to the study of various aspects of the novel.

Modern Chinese Literature

Modern Chinese literature began with the May 4th Movement, a massive student demonstration in 1919 against imperialism and feudalism. The Movement caught the imagination of the Chinese writers, who believed that literature could play a significant role in the battle against the evils of old society and their decadent forces. These writers, through their works, created a new literature which gave hope and strength to the Chinese people in their revolutionary struggles. The representative writers are Lu Xun, Guo Moruo, Mao Dun and Ba Jin.

By all consent, Lu Xun (1881-1936) was the father and standard-bearer of modern Chinese literature. He was a prolific writer and his numerous novels and essays have been greatly admired by the Chinese readers and literary critics and scholars. He had also translated 200 literary works of more than 90 foreign writers from 14 different countries. In 1981, the *Collected Works of Lu Xun* was published, consisting of 16 volumes. His works have now been translated into more than 50 languages in 30 countries.

In all his writings, Lu Xun has artistically revealed the Chinese heart and spirit. His biting satire opened the eyes of many readers to the injustices and cruelties of the feudal society that was the reality of China of his day. In *The True Story of Ah Q*, for example, he has created a hired hand who is the epitome of the peasants living under the yoke of feudalism in old China. Through Ah Q, Lu Xun has depicted the plight and resilience of the peasants, whose spirit can never be destroyed. Behind much of the satire is the urge that there should come drastic social changes in order to preserve the honour and dignity of mankind. Appropriately, the short story has been regarded as an immortal work in modern Chinese literature.

Socialist Literature

The founding of the People's Republic of China in October 1949 ushered in a new literary period. Before that, in the long course of complex struggles, the revolutionary literary movement had been gathering force and it had produced a contingent of promising writers. Mao Zedong's "Talks at the Yan'an Forum on Literature and Art" in 1942 had also provided the critical thinking behind literary and artistic creations. With the birth of a new country, every condition was ripe for the arrival of socialist literature.

The new spirit since 1949 has inspired numerous writers, young and old. Many excellent works have been produced, including those by writers of the older generation, such as *Builders of a New Life* by Liu Qing, *Great Changes in a Mountain Village* by Zhou Libo, *Sanliwan Village* by Zhao Shuli, *Steeled and Tempered* by Ai Wu, *Keep the*

Red Flag Flying by Liang Bin, *The Song of Youth* by Yang Mo and *Red Crag* by Luo Guangbin and Yang Yiyan. Poetry, too, has flourished and most commendable are the works of veteran and young poets such as Ai Qing, Li Ji, Wen Jie, Guo Xiaochuan and He Jingzhi.

After the social and political turbulence of the "cultural revolution" during the decade 1966-76, the Chinese literary world has gained a new vitality. A great number of young and middle-aged writers such as Wang Meng, Jiang Zilong, Chen Rong, Xu Huaizhong and Zhang Jie have now come to the fore. At the same time, many women writers have also distinguished themselves in the literary world.

Since 1976, thousands of novels and countless poems, short stories and essays have been published in more than 400 literary journals and magazines. The authors vividly describe the injuries they have suffered and their works constitute what critics and scholars now define as "scar literature". As the wounds have been healed, however, the writers look for new themes in their attempts at realistic reflection of contemporary life. While retaining the best of their literary traditions, the Chinese writers today have increasingly turned to foreign works in their efforts to improve artistic expression and achieve a distinctly individual style. Socialist literature will be taken to greater heights.

Theatre and the Cinema

Traditional Chinese opera has a history of more than 800 years. It is an art form which integrates singing, music, dialogue, acting and acrobatics. There are more than 300 different operatic forms in China. Among the local operatic forms staged nationwide are Beijing Opera, Pingju Opera, Shaoxing Opera and Henan Opera. The best-known is Beijing Opera, which has a history of more than 200 years. It originated in Beijing, then capital of the Qing Dynasty.

There are different schools, styles and forms of singing in Beijing Opera. In acting and acrobatic fighting, different roles follow different patterns, and their movements and gestures are stylized, suggestive and symbolic. For instance, the actions of opening a door, going up the stairs, rowing a boat or climbing a hill, are done purely through the dance-like movements of the actors with the help of props. String and percussion instruments also provide a distinct characteristic of Beijing Opera.

The most famous Beijing Opera actor is Mei Lanfang (1894-1961). Throughout his career, he sought to improve every aspect of the art of performance: singing, recitation, dancing, music, costumes and make-up. His innovations have been widely adopted and the style of the "Mei School" is greatly appreciated by the audience. Especially popular among Mei Lanfang's masterpieces are: *A Woman Feigning Madness*, *The Drunken Beauty* and *The Conqueror Bids Farewell to Lady Yu*.

Modern Chinese drama has developed under the influence of foreign dramatic literature and conventions. In the 1910's, drama troupes were formed in the country. The most popular plays staged in the 1930's and the 1940's are *Thunderstorm*, *Sunrise*, *Qu Yuan* and *Twin Flowers*.

After the founding of New China in 1949, great advances have been made in Chinese drama both in the quality of the script and that of stage production. *The Dragon-Beard Ditch*, *Cai Wenji* and *Guan Hanqing*, all well-written plays, have been well received by the Chinese audience. The best-known, however, is *Teahouse* by Lao She, which has gained increasing popularity abroad. Over the last few years, it has been staged in Western Europe and Japan. The play is about the changes of an ordinary Beijing teahouse over a period of several dozen years, and has a strong local colour. At the same time, however, it vividly recaptures the life and spirit of the people who lived under the past several regimes.

The influential playwrights in the movement of modern Chinese drama are Cao Yu, Tian Han, Guo Moruo and Lao She.

It was not until the eve of the First World War that China made its first film. Gradually the film industry developed. In the 1930's and the 1940's, a number of films were produced which realistically reflected contemporary life and problems. The best-known productions were *Wild Currents*, *The Great Road*, *Song of the Fisherman*, *At the Crossroads* and *The Spring River Flows East*.

The film industry made great advances after the founding of New China in 1949. Films such as *The Lin Family's Shop*, *Sons and Daughters of China*, *The White-Haired Girl*, *The Song of Youth* and *The Threshold of Spring* have attracted millions of movie-goers. New productions in recent years include the following popular feature films: *Happiness for All*, *Legend of the Tianyun Mountains*, *Tear Stains*, *Camel Xiang Zi* and *Neighbours*.

Animated films in China are shot in many different forms, but they all share the common characteristic of a national style. In their productions, the directors make good use of traditional Chinese painting, murals, New Year pictures, folk art and local operas. Consequently, many traditional Chinese paintings, for example, have come to life on the screen such as *The Tadpole Looks for His Mother* and *The Cowherd's Flute*, masterpieces of the distinguished 20th century artists Qi Baishi and Li Keran, respectively.

83

Many of the animated films have won prizes or awards at international film festivals.

China has business ties with 180 film distribution companies and agents in more than 20 countries and regions. Every year foreign films are introduced into the country and they are dubbed in Chinese. So far, the total number done since Liberation is more than 1,000.

There are altogether 19 film studios in China. Thirteen of these also have feature film studios, which produce at least 100 feature films a year.

Music and Dance

As early as the first century B.C., more than 80 different kinds of musical instruments were already in use. Among the historical finds of these instruments in Hubei in 1978 was a musical stand of 64 bronze bells. The bells have a considerable variation in pitch, and they were made more than 2,400 years ago. They can produce a range of five octaves, and that itself is ample proof of the extraordinary knowledge of music in ancient China.

Over the many centuries of feudal society, there were many periods during which musical culture flourished. Native and foreign music combined to produce a new Chinese music. The best-known works of Chinese classical music are *The Eighteen Airs for the Fife*, *Ambush on All Sides* and *Spring Moonlight and Flowers on the River*.

The 1930's and 1940's produced many patriotic musicians. Their emotional response to the fear of the breaking-up of the country led to the creation of many musical pieces which appealed to the people's hearts. The musicians hoped that through their notes and words they could arouse the people into action and together try to preserve the unity and sovereignty of their country. *March of the Volun-*

teers (words by Tian Han and music by Nie Er) unified all Chinese hearts and it is now the national anthem of China. At present, much work is being done by scholars in music departments of universities or special institutes. They collect and do research on classical and folk music. In 1983, an orchestra of ancient Chinese musical instruments that can produce eight tones has been set up and in its performances, the members use modern replicas of ancient musical instruments.

In recent years, Chinese musicians have paid a great deal of attention to the use of Western musical instruments, in their presentation of the sentiment which lies behind Chinese tales and themes. The violin concerto *Liang Shanbo and Zhu Yingtai,* for example, conveys, through Western music, the feeling of loss and the sadness of missed opportunities. From time to time, Chinese musicians will also give performances of Western masterpieces such as the Ninth Symphony of Beethoven.

At present there are a great many song and dance troupes, opera companies, symphony orchestras, choirs and traditional instruments orchestras. The musicians are trained mainly in the eight conservatories of music, which have their own primary and secondary schools, in Beijing, Shanghai, Shenyang, Chengdu, Tianjin, Xi'an and Guangzhou. These institutions and their schools provide music education at different levels from the very basic to the advanced. This comprehensive system has been working well. When a graduate from the secondary music school enters a conservatory, he or she may choose courses offered by various departments such as composition, folk music, vocal music, orchestral music and the piano. The Central Conservatory of Music and the Shanghai Conservatory of Music also have departments on conducting, musicology, and modern opera.

Most of the young musicians who have achieved outstanding results in national and international competitions have been trained by these schools.

Dance

The earliest depictions of Chinese dance are found in the three drawings on a pottery basin dating back more than 5,000 years, excavated in Datong County, Qinghai Province. In the Han Dynasty, Chinese dance was refined into an art with its own grace and beauty of movement. Traditional dance reached its peak in the Tang Dynasty, and it provided entertainment which was more artistic than before. *Prince Qin Storms the Enemy Lines*, for example, was a full-length dance portraying story and theme. It was frequently staged and deservedly earned its fame throughout the country.

Over the past 30 years or so, Chinese audiences have enjoyed the performances of traditional dances such as the *Dragon Dance*, *Lion Dance* and *Red Silk Dance*. In addition, many dances in dramatic productions have also provided popular entertainment. For instance, the full-length dance-drama *Along the Silk Road*, staged over the last few years, has produced the greatest impact on account of its artistic originality, quite apart from the attraction of the legendary story. Based on the dance movements portrayed in the Dunhuang cave murals, it recreates the elegant and graceful style of Tang dancing, while telling the story of how silk was introduced into the West. Another favourite is the *Flight to the Moon* adapted from a popular Chinese folk tale.

As China is a country of many nationalities, it is to be expected that there are many different kinds of dances which reflect different ethnic life and interests. At the Ethnic Minorities Theatrical Festival, held in Beijing in 1980, more than 140 dances were staged, such as the Yi *Bronze Drum Dance*, the Kazak *Lamb Snatching* and the Mongolian *Eagle*. All these ethnic dances had the distinctive features of their own.

Western ballet has also been popular in China. In 1959, the first ballet company was formed. This company, the Experimental Ballet Troupe of the Beijing School of Dancing, staged performances of famous European classical ballets such as *Swan Lake, The Fountain of Bakhchisarai* and *The Corsair*, and they were all well received. Over the years, efforts have been made in adapting Western classical ballet to Chinese dance. Such experiments have yielded good artistic productions such as the Chinese ballet of *The White-Haired Girl*, and *The Mermaid*.

Fine Arts and Handicrafts

Traditional Chinese fine arts are distinctly different from those of the West. In painting, for example, the painter uses his brush, and every stroke or dot has to be carefully made because of the instant absorbing nature of the soft-tissue paper. In the brush-work, he will also try to produce different shades of colour in order to achieve the artistic effect he wants to give.

As is to be expected, many masterpieces have been produced in the long history of traditional Chinese painting. Among these the best-known are: *The Spring Outing*, a landscape scroll by Zhan Ziqian of the Sui Dynasty, and *Riverside Scene at the Qingming Festival*, a vivid portrayal of social life in Kaifeng, by Zhang Zeduan of the Northern Song. These two paintings as well as many others have attracted numerous admirers who appreciated their artistic reflection of life and art.

Today, many artists still follow the traditional style of

Chinese painting. However, others have been exploring new techniques and visions. They try to free themselves from the traditional artist's objects of contemplation: mountains, waters, flowers and birds — popular since the Yuan Dynasty. These painters try to capture the spirit of the age through their art. The experiments with a new approach have resulted in many high-quality works, including paintings which have won gold medals such as *Snowstorm in the Wilderness* by Huang Zhou, *Two Lambs* by Zhou Changgu, and *Bringing Food on a Snowy Night* by Yang Zhiguang. The most celebrated painters of modern China are Qi Baishi, Xu Beihong, Pan Tianshou and Huang Binhong.

The fine arts are in a very healthy state in China. Apart from artists of traditional painting, there are numercus others who are engaged in oil painting, ink-wash painting, woodcut and cartoon.

China's handicrafts can be traced back to the painted pottery of the late Neolithic Age, about 5,000 to 6,000 years ago. Each of the past dynasties has produced its own special art work: the bronzeware and jadeware of the Shang and Zhou dynasties 3,000 years ago, lacquerware of the Spring and Autumn and the Warring States periods, silk fabrics and embroidery of the Han Dynasty, silver and gold artifacts and tricolour glazed pottery of the Tang Dynasty, porcelain and brocades of the Song Dynasty, carved lacquerware and cloisonne of the Ming and Qing dynasties.

There is a great variety of handicrafts produced in China today. The artistic design of each work and its production have also been much improved. The major handicrafts include sculpture, pottery, porcelain, embroidery, lacquerware, glassware, metalware, paper-cuts, woven and plaited articles. The best-known works are jade carving, embroidery, porcelain and cloisonne.

At present China has more than 2,000 handicrafts enterprises and together they employ 300,000 workers. There are 60 research institutes and 19 arts and crafts schools and colleges. Every year, China turns out 600 different kinds of arts and crafts of numerous designs. Since 1951, China has held 300 large-scale arts and crafts exhibitions in more than 100 countries.

Religion

The Chinese Government has made every effort to guarantee the freedom of religious belief. Buddhism, Islam, Catholicism and Protestantism all have their followers in China. Taoist believers are found mainly among the Han people.

The Buddhists, Moslems, Catholics, Protestants and Taoists all have their national and local organizations which handle their own affairs independently without any foreign interference. From time to time, these organizations send representatives abroad and arrange exchanged visits with their counterparts in other countries.

Buddhism

In the first century, Mahayana, or Greater Vehicle Buddhism, was introduced into China from India. It absorbed Confucian and Taoist thought and over a long period of time gradually took root in the country. The strong popular appeal of Buddhism and its ideas are amply reflected in the impact it has made on Chinese philosophy, morality, literature, and art.

In the long history of Chinese Buddhism there were many famous monks. Fa Xian of the Eastern Jin Dynasty and Xuan Zang of the Tang Dynasty, for example, had done much to the cultural flow between China and India. Both had been to India in quest of Buddhist truth.

Buddhism also has a wide influence in China's national minority areas. Lamaism, a Buddhist sect, has its followers mostly in Tibet and Inner Mongolia. Hinayana, or Lesser Vehicle Buddhism, finds its believers mainly among such nationalities as the Dai, Blang, Benlong and Va in Yunnan Province of south China.

Islam

Islam reached China in the mid-7th century. In the Tang and Song dynasties, with the increase in trade, Arab and Persian merchants came to China. They brought with them their religious beliefs and customs. Consequently, Islam spread and mosques were built. Among the best known are the Guangta Mosque in Guangzhou and the Qingjing Mosque in Quanzhou, which still retain their former splendour.

Today Islam has a large following among 10 of China's minority nationalities, the Hui, Uygur, Kazak, Tatar, Kirgiz, Tajik, Ozbek, Dongxiang, Salar and Bonan. These minority peoples live in compact communities mostly in northwestern China, except the Hui which are found all over the country.

Over the years the Chinese Islamic Association has organized pilgrimages to Mecca for many Muslims.

Roman Catholicism

Originally known as Nestorianism, Roman Catholicism reached China in the 7th century. It flourished for some 200 years before it declined. But the year 1601 saw the arrival of the Italian Jesuit missionary Matteo Ricci whose work eventually led to the revival of the religion. A Catholic cathedral was built in Beijing and Catholicism also spread in other parts of the country.

The Chinese Catholic Church was completely powerless for a long time when it was under foreign domination in the pre-Liberation days of China. In 1957, a national Catholic conference was held in Beijing, and the Chinese Patriotic Catholic Association was founded. The Chinese Catholic Church then became an independent church administered by the Chinese Catholics themselves.

Protestantism

Protestantism was introduced into China around the time of the Opium War of 1840. But in the old days Chinese Protestants, under foreign domination, faced the same problems as the Chinese Catholics. In 1954, a national Christian meeting was held in Beijing and the Three-Self Patriotic Movement Committee of the Protestant Churches of China was formed. It called upon both the clergy and the laity of Chinese Protestants to govern their own church, support it with their own economic means and do their own evangelistic work. This is how "Three Selfs" came to be known (self-administration, self-support and self-propagation in evangelistic work).

Taoism

Taoism is an indigenous religion dating back to the 2nd century. Taoists worship supernatural beings and believe that their particular regimen (including meditation, use of charms and spells, and ascetic practices) can help them to attain immortality.

Taoism in its earliest days had its popular appeal in many parts of China. But since the beginning of the Ming Dynasty, it has gradually declined. Nevertheless, it still has a number of followers today.

Tourism

Places to Go

There are many scenic spots in China because the country has numerous picturesque mountains and rivers. The Qinghai-Tibet Plateau, for example, is known as "the roof of the world". Many other lofty mountains such as Taishan, Emci, Huangshan and Lushan also have their own scenic splendours. The three gorges on the Changjiang River are a spectacular sight; so, too, is the scenery of Guilin in Guangxi and the West Lake in Hangzhou.

Likewise, the historic sites attract many tourists every year. Beijing is usually their first choice, for it has been the capital of the country for the past seven hundred years or so: the dynasties of Yuan (1271-1368), Ming (1368-1644), Qing (1644-1911) and since 1949, the People's Republic. The Forbidden City, in the heart of Beijing, is very much as it was in the past and it is the largest palace in the country. Not too far away from Beijing are the Summer Palace, the Ming Tombs, the world-famous Great Wall and Zhoukoudian, the home of the Peking Man who lived 500,000 years ago.

The ancient city of Xi'an, capital for 10 feudal dynasties, is another place of tourist attraction. Here they will see the tomb of the First Emperor of Qin (259-210 B.C.), where thousands of pottery warriors and horses are found. They will also see the Great Wild Goose Pagoda built in 648, and the Banpo Site where a primitive village once flourished

6,000 years ago. In addition to these, there are many other ancient tombs and ruins of ancient towns, which are well worth a visit.

Tourists are also attracted to the Mogao Grottoes at Dunhuang in Gansu Province, the Yungang Grottoes in Shanxi Province, the Longmen Grottoes in Henan Province, and the Dazu Grottoes in Sichuan which are commonly referred to as the four art treasure-houses of stone sculpture inspired by Buddhist belief. The Grand Confucius Mansion, Confucius Temple and Confucius Forest in Qufu in Shandong Province, the hometown of the world-famous educator and thinker Confucius (551-479 B.C.) are among the many tourist attractions in China, as are the Dujiangyan Dam, which was built over 2,000 years ago, and the world's earliest and largest man-made waterway, the Grand Canal.

Each of China's 56 ethnic groups has its unique culture and customs, which also attract the tourists. Chinese music, operas, dances, arts and crafts and the delicacies of Chinese cooking are of great interest to visitors from abroad.

Development

China does not regard profit as the only goal; rather, it sees tourism also as a means of expanding international communication and exchange and promoting understanding and friendship between the Chinese people and people in other countries. Tourism in recent years has witnessed a fast growth in China as a result of adopting the policy of opening to the outside world. In 1983, 120 cities and regions were open to tourism, and attracted more than 870,000 tourists from other countries. In the meantime, there has also been a gradual development of domestic tourism.

Many and diversified are the programmes organized for the tourists. Special trips bring tourists to the scenic spots.

On other tours, they also have the opportunity to observe the life and customs of people in various localities. Tourist activities like mountaineering are included and for their relaxation various courses are provided such as those in *Taijiquan* (shadow boxing) and Chinese cooking in order to meet the different interests and demands of the tourists.

Tourist Facilities and Service

To improve the service in the cities many modern tourist projects have been undertaken. More and more hotels have been built, which provide the tourists with suites as well as one-storey, bungalow-like houses. Many of these hotels have winding corridors in the characteristic style of traditional and national architecture in north China. The cave-dwelling hotels in Yan'an, Mongolian yurt hotels and bamboo stilt house hotels in Xishuangbanna, Yunnan, apart from providing modern facilities will also introduce the tourists to the different styles of distinctive local architecture and culture. For example, for many tourists, it is a rare and rewarding experience to go to subtropical Xishuangbanna in southwest China, to stay in a bamboo house and to join the Dais in their Water Sprinkling Festival.

Renovation and rebuilding have in recent years been carried out in some tourist spots including a section of the Great Wall at Badaling, the Tanzhe Temple, the Lamasery of Harmony and Peace and other prominent temples in Beijing. A cable line leading to the top of Mount Taishan in Shandong Province has been put into service, making sunrise-viewers' trip to the summit much easier.

As tourism is a new undertaking in China, much still remains to be done. Travel and tourist agencies and departments are making every effort to ensure that the tourists will leave China with happy memories.

95

Sports

Great attention has been paid by the Chinese Government to sports. Over the last 30 or more years, because of mass participation in sports many outstanding athletes have emerged. It is hoped that soon China will be a new force in world sports.

In recent years, the Chinese athletes have come to the fore in such events as table tennis, women's volleyball, badminton, gymnastics, sports acrobatics, diving and weightlifting. The impact has been increasing every year. By 1983, Chinese athletes had broken or surpassed 264 world records and won 122 world championship titles.

Table Tennis

Since Rong Guotuan won China's first men's singles title at the 25th World Table Tennis Championships in the Federal Republic of Germany in 1959, China has continued to maintain its lead in table tennis for the past 20 or more years. At the 36th World Table Tennis Championships held in Yugoslavia in 1981, the Chinese players captured all the titles in the seven events as well as all the runners-up in the individual events, something unprecedented in 55 years of world table tennis championships.

Badminton

This is another popular sport in China. Many world-class players have been produced. At the First World Bad-

Overpasses built in Beijing to solve problems of traffic jams.

An inside view of a courtyard house in Beijing.

Spring Festival celebrated in a small country town in Anhui
Province.

A giant "centipede" trailing high over Tiananmen Square. Kite making has a long history in China.

Herdsmen enjoying a feast of mutton.

The Mongolian herdsman milking a horse.

A "floating town" in south China.

T.V. sets and tape recorders are no longer a novelty to Chinese city dwellers.

A corner of the workers' residential quarters in the Shanghai Petrochemical General Works. In Chinese cities, housing is generally provided by the state and the rent is low.

Preparing a noonday meal for her husband.

Angling is a favourite pastime among the Chinese people.

The Hall of Prayer for Good Harvest in the Temple of Heaven Park, Beijing. It was constructed during the Ming and Qing periods (1368-1911) for emperors to come to pray and make sacrificial offerings.

The ruins of Yuanmingyuan (Park of Perfection and Brightness), a famous park with many architectural structures fully demonstrating the refinement of Chinese art. It was first constructed in 1709. In 1860, the Anglo-French joint forces set it to fire and destroyed it after their savage looting of all its treasures.

Mongolian yurts for tourists.

The camel's back provides relaxation and recreation for tourists.

minton Championships held in Thailand in 1978, the Chinese teams took four of the five titles. In 1982, the Chinese team competed for the first time at the 12th International Badminton Championships held in Britain and took the Thomas Cup by beating Indonesia's 7-times world champion team.

Volleyball

This is a sport that has brought the Chinese players much success. Particularly worthy of mention is the achievement of the women's team. At the 3rd World Cup Women's Volleyball Championship held in Japan in 1981, the Chinese women's team carried off the title for the first time after winning all the seven matches played. The following year, at the 9th World Women's Volleyball Championship held in Peru, it captured the crown by dethroning the Olympic champion team of the Soviet Union. Lang Ping has distinguished herself as a world-class spiker and is now ranked among the world's best.

High Jump

No spectacular results have as yet been produced by Chinese athletes in track and field events. High jump, however, is the exception. In 1957, Zheng Fengrong became the first Chinese woman to set a world record when she cleared 1.77 metres. Ni Zhiqin in 1970 broke the men's world high jump record by clearing 2.29 metres. At the 9th Asian Games held in India in 1982, the 19-year-old male high jumper Zhu Jianhua cleared the bar at 2.33 metres — the world's best performance for that event in that year. At the 5th National Games held in Shanghai in 1983, he set a new world record by clearing 2.38 metres. Zhu Jianhua's performances have attracted international attention. He was given a special award by the Italian Track and Field Association on October 24, 1983.

Diving

At the 10th World University Games held in Mexico in 1979, the 17-year-old Chen Xiaoxia dethroned the Soviet Union's ace diver Irina Kalinina and won the women's platform diving title. The chairman of the International Swimming Federation described her as "diving queen of the world". In 1981 and 1983, many gold, silver and bronze medals were taken by the Chinese star-studded diving team at the 2nd and 3rd World Cup Diving Championships, held in Mexico and the United States separately.

Gymnastics

In recent years, Chinese gymnasts have come into the limelight in competitions outside the country. The 15-year-old girl, Ma Yanhong, won the world title for the uneven bars at the 20th World Gymnastics Championships held in the United States in 1979. Two gold medals were won by Chinese gymnasts — Li Yuejiu on the parallel bars and Huang Yubin on the rings at the 5th Gymnastics World Cup held in Canada in 1980. At the 21st World Gymnastics Championships held in the Soviet Union in 1981, Li Yuejiu and Li Xiaoping won gold medals for the men's floor exercise and pommel horse respectively. At the 22nd World Gymnastics Championships held in Hungary in 1983, the Chinese men's team carried off the championship title from the Soviet Union's team which had hitherto dominated all world gymnastics competitions. In the competition, the Chinese team won three gold medals, two silver medals and three bronze medals.

Wushu

Wushu (known abroad as *kung-fu*), or martial arts, is a popular sport with a long history in China. It is practised both for physical training and self-defence. Back in the 3rd century, the famous surgeon Hua Tuo devised the *wuqinxi* (meaning "five-animal exercises") for curing diseases and physical training, which has been handed down to the present day.

Wushu is practised in various types of set exercises, either barehanded or with weapons such as swords, spears and clubs. There are also exercises in pairs, armed or unarmed, or with weapons against a barehanded opponent.

The art of *wushu*, which contains many beautiful, natural body movements, has been adopted in Chinese opera for the fighting scenes on the stage. Chinese acrobatics have also absorbed the best of the basic *wushu* movements.

There is a national *wushu* association in the country. *Wushu* courses are offered in all institutes of physical education; there are training classes in coaching centres in many parts of the country; and a national *wushu* competition is held every year.

(1) Conversion Table

Length

---

1 kilometre (1,000 m) = 2 *li* = 0.621 mile = 0.540 nautical mile
1 metre (m) = 3 *chi* = 3.281 feet

---

1 *li* = 0.5 kilometre = 0.311 mile = 0.270 nautical mile
1 *chi* = 0.333 metre = 1.094 feet

---

1 mile = 1.609 kilometres = 3.219 *li* = 0.863 nautical mile
1 foot = 0.305 metre = 0.914 *chi*

---

1 nautical mile = 1.852 kilometres = 3.704 *li* = 1.150 miles

---

Area

---

1 hectare = 15 *mu* = 2.47 acres

---

1 *mu* = 6.667 ares = 0.164 acre

---

1 acre = 0.405 hectare = 6.070 *mu*

Weight

---

1 kilogramme = 2 *jin* = 2.205 pounds

---

1 *jin* = 0.5 kilogramme = 1.102 pounds

1 pound = 0.454 kilogramme = 0.907 *jin*

Capacity

1 litre (metric system) = 1 *sheng* = 0.220 gallon

1 gallon (English system) = 4.546 litres = 4.546 *sheng*

(2) Chronological Table of Chinese History

Xia	c. 21st century-16th century B.C.	
Shang	c. 16th century-11th century B.C.	
Western Zhou	c. 11th century-770 B.C.	
Eastern Zhou	Spring and Autumn Period	770-476 B.C.
	Warring States Period	475-221 B.C.
Qin		221-207 B.C.
Western Han		206 B.C.-A.D. 24
Eastern Han		25-220
Three Kingdoms (Wei, Shu and Wu)		220-265
Western Jin		265-316

Eastern Jin	317-420
Southern and Northern Dynasties	420-589
Sui	581-618
Tang	618-907
Five Dynasties	907-960
Song (Northern Song and Southern Song)	960-1279
Liao	916-1125
Kin	1115-1234
Yuan	1271-1368
Ming	1368-1644
Qing	1644-1911
Republic of China	1912-1949

The Truth

TRIUMPH
BOOKS

Copyright © 2009 by Peter Handrinos

No part of this publication may be reproduced, stored in a retrieval system, or transmitted in any form by any means, electronic, mechanical, photocopying, or otherwise, without the prior written permission of the publisher, Triumph Books, 542 South Dearborn Street, Suite 750, Chicago, Illinois 60605.

Triumph Books and colophon are registered trademarks of Random House, Inc.

Library of Congress Cataloging-in-Publication Data

Handrinos, Peter.
 The truth about Ruth : Yankees myths, legends, and lore / Peter Handrinos.
     p. cm.
 ISBN 978-1-60078-192-6
 1. New York Yankees (Baseball team)—Anecdotes. I. Title.
 GV875.N4H36 2009
 796.357'64097471—dc22

                                2008045501

This book is available in quantity at special discounts for your group or organization. For further information, contact:

  Triumph Books
  542 South Dearborn Street
  Suite 750
  Chicago, Illinois 60605
  (312) 939-3330
  Fax (312) 663-3557

Printed in U.S.A.
ISBN: 978-1-60078-192-6
Design by Patricia Frey
Photos courtesy of AP Images

CONTENTS

Aristotle was not Belgian, the principle of Buddhism is not "every man for himself," and the London Underground is not a political movement. These are all mistakes, Otto. I looked them up.

—Wanda Gershwitz, *A Fish Called Wanda*

INTRODUCTION

The Urban Legends

The New York Yankees have long been the most storied franchise in sports. But not all of the stories are true.

No, even the most famous of teams has been misremembered, misrepresented, misunderstood, and otherwise mis-ed through history's many tellings and retellings. All along, the fictional has coexisted with the factual, rumors have mingled with reality, exaggerations have mixed with exactitudes.

Much of the mis-ing problem comes from the fact that Yankees lore traces well back into the 1920s and 1930s, an era with very different standards of journalism. From that long-bygone time until at least the 1960s, baseball was treated more as entertainment than as news, and otherwise bored beat reporters felt perfectly free to craft semifictional tales to sell the game through some measure of color, humanity, humor, or what have you. Long-retired chroniclers freely confessed that they polished quotations beyond all recognition, covered up unpleasant incidents, concocted others, and generally acted as public-relations flacks without portfolio.* They were more storytellers than straight-up newswriters.

---

*My favorite example of the old ways: years afterward, it was revealed that sometime in the 1920s, a married player ran through the aisle of a crowded railroad car, naked, trailed by an equally naked woman clutching a knife.

Who was she? What was with the cutlery?

Who knows?

The "reporters" at hand glanced up, chuckled, and promptly went back to their poker round. They'd never heard of Woodward and Bernstein.

Just as long as they didn't shade matters so much as to be completely implausible—an iguana escape couldn't be passed off as a Godzilla rampage—the media members saw their forays into creative writing as a means to go about the ultracompetitive business of selling newspapers and books in New York, the most ultracompetitive city of them all.

That long legacy of less-than-scrupulous reportage meant that Yankees images were, very often, "legendary" in the original sense of the term: their essential realities were grafted onto elements of the fanciful, the made-up. They contained some truth all right, but it was rarely just the truth, the whole truth, and nothing but the truth. Mickey Mantle wasn't just blessed with immense strength and speed, but with nearly superhuman powers. Yogi Berra wasn't just the author of a handful of memorable quips, he was something like a one-man comedy festival. And so on. Almost always, the original depictions were focused on selling, selling, selling, then took on lives of their own because those who should have known better basically 1) didn't know better, 2) didn't care, or 3) didn't want rock the boat.

Another significant factor in the creation of Yankee mythologizing was the extreme nature of the franchise itself. It goes without saying that, for nearly 90 years, it has been the National Pastime's true flagship: home to the most championships, the most Hall of Famers, most familiar touchstone to everything from personalities and rivalries to traditions and virtually everything else that makes baseball baseball. Surely the Yankees own the all-time franchise record for all-time franchise records, so when commentators attempt to put a new spin on the club's already stupendous essentials, they've been tempted to puff them up into something even larger than life.

Babe Ruth, for instance, possessed a personal charisma and cultural impact to match his on-field accomplishments, so it's no wonder that he attracted all manner of wild rumors, controversies, and claims in the way that magnets attract steel. Much of it has endured because it tapped into the public's ready fascination with his entire persona. Lou Gehrig, similarly, has always been linked to figures such as Wally Pipp and Cal

Ripken Jr. because the connections, however misconceived, seemed to highlight Gehrig's essential qualities. Closer to the present day, Reggie Jackson's undeniable flair for the dramatic and Derek Jeter's sense of cool have provided a hook for more punched-up copy.

This book is a long-overdue attempt to deal with all that non-truth, to retire some sacred cows, to knock over a few apple carts, to bull-rush a couple of china shops, to crash a few conventions. Its skeptical spirit seems long overdue but might invite some other questions of its own, so it's best to get them out of the way right away.

For one thing, a few fans might simply prefer their team's history as is, and that's fair enough. This book is not for them. The following chapters are all about revisiting the Yankees' retrospectives and, where appropriate, replacing them with something more sound and reliable; it's just the kind of thing hard-line traditionalists will hate. They should stick with Santa Claus.

Others might see a critique of Yankees myths as a veiled attack on the team itself, as an indirect means to "cut them down to size." Not so. For the record, I'm a big Yankees fan. I have been ever since Dad took me, at age five, to see the "Bronx Zoo" team of 1977. Researching the Yankees' miscellaneous myths has only made me admire the franchise even more. I've found that, in more than a few instances, their most memorable moments have been *even more* wondrous than we've been led to believe and, even when that wasn't the case, it was all right. The Yankees aren't so very delicate. They don't need old wives' tales to make them the most extraordinary team of them all—they're all that without the extra hoo-ha, thankyouverymuch. Always have been, always will be.

Finally, there's the question of accuracy. A skeptic/reader has every right to say "Well, Mr. Smarty-Pants Author who I've never heard of, how do you know *your* answers are so 100 percent reliably exactly right?"

To that, the only honest answer is: "I don't."

In most every instance, some measure of credible evidence and stats provide solid rejoinders to some pretty flimsy notions. There are objective facts and black-and-white numbers that tell us that the '79 Yankees did not collapse after Thurman Munson's death and that Yankee Stadium was, in all but name, demolished long ago. These may be inconvenient facts and ignored numbers, but they do exist, and they declare that what most commentators and fans think they know just ain't so.

Beyond that, admittedly, there are some cases that will never be completely closed. Much has been lost in the mists of time, so it is, indeed, within the realm of possibility that the Pittsburgh Pirates were really swept in the 1927 World Series because they were demoralized by their opponents' pregame batting practice. I wasn't there—not even my grandpa was there—so I can't claim with metaphysical certainty what went down on that particular day. Grandpa and I weren't witnesses to the Babe's "called shot" incident, either. And in the world of worlds, I acknowledge there is the slimmest of chances that Reggie Jackson possesses a 160-point IQ. That sort of thing. There's no firsthand, ironclad information on those issues and many more besides, so the cases against them, no matter how persuasive, have to be circumstantial in nature.

Still, even where it's been impossible to come up with definitive answers to everything, it's often been possible to produce some significantly better answers to a lot. That's what this book is about. It's for anyone who wants to examine, reexamine, think, and rethink what's behind the New York Yankees' most popular myths, legends, and lore.

C'mon. Let's go.

Popular Myths, Legends, and Lore

CHAPTER 1

The Truth About Ruth

Like the team that he helped launch into greatness, Babe Ruth was, in many ways, far more celebrated than he was well-known.

The general outlines of his image are still clear enough. The guy was fat. He may or may not have been part-black. His numbers were probably inflated by the fact he didn't have to play against Negro Leaguers but did get to play with a short right field porch at Yankee Stadium. He swung immense bats. One time, he visited a sick kid in the hospital. People called him the Sultan of Swat and blamed him for the Curse of the Bambino. All of this would be well and good except, unfortunately, that none of it is true.

ABSOLUTELY FLABULOUS

Casting a tub o' goo like John Goodman in a 1992 Babe Ruth biopic was a big, fat insult to the Bambino's athleticism. From the looks of him, the on-screen Goodman was well north of 300 pounds, but his real-life counterpart wasn't anywhere near that. The 6'2" Ruth reported to Yankee spring training camps of the 1920s and 1930s tipping the scales at anywhere from 215 to about 235 pounds. It was said that, most of the time, his fairly massive, 42-inch upper chest was matched to a 40-inch waist. He wasn't skinny, especially in those days, but he was no more than stout, either. Even at his heaviest, nearing age 40, the Babe probably weighed less than modern-day players such as Jim Thome and Frank Thomas.

He was significantly more conditioned than the average major leaguer of his day. Although his competition was forced to take blue-collar jobs during the winter months, Ruth was, very often, rounding

Babe Ruth with Hank Wilson (left) and Lou Gehrig (right). Even in the latter years of his career, Ruth was not all that heavy of a hitter.

himself into game shape by hitting the weights and going through the exercise paces. He was one of the rare stars with enough money to hire an off-season trainer, Artie McGovern, and he patronized an exclusive gym at East 42nd Street. Although it doesn't exactly jibe with his reputation as a complete natural, the Bambino was known to work and sweat and strain as much as any ballplayer of his generation.

It was well known that Ruth mastered the arts of both playing well and living large. Many witnesses have recounted numerous nights when he would drink beer by the pitcher and eat spare ribs by the rack. Those piggish habits would have rendered nearly anyone else into a blimp, but Ruth's turbocharged metabolism and hectic schedule (he routinely ran around for up to 20 hours per day) evidently served to burn off sufficient calories to neutralize the meals, at least in the playing months during his career.

Despite it all, he was still considered a heavy hitter, so to speak. Several factors fed into it, so to speak.

Ruth did have one truly out-of-control year, in 1925, when he suffered the "Bellyache Heard Around the World," a serious medical episode that was officially blamed on overeating. It cemented what was an already well-established image, but few realized that his hospitalization prompted the scared-straight Babe to hook up with McGovern's gym, practice some girth control, and, for the most part, clean up his act.

Finally, there's no denying that Ruth kind of *looked* like a fat guy. He had a moon-shaped face and, like Pops Stargell and Roger Clemens, never quite lost that double-chin look, no matter how hard he worked out. His height and super-sized playing achievements may have helped contribute to his enduring reputation for horizontal vastness, but it simply isn't matched by his physique.

BACK TO BLACK

When Babe Ruth was playing in the major leagues from 1914 to 1935, white Americans had, to put it delicately, a very different outlook on race relations. They were...a bit less enlightened back in those days. Which is to say, at the time, there was some harshness, racial-wise.... OK, they were out-and-out racist.

Ruth probably heard some of the worst of the worst epithets ever heard on a major league diamond before the days of Jackie Robinson. Players such as Ty Cobb and Smoky Joe Wood thought nothing of openly calling him a n——. Hecklers compared him to an ape or a monkey, saying Ruth's flat nose and big lips aligned with "African" looks. Even some Negro Leaguers supposed that the Babe was, secretly, one of them—if only because he was so athletic.

Leaving aside those absurdities of racial classification, we know also that the Bambino was the spitting image of his father, George H. Ruth Sr., and that his paternal family hailed from either Pennsylvania Dutch country or Germany. We know that his mom, Katie Schamberger Ruth, was the daughter of German immigrants. We know, also, that their only son's skin was pale enough, at least when he wasn't tanning his way through nearly 200 day games and exhibitions per year. Ruth was about as German American and lily-white as anyone who's ever played major league baseball.

BLACK BALL

When Barry Bonds was storming after Babe Ruth's career homer total a few years ago, the debate over Bonds' potential asterisk sometimes strayed into a debate over Ruth's unfair advantages. After all, the Babe may not have had access to steroids, but neither did he compete against some of the best players of his day. If he faced the Negro League's pitchers, his numbers might not have looked quite so good.

Ruth however *did* compete against great Negro League ballplayers during dozens of off-season barnstorming exhibitions. The ballgames may not have counted in the official record books, but they surely counted to the paying customers who thrilled at the chance to seize bragging rights. The games especially counted to all the black pitchers and fielders involved who wanted to show what they could do against the most fabled slugger of them all, and on those occasions, Ruth was Ruthian. He was an equal opportunity batter.

When the Babe visited Cuba after the 1920 season, he went 11 for 32 with a .839 slugging percentage in 10 ballgames, and in 55 documented at-bats against Negro Leaguers in the 1920s and 1930s, he had a .400 batting average to go with 1.000+ slugging. Ruth faced the great Satchel Paige once, in 1938, and he launched one of his patented long-distance homers, despite the fact that the Bambino was 43 years old at the time.

The same Negro Leaguers who routinely beat all-white major league barnstormers couldn't touch Ruth. Judy Johnson, the Hall of Famer who played in many of Ruth's integrated games, always dismissed the notion that his fellow African Americans could have stopped the Bambino, saying, "We could never seem to get him out, no matter what we did."

(One last note on the subject of segregation: it's often been said that the white hitters of their time looked better than they were because they never had to face black pitchers such as Paige and Bullet Rogan. True enough, but the argument goes both ways. Paige, Rogan, and others wouldn't have looked quite so good if they had faced "Murderers' Row" on a regular basis, either.)

THE HOUSE BUILT FOR RUTH

In a certain, little-noticed way, Yankee Stadium was designed to favor the Babe. It was laid out on its north-south axis so that the late summer's afternoon shadows fell on the Babe's customary position in right field, thus ensuring that the club's biggest drawing card would stay shaded and cool while the stadium's left fielder struggled with one of the toughest sun fields in the majors.

That was about the only way in which "the House that Ruth Built" was "the House Built *for* Ruth," however. When author Harvey Frommer writes that the stadium's dimensions were "tailored for Ruth's left-handed power," he's repeating a myth.

In Ruth's playing days at Yankee Stadium from 1923 to 1934 the right field line was, indeed, a mere 296 feet from home plate, but people forget how that cozy distance sharply dropped away to 407 feet in right-center field and a distant 461 feet in dead center. The very friendly "Ruthville" section next to the foul line quickly made way for a highly hostile "Death Valley" area right next door so that, on balance, the ballpark was extremely tough for Ruth—not to mention anyone else with power to all fields.

What would have happened if Ruth had played with more modest dimensions back at home? He probably would have hit even more homers. A lot more. Author Bill Jenkinson recently made an exhaustive study of Ruth's long balls from 1923 to 1934, finding that the Bambino hit 56 center-field or left-center homers on the road *but only a single one of those shots in the old stadium.* Thus Ruth was consciously going with a more natural, all-fields approach on the road and adjusting into a more extreme, dead-pull approach for the short right porch back in the Bronx. If Yankee Stadium had played like the typical road ballpark, Ruth would almost certainly have hit another 50-plus more career homers—more than enough to ensure that he would have been the all-time home-run king to this day.

THE BIG STICKS

48 ounces? 52? 54? Just how big were Babe Ruth's game bats? Although the Babe undoubtedly swung lumber much, much heavier than the whip-handled 32- to 34-ounce jobs we find today, no one's completely sure of how big of a bat he used in game action.

In the early 1920s the Bambino placed orders for Louisville Sluggers weighing more than 50 ounces, but, contrary to reports from Grantland Rice and others, there's no reliable evidence that he ever used those models for anything other than batting practice. Bat weights weren't introduced for another 50 years or so, so the big sticks may well have been the functional equivalent of warm-up aids, used strictly to build up the big guy's vaunted hand/wrist/forearm strength.

The Babe with boxer Jack Dempsey. Not a game bat.

We do know that, in his 60–home run year of 1927, Ruth mostly swung a Black Betsy model weighing 44 ounces, so it's safe to say that he probably never used anything close to a 50-ounce club in competition. Besides, have you ever seen one of those things? It's not a big bat; it's a small telephone pole.

THE BABE AND THE KID

There's an old story that says that Babe Ruth once promised a sick little boy he'd hit a home run for him, then went out and did it. The reality was even better.

9

When Johnny Sylvester, the 11-year-old in question, fell from a horse in 1926, his well-connected family asked the famed Babe Ruth to convey get-well wishes. The Babe obliged with a signed baseball and a note promising, "I'll hit a home run for you in Wednesday's game." Ruth then proceeded to hit a home run in "Wednesday's game"—that is, Game 4 of the 1926 World Series—then added another couple long balls for good measure. It was the first time anyone had ever hit three homers in a World Series game. It seems that the Bambino couldn't do *anything* in a small way.

Babe Ruth and Baby Ruth

Imagine it's 1920. You're a lawyer for the Curtiss Candy Company. You need a highly positive, highly commercial name for a tasty chocolate, nougat, and peanut concoction you're preparing for the consumer market. You want to label the product after the most exciting, most beloved athlete in America, but there's one problem: the company execs don't want to shell out a penny for the celebrity endorsement. You, the Curtiss lawyer, come up with an ingenious solution: forget the endorsement altogether and name the candy bar after...Ruth Cleveland.

Ruth Cleveland?

Ruth Cleveland, the baby girl born to President Grover Cleveland and his wife back in 1891. Sure, poor little Ruth had died way back in 1904, more than 16 years before, and the general public didn't know about her when she was alive. And yes, there's a slight resemblance between the names "Baby Ruth" and "Babe Ruth."

You somehow hoodwink a federal court to overlook all these facts too, and cut the Bambino out of a nifty little royalty check. Then, as a topper— the metaphorical chocolate over the peanuts and nougat—you successfully sue Ruth when he tries to introduce his own candy bar a few years later. You claim that the new bar would cause confusion with your own bar, the one that supposedly has nothing to do with Babe Ruth in the first place. You do all this while keeping a straight face.

All this makes you a very successful, if dishonest, lawyer, but if that candy was named after Ruth Cleveland, then I'm Ruth Buzzi.

THE SULTANATE

It's said that God has 1,000 names, and the most godlike of baseball players had almost as many nicknames.

As most fans know, the breathless newspaper accounts of the 1920s and 1930s habitually tagged Babe Ruth as "the Sultan of Swat," "the Caliph of Clout," "the Behemoth of Bust," "the Prince of Pounders," "The Wizard of Whack," and on. There were a dozen variations on that gimmick.

When George Herman Ruth Jr. debuted in the Majors in 1914, minor league teammates had already dubbed him "Babe," because the 19-year-old was just a babe in the woods. Later, the Italian version of the nickname (Bambino) gained popularity, so, for variety's sake, some friends took to calling him "Bam" or "the Big Bam." Some childhood acquaintances called him "Jidge," a rejiggering of his birth name.* But outside of the funny papers, there were never any mentions of Ruthian Sultans, Caliphs, or Behemoths.

THE PINSTRIPERY

Robert Creamer's best-selling *Babe* contains a pretty startling passage explaining how the Yankees' iconic look was inspired by its most iconic figure.

> *Because of Ruth's bulk, [owner Jacob] Ruppert decided to dress the Yankees in their now-traditional pinstripe uniform. The natty, clothes-conscious Ruppert felt the new uniform would make Ruth look trimmer.*

---

*As far as research shows, no one but his parents and, possibly, his first wife, ever called him George.

It's a notion that's been subsequently picked up by Pulitzer Prize winner Richard Ben Cramer and others, but there are at least three problems with this chestnut:

1. The pinstripes first showed up on team uniforms in 1912 and became a permanent fixture in 1915, five seasons before Ruth's contract was sold to New York;

2. As noted above, Ruth wasn't particularly rotund, especially when he started out with the Yankees;

3. Pinstripes can't make fat people look thin, anyway. Just ask David Wells.

TRAIN IN VAIN

The Babe grew up a Baltimore street urchin and never did lose his childlike sense of adventure. After hitting a home run, he tended to hop and skip and salute and laugh all the way around the bases. During poker games, he never folded his hand. He treated money like so many pieces of paper, routinely tipping bellhops with fifties and thoughtlessly handing over $500 bills to friends in need. Once, at a swanky DuPont estate party, he demonstrated his famous swing with a handy stick of celery. When he appeared at a 1921 ceremony with Generalissimo Ferdinand Foch, formerly of the Allied and Associated Powers for the Western Front, the Babe took one look at the Generalissimo's chestful of medals, then breezily said, "I suppose you were in the war."

There was an amiable recklessness in Ruth, but no real malice. Apart from a handful of fistfights on the ballfield, Babe Ruth never found himself in violent situations, and there's certainly no credible evidence that he ever dangled his manager, Miller Huggins, off the railing of a speeding railroad car. As much as he may have rebelled against Hug, no one ever saw him do anything that stupid or dangerous. Indeed, the only Ruth-era player to repeat the story was the widely despised Leo Durocher, a pool shark–turned–utility man once accused of stealing the Babe's watch.

To the extent that the train tale had any ring of truth, it was probably borne from stories of the Yanks' wild railroad trip back from St. Louis

Ruth, the merry prankster, in disguise before an exhibition game in 1933.

following the 1928 World Series. The Babe, dressed in nothing but his custom silk underwear, made his way amid his triumphant teammates that night, drinking and dancing, striking up group sing-alongs of "The Sidewalks of New York," enlisting Lou Gehrig to help him lead a winding conga line through the railcars. Ruth developed a certain technique for smashing the top out of straw hats and yanking/ripping dress shirts, and almost all the world champions ended up naked from the waist up. It was a heckuva scene, apparently.

When Ruth came across Huggins in the midst of the revels, he didn't dangle him anywhere—though he did try to stuff the jockey-sized (5'6", 140 pounds) manager into one of the railcar's overhead compartments. The next morning it was reported that Hug's dentures were missing and—no one knows how or why—his tiny dog had a hangover.

No arrests were ever made in the Case of the Drunken Chihuahua, but there was one prime suspect.

Managing Myth

The Babe's widow, Claire Hodgson Ruth, often said that one of her late husband's greatest regrets was that he never had the chance to work as a big-time manager. The picture she painted was of the pastime's foremost player, forlorn and forsaken, waiting for a front-office phone call that never did come.

Not quite true. The Babe did want to give managing a go, at least in some vague way, but he never wanted a job enough to actually follow through on it. In the early 1930s, the Yankees offered him the managing job for their top farm club, the talent-rich Newark Bears. He declined. He also turned down several other minor league clubs who offered one- and two-year trial opportunities. In the 1933 off-season, the Detroit Tigers wanted to arrange an interview for their top job; the Babe wanted to take a three-week Hawaiian vacation first. By the time Ruth ventured back from the luau, Detroit had hired someone else.

Curses!

Babe Ruth loved Boston. It was the team that fulfilled his dream by bringing him to the big leagues. It was the city where the masses cheered his first homer titles and celebrated his first championships. He met his wife there, partied there, joined the Knights of Columbus there. Just as soon as he had the necessary money, he settled down in a Sudbury farm during the off-season. When he heard that he'd been (quite involuntarily) sold to the Yankees in 1920, he was quoted calling his former boss a "cheap son of a bitch" and saying, "My heart's in Boston." Leaving aside that Babe Ruth's ever-forgiving, kind heart would forbid him to curse any franchise, he certainly wouldn't have cursed his favorite town's ballclub.

To be sure, Boston and the Red Sox saw more than their share of misfortune in the 80 or so years after the Babe made his way down Old Post Road, but their hardships were hardly Ruth-related. Maybe Dan Shaughnessy called it "the Curse of the Bambino" because "the

Curse of the Racist Owner, Crony-Riddled Front Offices, Incompetent Managers, and Bad Players" wouldn't fit on the book cover.

"THE MOST COMPLETE BALLPLAYER OF ALL TIME"

A lot of people who know almost nothing else about the national pastime believe that Babe Ruth was, without any question, the single most astounding player ever to play the game of baseball. A lot of people are exactly right. With all due respect to the late Ted Williams, only Ruth could walk down the street and have others rightfully declare, "There goes the greatest hitter who ever lived."

Scores of statistics could illuminate that fact, but my favorite one goes to his impact over the entire game. For a modern-day hitter to dominate the 2007 American League like Babe did in seasons such as 1920 or 1927, he would have had to hit anywhere from *315 to 338* home runs on the year. What's more, despite his sweeping, all-or-nothing swings, the Babe was an accomplished contact hitter as well, finishing with a .342 batting average that still leaves him in the top 10 of all time, third highest among those who played most of their games in the post-1920 era. It's an average so astronomically high that he could've finished his career with a 0-for-1,100 slump and *still* retired as a career .300 hitter.

Almost as incredible, Ruth was absolutely lights-out as a starting pitcher, putting up a 94–46 career record along with a stingy 2.28 earned-run average. He ranks among the all-time MLB leaders in winning percentage (he was at 10th place with .671 at the start of the 2008 season) and ERA (14th place). Winning 67 ballgames by age 23, Ruth was on a pace just barely behind Walter Johnson (417 career wins) and Christy Mathewson (373).

Babe Ruth gave up pitching only because his superstardom in the pitching rotation yielded to something like super-duper-stardom in the everyday batting lineup. He was the ultimate—the one man who could outhit all the hitters, then turn around and outpitch all the pitchers. There'll never be another.

Saying that he was the *greatest* ballplayer of all time isn't exactly the same as saying he was the most *complete* player of all time, because the latter term demands production in areas such as fielding and base running. When it came to those somewhat lesser skills, Ruth was all too human.

Blame it on his notoriously short attention span, but in six of the 17 years during which he played at least half a season as a position player, the Babe's fielding percentage was lower than the American League average, and he made enough errors that his career .968 fielding percentage barely outpaced the .966 major league average. Even worse, Ruth had horrendous putout and assist numbers, finishing with a 2.07 range factor, far below the average AL outfielder's 2.22. Statistic guru Bill James gave the Babe an overall "C–" rating with the leather.

Another personal shortcoming, recklessness, might have been responsible for Ruth's weakness at stealing bases. While prolific base stealers like Tim Raines might expect to steal bases with a better than 80 percent success rate, Ruth stole his 123 career bags at an anemic 51 percent rate, one of the worst percentages ever recorded for those with as many as 100 career attempts. The list includes Duane Kuiper and Buddy Bell—not fast company.

In my opinion, the Babe wasn't nearly as complete of a ballplayer as the Mick. Although it's true that Mickey Mantle couldn't pitch or match Ruth's lefty power or batting average, he did have right-handed power Ruth couldn't touch, not to mention multiple years with Gold Glove–quality fielding and league-leading stolen-base totals. Ruth was incredible in what he could do, but only Mantle could do it all.

CHAPTER 2

"Yankee Stadium is 'The House that Ruth Built'"

Babe Ruth seemed to change everything.

Before he arrived in 1920, the Ruth-less Yankees were, in relation to New York's well-established Giants and Dodgers, an afterthought to the afterthought. They first staggered into town in 1903, the shell of a bankrupt Baltimore franchise, and had just seven winning seasons in their first 19 years. Their bare-bones lineup featured "hitters" such as Doc Cook, Harry Wolter, and Birdie Cree* and, though they played in the biggest city in the country, their attendance rarely strayed out of the second division. Befitting their status as the Giants' junior varsity, the Yankees were rent-paying tenants at the older club's Polo Grounds.

Then, with Babe Ruth, suddenly night became day, down was up, and bologna was sirloin. In the Babe's first season, the Yankees put up their highest-ever win total and never looked back, turning in 14 winning seasons in 15 years and gathering seven pennants and four world championships along the glorious way. Attendance soared well over the magical one million level, double and triple previous marks. When the 1923 Yankees opened their new ballpark, the biggest and richest one in the world, of course they called it "the House that Ruth Built." Ruth was the one who turned it all around.

It seemed that way. But it wasn't.

---

*I'd never heard of them, either.

After all, as incredibly skillful and beloved as Ruth may have been, he was just one ballplayer, and all individual ballplayers, no matter how incredible, are ultimately at the mercy of forces larger than themselves. You could ask Robin Roberts, Harmon Killebrew, Juan Marichal, Fergie Jenkins, and dozens of other Hall of Famers how many championships and capacity crowds any one performer could win with an otherwise weak team. They'd say zero because they'd know that, in baseball, nothing was more common than a lone superstar losing out to the kind of strong, top-to-bottom rosters fielded by superior organizations.

Not even Babe Ruth was exempt from that rule of baseball life, and not even Babe Ruth could deliver it to the Yankees. The one who did, the one who truly changed everything, was Colonel Jacob Ruppert Jr.

Ruppert bought the Yankees in 1915, five years before Ruth arrived in New York, and began laying the groundwork for a new era almost immediately. In 1918, he saw something special in a failed Cardinals manager and hired Miller Huggins as his new skipper. Just over two years later, he saw another something special in former minor league promoter/Red Sox skipper Ed Barrow and hired him as his new general manager. Starting off with those two future Hall of Famers in the dugout and front office, Ruppert soon turned his attention to the personnel he'd need on the field, financing big-money acquisitions such as the celebrated Mr. Ruth and spending freely on amateur free agents such as Lou Gehrig and Tony Lazzeri.

Back in the '20s, as in the 2000s, the Yankees were accused of buying their championships, but what distinguished Ruppert wasn't the quantity of money spent but the quality of decisions made. After all, virtually any owner in the majors could have availed himself of the big-money contracts that the Yankees picked up, but only Ruppert had the guts to risk such investments. Any baseball businessman might have flinched when bonus babies such as Lyn Lary and Jimmie Reese flopped, but Ruppert had the patience to emphasize the many deals that did work out. He had the savvy to see how big investments were recouped in the form of goodwill and team pride.

It may have seemed like Ruth's outrageous talent was contagious, but the reality was a bit less mystical—it was because his owner found the best manager and executive in the business and possessed the financial savvy needed to surround the Bambino with talent up and down the roster. Before long, Ruppert created a nonpareil scouting and development network, run by Barrow and junior exec George Weiss, kick-starting a well-oiled machine that would supply Yankee lineups and staffs for three decades after the Babe's 1935 retirement.

If Ruppert was able to create a dominant Yankee organization because he was both richer and smarter than the rest, it was hardly the end of his capability. Unlike most wealthy owners, he also knew how to step back and leave well enough alone. He was humble enough to keep out of the limelight, leaving Huggins and Barrow to do their jobs without any second-guessing and, when his junior partner tried to elbow in, Ruppert simply bought out the guy's shares. Lest anyone else get any ideas about undermining Hug and Barrow from then on, Ruppert refused to set foot in the players' clubhouse, limiting most of his personnel interaction to one-off negotiating sessions at his Knickerbocker Brewery offices on 92nd Street.

The Colonel's famed air of detachment was especially useful when it came to his most important player. Ruppert acquired Ruth from the Red Sox largely because Huggins was confident he could handle the Babe's bad habits, and with Ruppert's steady backing, the "Mighty Mite" did just that. The skipper benched, fined, and suspended the big man whenever his carousing started to interfere with his performance on the field. Huggins was secure in the knowledge that Ruppert would stand firm against the most powerful athlete in the country. Faced with a united front, Ruth inevitably chose to calm down, apologize, and return to making news through binges involving nothing more than home runs.

Finally, beyond the intelligence and cool that first made the Yankees the Yankees, Ruppert was also the true father of the franchise's home. Make no mistake, he was the founding father of Yankee Stadium. River Avenue and 161st Street is the address for "the House that Ruppert Built."

When Ruppert's early maneuvers helped the Yanks to outgrow the Polo Grounds, he scouted out a future ballpark locale in an out-of-the-way Goatville neighborhood across the Harlem River. After buying the Bronx property from the estate of William Waldorf Astor in early 1921, the Colonel approved a truly audacious plan for a ballpark, one that would introduce the first-ever three-deck structure, seat a record 58,000-plus, and leave a footprint almost twice the size of the second-biggest ballpark to that date. For his grand finale, "the Master Builder of Baseball" actually brought the mammoth project in on time and on budget.*

The stadium was the single biggest success in a career full of them, and, in that way, Jacob Ruppert may have guaranteed that, apart from a seldom-visited plaque in Monument Park, he'd be largely forgotten. You see, by the time the Colonel died in 1939, the Yankee franchise had been so thoroughly transformed and had remained dominant for so long that few could fully understand just how far they'd come. It was almost impossible to imagine that they could have ever been the third team in a three-team town. Or that Miller Huggins and Ed Barrow could easily have gone down as a failed manager and some other guy. Or that Babe Ruth might have been known as the out-of-control sort with the potential to wreck a franchise, not save it. Or, God forbid, that Goatville might have continued to host the western Bronx's finest garbage dumps and not "the Cathedral of Baseball."

It was hard to believe that one man could have set so much into motion, but, believe it or not, he did. Ruppert, not Ruth, changed everything.

---

*For those unfamiliar with New York City politics and construction trades, this feat is roughly comparable to piloting a moon mission while simultaneously fiddling a Bach concerto.

CHAPTER 3

Four Facts and One Theory on Jake Ruppert

THE FATHER OF YANKEE STYLE

When Colonel Ruppert first bought his ballclub in 1915, it was still known as the Highlanders in some quarters. He insisted they be known as the Yankees from then on. He took the club's thicker, black pinstripes and had them replaced with the now-iconic thin, blue variety, ordered that the interlocking "NY" be adopted as a uniform feature, and, in 1929, made the Yankees the first club to wear numbers on a regular basis.

You know the elegant frieze that still tops the outer wall beyond center field? The thing that looks like an upside-down white picket fence? Ruppert also commissioned that one, through the designs for the original Yankee Stadium.

In sum, the Colonel helped introduce the most famed team name, uniform, and ballpark decoration in sports. Forget Cooperstown—the man deserves a plaque in the Museum of Modern Art.

THE HIGHER LEAGUE

Jerry Coleman once said that, when he was growing up on the West Coast in the 1930s, there were the major leagues, and then, somewhere above the rest, there was another ballclub. For generation after generation, it was the same story. The Yankees had more wins, headlines, and money than the other teams, but what really set them apart was the special way they carried themselves.

Ruppert had something to do with that. He addressed his employees as business associates, calling Red "Mr. Ruffing" and Lefty "Mr. Gomez," for example. His players always stayed at first-class hotels, ate at gourmet restaurants, and traveled the railways in luxury sleeping and dining cars. Their spring-training base was the four-star Don Cesar Hotel. The Yankees were, literally, cleaner, brighter, and classier than the rest of the league, because they were the first team to use four sets of home and road uniforms and the first to dry-clean them on a daily basis.

Backed, as always, by Ruppert's management acumen, that kind of professional style tended to turn into substance. By the 1930s, skipper Joe McCarthy was telling his men, "You're Yankees. Act like it."

RUPPERT PARK

Ruppert made another completely forgotten contribution to his franchise, and that was in his refusal to take the spotlight at the team's gleaming new venue.

Ego-tripping nomenclature was all the rage back in the ballpark boom of the 1910s and 1920s. Fat-cat owners either named the buildings after themselves (Ebbets Field, Crosley Field) or their related business interests (Fenway Park, Wrigley Field) but, as always, Ruppert was bigger and more unconventional than all that. It was decided that his building would honor not any single person or business but the team itself. In addition, it wouldn't be labeled as just as a field or a park, but as a stadium, the first with that label since the time of the ancient Greeks and Romans. Thus the Colonel ensured that the world would be spared a "Ruppert Park" but would see a "Yankee Stadium," a label that still survives in an era where naming rights are sold to the highest corporate bidder.

DON'T BREAK UP THE YANKEES

Harping opponents cried, "Break up the Yankees" starting in the mid-1920s, and the complaint became a virtual chorus after the '27 club steamrolled through the season. The owner who made the dynasty

Owner Jacob Ruppert (second from left) celebrates the Yankees' 1937 World Series championship. His employees, from left to right: manager Joe McCarthy, Lou Gehrig, and Tony Lazzeri. And a young Joltin' Joe in the front row.

happen didn't want to hear it; Jake Ruppert was the founding father of Yankee swagger.

The Colonel expected his club to win every game. "Why shouldn't they?" he'd ask. He hated close wins, much less losses, and once said that his idea of a perfect day at the ballpark was when "the Yankees score eight runs in the first inning and slowly pull away." When he signed Lefty Gomez after a 26-win season, the owner barked, "Now go out and win 30 games!" When his landlords wanted Ruppert out of the old Polo Grounds, he set off with the parting words, "Yankee Stadium was a mistake. Not mine, but the Giants'." Jake once turned down a chance to buy the Cubs, explaining that he wouldn't be interested in "anything so far from Broadway."*

---

*Take that, Chicago!

As for those who thought maybe the Yanks should take it a little easy on the pretenders to their throne, Ruppert could only grin. He once said, "There is no charity in baseball. I want to win the pennant every year, and the bigger the margin of victory, the better."

Steinbrenner would have loved the guy.

Separated at Birth?

Jake Ruppert was well-rounded (in the bodily sense of the word), sported a bushy white mustache, smoked cigars about the size of babies' arms, and always dressed the part of a wealthy playboy, right down to the immaculate suit and bow tie. He would be in his natural element at a high-society event in a top hat and tails. Ruppert fit the image of the old-time robber baron cliché so well that he may have become its face, serving as the unwitting model for the Rich Uncle Pennybags (also known as Mr. Monopoly) character from the Monopoly board game. It's impossible to know for sure, because no one knows just which artist drew the character in the first place, but we do know that Rich Uncle Pennybags first showed up on the Hasbro games in 1936, when Ruppert was the highly visible leader of the most highly successful sports franchise in the country, the one that played in the media capital of the country. He would have been the obvious pattern for a 1930s plutocrat cartoon, much like Bill Gates would be the obvious model for a new millennium cartoon depicting a computer geek/billionaire.

Some say that the anonymous Monopoly artist may have been channeling J.P. Morgan for inspiration, but Morgan was infamous for his red bulb of a nose. Besides, in 1936, Morgan had been dead for more than 20 years. Call me crazy, but I think Mr. Ruppert may have been Mr. Monopoly.

CHAPTER 4

Wally Pipp's "Headache"

Nobody remembers that Sammy Vick, the 1919 Yankees' right fielder, was replaced by Babe Ruth. Nobody recalls the momentous decision that replaced Gus Niarhos with a young Yogi Berra. And nobody particularly cares that Bob Porterfield lost his spot in the rotation when Whitey Ford showed up. But everybody knows that Wally Pipp was succeeded by Lou Gehrig at first base. That's because Pipp had what the others didn't—he had a story.

It was often said that Mr. Walter Clement Pipp, age 32, was going about his routine for the 1925 Yankees when, one fine day, he was foolish enough to beg out of the lineup, explaining that he had a mild headache. Manager Miller Huggins reluctantly penciled in a rookie, Lou Gehrig, who never did give Pipp a chance to win his job back, seeing as how the Iron Horse didn't miss a day of work for the next 14 years and 2,130 or so ballgames. It was a memorable story. Fictional, but memorable.

Newspaper accounts of 1925 never mentioned anything about a Pipp headache, but they did have plenty of mentions of his terrible slump. He was hitting .244 and had a measly three home runs two months into the season. Pipp had nose-dived into .181 average over the three weeks immediately preceding Gehrig's start on June 2 and was particularly useless against lefties like that day's starter, George Mogridge of the Senators. The Yanks were 15–26, and Pipp wasn't helping a whit.

Pipp was yanked because his poor performance was giving *Huggins* a headache. The skipper was desperate for production at first, probably desperate enough to start Lou Merloni, forget Lou Gehrig.

25

Pipped

Very often, the story behind a story can be more interesting than the story itself. Such is the case with the "headache" myth.

As it happens, the guy most responsible for popularizing the Wally Pipp story is Wally Pipp himself. After he retired from the game in 1928, the former Yankee repeated the tale before dozens of banquet gatherings, later translating the publicity into decades of sportswriting jobs. He worked for a fledgling *Sports Illustrated* in the 1950s. He was famous. Aside from members of the 1927 Yankees, he was virtually the only former teammate invited to Lou Gehrig Appreciation Day in 1939. The story even made it into *Pride of the Yankees*, the (factually liberal) film version of Gehrig's life story.

Why did the story gain traction? Almost certainly because its underlying message fit so well in desperate times. It worked as a cautionary tale to those who'd lived through the worst of the Great Depression's mass unemployment. It said, "Always show up for work or you may find yourself out of a job for the duration. Be careful, or you could be Pipped."

The story may have made Pipp look a little soft, but portraying oneself as slightly less durable than Lou Gehrig has to be the mildest imaginable put-down. I mean, who would feel bad about losing a talent show to the Beatles? Anyway, it was a small price to pay for ensuring that baseball would always (mis)remember Wally Pipp.

One more thing about the headache story: it's often been "debunked" in a way that should itself be debunked. Author Ray Robinson and others have said, "Wally Pipp didn't beg out with a headache, but he did have a skull fracture. That's how Gehrig got his chance." Not true. Pipp was, indeed, hit in the head by a wild batting-practice fastball from Charlie Caldwell, but the resulting concussion didn't happen until *July* 1925, almost a month after Wally had been pushed out of the lineup. Gehrig was already establishing himself as an everyday player at that point, and the Yankees were well on their way to saying goodbye, Mr. Pipp.

CHAPTER 5

Getting Tough with the '27 Yankees

Rolls Royce. Rolex. Cartier. The 1927 Yankees. Some brand names have become synonymous with excellence. While Rolls Royce and Rolex were known for their first-class engineering and Cartier for their superlative jewels, the '27 Yankees were known for their pairing of mighty offense and stingy pitching. Long before they had won 110 games or swept their way through the World Series, the club was widely hailed as epic, historic, the single best team of them all. More than 80 years later, it's still true.

Still, like a lot of superlative claims, it is more often repeated than fact-checked. To see how the "Murderers' Row" Yankees hold up, let's put them up against the Yankees of 1939 and 1998, the only other New York squads to compile a .700+ winning percentage and sweep their way through a World Series.

1) Winning

Hall of Fame manager John J. McGraw once said, "The main idea is to win," and the '27 Yankees did that like no Yankee club before or since. Here is a comparison of the '27, '39, and '98 Yankees in terms of winning percentage, actual record, how their winning percentage translated from a 154-game season to a 162-game season, and their final advantage over their league's second-best ballclub:

Team	Win %	Record	Raw Record Translated	Games Ahead
'27	.714	110–44	116–46	19
'39	.702	106–45	114–48	17
'98	.704	114–48	—	22

Not much to say here. The '98 Yankees did finish with a slightly bigger gap over the second-place Red Sox (and every other team in the AL), but only the '27 Yanks were in first out of the gates and stayed at a Secretariat-like pace throughout the entire season.

Edge: '27

2) Domination

For ordinary mortals, all wins count the same in the standings, but to be considered an all-time team, one has to pulverize the weak (losing record) sisters of the world while also dominating the good (.500+ winning percentage) teams.

Left to right: Lazzeri, Ruth, Gehrig: The kingpins of Murderers' Row.

Here's how the candidates did in their season series against both the AL's losers and winners:

Team	Win % vs. Losers	Win % vs. Winners	Losing Series
'27	.772	.636	0
'39	.788	.635	1
'98	.776	.593	1

Again, the '27 Yanks stand alone. The '39 and '98 Yankees ran up bigger shares of their final win totals against losing ballclubs, if just barely. They both lost a season series each, so congratulations to the plucky 1939 Red Sox and 1998 Angels.

Edge: '27

3) Offense

Apart from the all-important runs-per-game number, the best measures of team offense involve the ability to get on base and hit for power. A handy on-base-plus-slugging average (OPS+) stat combines the two measures while also adjusting for the league's overall offensive level and the team's home ballpark (performance is measured by a club's ability to rise above the "100" norm):

Team	RPG	OBP	SLG	OPS+
'27	6.29	.381	.489	137
'39	6.36	.370	.451	117
'98	5.96	.362	.460	117

Granted, comparing a lineup with guys like Babe Ruth and Lou Gehrig plus Tony Lazzeri and Earle Combs to a lineup featuring Joe DiMaggio and Bill Dickey plus Charlie Keller and George Selkirk is sort of like comparing diamonds to…diamonds. The crowd was the photo-negative of the '62 Mets—*everybody* here could play this game.

Still, one was even more outstanding than the other. The Murderers' Row lineup may not have scored quite as many runs per game as the '39 Yankees, but it outdid the latter in terms of on-base and slugging and, because the '27 league norms represented lesser offensive production, their final OPS+ number is even more impressive.

One final note: among the intriguing "what ifs" in Yankee history involves Lou Gehrig's untimely death. If the Yankees hadn't had to replace the Iron Horse with Babe Dahlgren (.235 batting average, .312 on-base, .377 slugging) early in the '39 season, they would have established a far more explosive lineup, maybe explosive enough to overcome the '27 club. As it is, though...

Edge: '27

4) Pitching

Any franchise nicknamed the Bronx Bombers might slight the pitching side of the game from time to time, but the Yankees' best clubs couldn't have reached their pinnacles without some outstanding performances on the mound.

Here's how the candidates did in terms of earned runs per game, the strikeout-to-bases-on-balls (K/BB) ratio that indicates a domination of the strike zone, and the walks-plus-hits-per-innings-pitched (WHIP) number that indicates how well they shut down base runners. A final ERA+ stat adjusts earned-run average for the league's offensive level and home ball-park conditions (as with OPS+, 100 is set as the historic average):

Team	ERA	K/BB	WHIP	ERA+
'27	3.20	1.05	1.30	120
'39	3.31	1.00	1.32	131
'98	3.82	2.32	1.25	116

The plot thickens.

The '27 Yankee staff had, in Waite Hoyt and Herb Pennock, two future Hall of Famers sporting ERAs of 3.00 or below, plus the American

Lefty Gomez could dominate the league with one leg tied behind his back.

League's best reliever, Wilcy Moore, who played like a Hall of Famer in his single career year. Even the fifth starter, George Pipgras, went 10–3 and finished fourth in the AL in strikeouts per nine innings.

But...the '39 Yankees had Red Ruffing, Lefty Gomez, and friends leading the AL in complete games, shutouts, and saves while throwing at an ERA that was more than 1.30 runs per game better than the average club. That 1939 staff's raw numbers may have been a shade lower than the '27ers in strikeouts-to-walks and just a shade higher in WHIP, but 1939 was a significantly more offense-friendly season than 1927, one where the average AL club was scoring 0.3 more runs per game. Because it adjusts for that fact, the staff's ERA+ stat looks significantly better.

Edge: '39

5) Fielding

Fielding can be broken down into fielding percentage, the number of unearned runs per game, and a Bill James–engineered innovation called defensive efficiency. That last one estimates fielders' ranges by measuring how often batted balls are converted into outs (the more efficient the defense, the better).

Team	Fielding Percentage	UR/G	Defensive Efficiency
'27	.969	.66	.701
'39	.978	.35	.730
'98	.984	.23	.707

Scott Brosius: good fielder, great leaper.

When there superstars all up and down the lineup and rotation, it can be a bit tough to concentrate on the subtle art of fielding, as the '27 Yankees knew all too well. They were fairly—dare I say it?—*bad* in terms of miscues, unearned runs, and inefficiency. At shortstop, Mark Koenig led the AL in errors.

The 1939 Yankees were superior to the '27 club, but the 1998 team was better still, largely due to solid glove guys such as Scott Brosius and Chuck Knoblauch. (This was before Knoblauch began tossing his throws from second base to the box seats.)

Edge: '98

6) Depth

Stars are all fine and good, but baseballs ultimately a team game, one that relies on second-line players doing their share if a ballclubs going to succeed over the long, long, long regular season. The following lists how many reserve contributors could be found on the respective Yankee teams. The position players involved were nonstarters who nonetheless picked up at least 100 at-bats with an above-average OPS and the pitchers weren't #1 to #5 starters nor primary relievers but did pitch at least 50 innings with a better-than-league-average ERA:

Team	Bench Contributors	Contributing Pitchers
'27	1	0
'39	1	3
'98	2	2

Maybe it was the front-liners' dazzling performances, but the '27 Yankees didn't have much bench strength or bullpen depth to speak of. Only 25 players got into games on the year, and among the second-liners, only Mike Gazella made any kind of an impression, hitting .278 in 54 games as Jumpin' Joe Dugan's backup at third base.

The other New York teams, on the other hand, both had several strong players to spare. Tommy Henrich contributed 57 RBIs and good fielding to the 1939 Yanks, while hurlers Steve Sundra (11–1 in 121 innings), Oral Hildebrand (10 wins, 127 innings), and Marius Russo (2.41 ERA, 116 innings) could have been front-end starters on any other team. The 1998 Yankees, for their part, had the aging-but-useful Tim Raines and Chili Davis as subs, plus Ramiro Mendoza and all-but-forgotten Darren Holmes coming in relief.

It's incredibly tough to choose between them, but give the incredibly thin edge to the '39ers, if only because they may have been only team ever to grab more than 300 quality innings from guys relegated to spot starts and middle relief. Even in this bunch, that's unbelievable.

Edge: '39

7) The Time Machine

To recap, the 1927 Yankees won over the competition like no one before, mostly because they had Ruth, Gehrig, and their fellow sluggers dominating the league in offense. Meanwhile, the 1939 Yankees boasted better pitching and a deeper roster, and the 1998 Yanks had fielding on their side, at least. There's one final thing to consider: the time machine factor.

Suppose you could build a contraption to transport you back and forth through the eons. This machine is limited to the national pastime, sadly, so you couldn't use it to say, cure the bubonic plague or kill Hitler or stop George Lucas from making *The Phantom Menace*. You could use the time travel only to pick up old ballclubs from their own era, transport them all into, let's say, 2009, and then compare how they'd play out under the exact same conditions. Who'd win out?

The time-travel thing, of course, ultimately comes down to a question of historical progress. If the game of baseball has gotten easier over the years, you'd expect the old-timers to have the edge over the newer guys. If, on the other hand, the game has become harder and harder, the new players have the advantage.

Well, baseball has gotten harder. Without a question, everything has gotten harder. The 1927 Yankees and, mostly, the 1939 Yankees lived in an entirely different baseball world than the 1998 Yankees. Back then, player conditioning included lifting beer cans and bending elbows at the bar; most players smoked on a daily basis. Studying film was unheard of, the crush of 24/7 media scrutiny unfathomable. Scouting operations barely stretched past the Mississippi River, so no one competed against a global talent pool stretching from Santo Domingo to Sacramento to Seoul. On that basis, if nothing else, the time machine factor must give a big advantage to the 1998 Yankees.

Edge: '98

The Final Tally

Years	1927	1939	1998
Winning	X		
Domination	X		
Offense	X		
Pitching		X	
Fielding			X
Depth		X	
Time Machine			X
Totals	3	2	2

So who comes up on top? Flip a coin. (Three-sided?)

CHAPTER 6

That Scary Batting Practice Story

The ['27 World] Series opened at Pittsburgh's Forbes Field. The day before, the Pirates had made the grave mistake of watching the Yankees take batting practice. Indeed, seeing the entire Yankee lineup pepper all corners of Forbes Field only exacerbated the Pirates' worries about taking on Murderers' Row.
   —Les Krantz, *Yankee Stadium: A Tribute*

Legend has it that the Pirates were spooked before the Series even began when they watched the mighty Yankees pound the ball in a batting practice display.
   —Richard Bak, *Lou Gehrig: An American Classic*

Batting practice. What a lovely sight. Typically, the sun is shining on a lush, green diamond as some old coach is out on the mound, tossing room-service fastballs right down the center of the plate. The batter is in the box, digging in, getting his feel and rhythm. Some fielders might be out in the distance, shagging flies, while the rest of the club is milling around the cage or the dugout, chatting away, trading some jokes. It's prep time, all right, but it's also a joyous rite of the game.

Except once. Once, we're told, it was a tactic. That the '27 Yankees once held a pregame batting practice display that was so impressive that it completely demoralized the opposing Pirates, who subsequently lost the World Series in four straight games.

Possible, but unlikely.

There were no mentions of the fearsome BP in the newspapers of the day, and beyond that, those who were supposed to be so affected by the incident steadfastly denied it. Paul and Lloyd Waner of the '27 Bucs may have said, in passing, something like, "They sure are big, aren't they?" but they always scoffed at the notion that they would be terrorized by a batting practice session.

When you think about it, that makes perfect sense. Batting practice is, after all, practice. Of course New York looked good against the soft-tossing—everybody does. It's easy. It's *supposed* to be easy. A major leaguer getting scared over someone else's run-through would be like an NBA star fearing the way his opponent practices free throws. It wouldn't happen to a professional. Wouldn't happen to a half-decent amateur, even.

The old myth must have less to do with the scenario itself and more to do with the Yankees' power. If the batting practice itself didn't scare the Bucs, maybe it was the Bronx Bombers who did the trick. Here was a team that had Babe Ruth, Lou Gehrig, Tony Lazzeri, Earle Combs, or Bob Meusel at or near the top of every major offensive category. Here was a team that bludgeoned the opposition, hitting almost three times as many home runs as the Pirates (158 vs. 54). Here was a juggernaut that went 110–44, a full 16 games better than Pittsburgh. Here was… **THE 1927 YANKEES.**

All that was true, and the Bronx Bombers did prove to be all-time greats, but in the moment, the '27 Pirates didn't necessarily have to take one good hard look at their opponents and see **THE 1927 YANKEES.** They weren't necessarily facing invincibility. Quite the opposite. They were, potentially, facing vincibility.

After all, it was the Bucs who had actually won more regular-season games than the Yanks over the previous three seasons (273 vs. New York's 270). They had also taken the more recent championship, just two years before, when they beat the 96–game-winning Washington Senators in the World Series. What's more, on the eve of the '27 Fall Classic, Pittsburgh had already beaten the reigning champion Cardinals to take the National League pennant. That is, the very same Cards team that had shocked the heavily favored Yankees in the previous year's World Series.

To be sure, the Pirates knew that the Yanks were huge power hitters and had a superior won-lost record on the year, but they also knew something else: it didn't necessarily matter. That had been the case in all of the Bronx Bombers' pennants to that date, and, heck, the Yankees had lost only three of the four.* In a short series, they could definitely be taken. They *had* been taken, again and again and again.

In the end, of course, it didn't work out for Pittsburgh. In Game 1 of the World Series (right after they were supposedly scared out of their wits) the Pirates lost a tough one-run game. They let the next couple of contests get away from them and dropped the last game by one run in the late innings. If there were a couple consolations in the sweep, it must have been in the fact that the Pittsburgh staff held those mighty New York sluggers to just two home runs while the Waner brothers hit well.

In the end, the Pirates didn't play scared. They just got beat.

---

*Hard to believe, isn't it? Babe Ruth had a single (1923) World Series championship to show for his first seven years in pinstripes, 1920 through 1926.

CHAPTER 7

"Babe Ruth Called His Shot in the '32 World Series"

This much is certain: on October 1, 1932, the New York Yankees were visiting the Chicago Cubs to play Game 3 of the World Series. New York had won the first two games, but the teams were knotted at 4–4 with one out and the bases empty in the fifth inning. Babe Ruth came up to the plate against Cubs starter Charley Root,* then worked a 2–2 count as players from Wrigley Field's home dugout conveyed multiple comments on the Bambino's parents, sexual habits, age, and looks. They were all unkind comments.

From here, accounts diverge. Several witnesses declared that Ruth merely gestured to the dugout and to Root while mouthing something like "one strike left" or "it only takes one to hit it." Others swore that, to the contrary, the Babe was actually pointing beyond the mound and out to center field, as if to mark the direction where he intended to blast a ball out of the park. On that next pitch, the Babe *did* hit a booming homer, which had to mean—didn't it?—that he'd just called his own shot.

---

*Maybe the most memorable batter/pitcher confrontation of all time, and it goes down as Ruth/Root. Weird.

Yankee teammates such as Lou Gehrig (who was the on-deck hitter), Joe Sewell, and Bill Dickey, as well as spectators such as Ray Kelly (a close friend of the Babe) all backed the "called shot" view. Cubs opponents like Gabby Hartnett (the catcher), Woody English, Charlie Grimm, and Burleigh Grimes were just as vehement that the gesture never happened. Predictably, the version that has held up over time is the most dramatic, the one that makes the Babe look most heroic.

Other accounts, however, cast considerable doubt on the "called shot" view. The Yankees were hardly unanimous in backing Ruth, for one. Ruth friends Mark Koenig and Frank Crosetti plus straight-shooting manager Joe McCarthy all denied that the Babe pointed out to center field. When interviewed shortly after the game, Ruth himself refused to make the claim, instead saying, "Why don't you read the papers? It's all there." Also, only a single on-site reporter, Joe Williams of the *New York World-Telegram*, supported the story on the day of the game, though it caught fire quickly afterward.

Common sense says that, if something as extraordinary as a batter calling his shot: *a home run...to center field...in a World Series game...in front of a huge crowd of spectators*, it would have been banner headline material like, "MAN WALKS ON THE MOON!" If ESPN had been around in 1932, it probably would have looped the replay for days, weeks. Certainly, Yankees, reporters, and thousands of spectators would have affirmed it on the spot. The fact that they *didn't* do that strongly indicates that Ruth jabbered and gestured to Root in some way that may have left itself to interpretation after the fact, with more overexcited Ruth fans (and their allies) seeing what they wanted to see while more sober observers saw the average batter's gesticulation.

If all that isn't quite enough to cast a dark shadow of a doubt on the "called shot" story, put yourself in Root's cleats in the moment. If the Chicago starter had indeed seen Ruth promise a home run shot to center field, he would have read it as an unforgivable insult between two honorable opponents. The stunt would have been absolutely infuriating if the pointer had been playing a run-of-the-mill game at home. The fact that it was a World Series and in Chicago's house would have come across as something beyond infuriating. Additionally, Charlie Root had finished in the top 10 in hit batsmen seven times in the nine seasons between 1926 and 1934; if he'd truly seen such a declaration, his only decision would have been whether to stick the next fastball in either Ruth's ear or his ribs. The fact that Root responded to the Ruth gesture not with a bean ball but with a hittable strike, speaks to the strong likelihood that the Babe didn't cross a line that demanded retaliation.

When you think about it, though, the enduring appeal of the story isn't about what Ruth may or may not have done one time a long time ago, but about the man's status as an incomparable slugger, a world-class showman. Regardless of what happened in the particulars of the Root at-bat, the "called shot" resonated because he was regarded as the kind of crowd-pleaser capable of fulfilling bold, fate-tempting predictions.

And you know what? He was. His truth was stranger than fiction.

Quite apart from Ruth's almost humdrum, daily greatness as a hitter, there *were* occasions when multiple witnesses saw the Babe openly forecast his next home run. Recent biographies by authors Bill Jenkinson and Leigh Montville recount several of them:

- **Polo Grounds, May 1918:** While still a full-time pitcher for the Red Sox, Ruth hits a tremendous line drive down the right field line. When umpire Billy Evans calls the ball foul, the Babe is heard to say, "I'll hit this [next] one right back and there'll be no doubt about it." And he did.
- **Comiskey Park, May 1923:** As the Yankees–White Sox game dragged into the fourteenth inning of a 1–1 tie, the club's traveling secretary, visibly nervous, mentioned that the ballclub was in danger of missing the train home. Ruth said, "Is that all? Watch!" and immediately hit a home run. When the Sox were retired in the bottom of the inning, the team made it aboard the 20th Century Limited with time to spare.

- **Toronto, August 1923:** In a scenario that would've fit well in the supernatural plot of *The Natural*, Ruth makes a pre-game prediction that he would swat a ball off a center-field clock tower during an exhibition match. Moments later, he hit a batting practice shot. Directly. Off. The. Clock.
- **Sportsman's Park, October 1926:** As noted previously, Ruth promised a sick little boy that he'd hit a home run in Game 4 of the 1926 World Series, then came through with *three* four-baggers in St. Louis.
- **Yankee Stadium, June 1927:** On the eve of a scheduled visit from aviator Charles Lindbergh, the Babe cut short his batting practice, explaining that he felt a homer coming for game time. Then, in the third inning, he...oh, you already guessed.
- **Sportsman's Park, October 1928:** In the seventh inning of Game 4 of the 1928 World Series, Ruth exchanged angry words with Cardinals pitcher Willie Sherdel, who had won 21 games on the year. He said, "Put one right here and I'll knock it out of the park for you," and on the very next pitch, did just that. (Just to make the incident a bit more spectacular, the dinger happened to be Ruth's third of the game.)
- **New York, September 1932:** Even on the eve of the '32 World Series, Ruth may have been "calling" his immediate future, sort of. Just before the Fall Classic began, the Bambino told Ray Kelly, his young friend, to travel with the team over to Chicago because he thought the Yankees would sweep the Cubs in four straight. They did.

Now, credibility can be a slippery thing, so maybe one of those incidents was overblown. Maybe more than one, but not *all* of them. It should be noted that even Koenig, who said the "called shot" never happened, did confirm similar incidents: "He would come into the dugout on some days and say, 'I feel good, I think I'll hit one,' and, by

God, he always did." McCarthy recalled the Babe similarly predicting a homer in May 1933. "He said, 'I feel good. I think I'm going to bust one today.'"

So, in the end, so what if Babe Ruth's called shot was a myth? Babe Ruth was always capable of summoning something magical, and *that's* no myth.

CHAPTER 8

Cal Ripken = Lou Gehrig

For as long as fans talk about baseball, they'll talk about Lou Gehrig and Cal Ripken Jr. The two will always be linked. Both came up as heralded two-way prospects, stars in both hitting and pitching who had enough surplus talent to excel in other sports. Both signed with their hometown organizations—Gehrig with New York and Ripken with Baltimore—and stayed there for their full careers. Both played through multiple MVP, All-Star, and pennant-winning seasons. Both were first-ballot Hall of Famers.

Above all these similiarities, Lou and Cal were known for their talent, work ethic, and good luck in playing consistently throughout every year. When Gehrig set a record by playing 2,130 consecutive games from 1925 to 1939, most people said that the mark would never be broken. It wasn't until Ripken surpassed it in 1995, an occasion marked by a presidential visit, exploding fireworks, unfurled banners, orchestral music, a tearful tour around Camden Yards, and a mini-speech acknowledging Gehrig's legacy. The ovation alone lasted nearly 20 minutes. Years afterward, a poll sponsored by Major League Baseball named the Gehrig/Ripken ceremony the number five most memorable moment in the game's history.

As long as baseball is baseball, it's fair to say that the Iron Horse and the Iron Man will represent the gold standard of durability in the sport with the longest, most grueling schedule. But the two stars had many more differences than similarities. The closer you examine them, the more you see that they were neither comparable players nor were their streaks comparable feats.

The first point of departure for the two is in their hitting. Ballplayers sometimes call number four the "hard number" and the Yankees' only No. 4 put up a lifetime's worth of hard numbers.

Gehrig was, if not the single greatest hitter who ever lived, among the handful of top contenders for the title. He was good enough to finish behind only Babe Ruth and Ted Williams in 20th-century on-base percentage and slugging. In the 12 years following his rookie year in 1926 to his last fully healthy season in 1937, he was all over the American League leader boards in everything from batting average to bases on balls and homers. His achievements were so superlative that his *worst* season numbers included a .300 batting average, .420 OBP, and the .549 slugging that came from 83 extra-base hits.

Though Ripken was considered a very good hitter, Gehrig's numbers were light years ahead. Lou's superiority to Cal in everything from career batting (.340 vs. .276), on-base percentage (.447 vs. .340) and slugging (.632 vs. .447) generates the same marked difference that separates Ripken from Mario Mendoza (.215/.245/.262), who's generally acknowledged as the worst major league hitter since the 1960s with more than 1,000 at-bats.

Rip did end up with more than 3,000 career hits and 400 homers, which is very nice and all, but the totals are a function of being good for a long, long (more than 3,000 games played) time.

In a wider context, Gehrig's raw numbers actually tend to understate his real importance. As the Yankees' cleanup hitter *par excellence*, he delivered a double benefit to the club. His talent at the plate forced pitchers' hands; they had to go after Babe Ruth with strikes and fastballs, lest they face Gehrig with a runner on base. Even in the rare times when Gehrig might have been slumping, his epic reputation was enough to force opposing pitchers to press, setting up the hitters before and after his cleanup spot. He was an RBI threat, a Ruth bodyguard, and a home-run machine, so his absence would have meant significant team losses in both power and protection.

Sure, Rip won a couple of Gold Gloves and put up sterling numbers in fielding percentage and range, but the difference between his fielding and the league average worked out to about one extra error for about every 100 plays, perhaps one-third of an extra assist or putout per game, and a fractional increase in the likelihood of a double play. He was a good glove man, but even a good glove man's contribution doesn't compare to the slugger who delivered a major league–record .92 RBI for every game played.

What do Gehrig's superior numbers and team impact have to do with his consecutive games streak? Everything. They meant that his everyday play was linked to everyday winning, and it was true even when he was quite clearly hurt. As some historians have noted, the Yankee captain nearly skipped out on several games in 1934 due to concussions and a severe cold and flu, but even in those moments, Gehrig was still Gehrig—he produced six hits in six at-bats in the "concussion games" and he hit two homers, two doubles, and tallied seven RBIs. Even at his weakest and worst, Lou was still capable of helping the team.

The fact that Ripken couldn't claim Gehrig's level of day-to-day productivity means that his lineup spot didn't have the same impact. There were plenty of days when Ripken's performance dictated that he could have or should have been benched in favor of a hotter hitter. Take his matchups against the following right-handed pitchers, for instance:

	AB	BA	OBP	SLG	OPS
Jaime Navarro	52	.192	.232	.308	.540
Juan Guzman	41	.171	.222	.268	.490
Eric Plunk	36	.139	.205	.222	.427
Chad Ogea	31	.097	.200	.129	.329
Rick Helling	30	.167	.194	.267	.461

Better yet, take the following four months:

	AB	BA	OBP	SLG	OPS
September 1988	118	.216	.314	.255	.568
September 1989	116	.198	.284	.356	.641
July 1992	126	.178	.286	.215	.501
August 1992	120	.218	.267	.255	.521

That September '89 mark is particularly interesting, as Ripken's late-season meltdown coincided with the Orioles' tumble from first place to two games out in the standings.

Virtually every hitter (except Lou Gehrig) has some matchups and endures slumps when he just can't buy a base hit, and the team-first choice is to move in capable substitute, at least for a game or two. Ripken should have been no exception, yet he kept on playing.* And playing. And playing.

Now, I'm no major league manager, but if I saw that my shortstop couldn't hit his weight in a certain matchup or over a certain month, I'd give him a little breather and use someone, *anyone* else. I'd put in Manny Alexander and hope for the best. I'd play Jeff Manto and clutch my lucky horseshoe. Tim Hulett. The bat boy. Volunteers from the grandstand.

Rip said that, like Gehrig, he was a team-first, lunch pail–to–work kind of fellow. "I've always felt that you came to the ballpark and my responsibility to the team was to be available to play." "It was a result of the determination to keep as much of my destiny as possible in my hands." "I had showed up and honored the game of baseball by playing as well as I could and as often as I could." "It was just about being reliable and professional, going out to play every day."

The humble talk well enough, at least to those who desperately wanted to believe the autograph-friendly hometown hero had made

---

* Bud Selig once exclaimed, "Who would they rather have had playing shortstop? That's the question." Glad you asked, Commissioner.

good, maybe even saved the national pastime from its collapse after the '94 strike. Very few have questioned the exalted St. Calvin's motives.

But how about a tiny little reality check? Plenty of tough guys have come along the pike with a Ripken-like commitment to playing and winning every single day, no matter what. To name just three, Brooks Robinson, Frank Robinson, and Pete Rose all played 95 percent or more of their teams' games for a decade or more. All three eventually decided that a brief rest, maybe a half-dozen games per year, was needed for their productivity in the long term. It was only common sense. No amount of bounce-back ability can make up for the pounding that goes into playing a near-daily six-month season—especially when a given contest is, say, the 13th ballgame in two weeks, a 100-degree day game in Texas, the second game of a doubleheader, or a day game following a night game. All ballplayers (and their managers) know how crucial a day of rest can be to a wearied player.

The smart move is to take a step back, then take a couple steps forward.

The unstated but unmistakable claim is that Ripken was, by some mysterious means, an exception to all that wear and tear, that he kept on keeping on because he was somehow tougher, more willful, and more joyous than the rest. Hmmmm. Tougher than Brooks Robinson, who played through enough bumps and bruises, stiffness and soreness, strains and sprains, and tweaks and tears to fill one of Dr. Bobby Brown's medical textbooks? More willful than Frank Robinson, who played like a man possessed, even after a 1967 second-base collision left him with persistent double-vision and vertigo? More joyous than Rose, the MLB career leader in showing up first and leaving last every day?

As Jim Bouton once said, "Yeah, surrre."

No, what really set Ripken apart from Gehrig, and virtually everyone else who played major league baseball, was the fact that he had the leverage to impose his consecutive game streak on his ballclub. The Iron Man was, in effect, the Teflon Man. He was bigger than the Orioles, and he had no problem with repeatedly proving it, either.

Try to imagine Lou Gehrig taking his own private limo service from the team plane or staying apart from the team in a separate road hotel. Imagine him calling pitches without his manager's knowledge, much less permission. Or forming a faction of clubhouse cronies and freezing out would-be job challengers. Or inviting a traveling circus full of record-fawning reporters into his clubhouse for months on end. Gehrig would have eaten his first baseman's mitt before he tried any of that prima donna bull. But Ripken did it all and had a lot more pull besides.

In May 1996, for instance, when manager Davey Johnson pulled him in the late innings for a pinch runner, the silent, stone-faced Ripken sat on the bench with his arms crossed, responded to postgame media queries with an icy "no comment," then gave Johnson the silent treatment as the Cal-centric media roasted the skipper. In September 1999, the Pride of Baltimore tried to get the team plane delayed because he was held up in traffic, and when general manager Frank Wren ordered the team to leave without him, it was Wren who was reprimanded, then fired. Oh, also, someone by the oddly familiar name of Billy Ripken hung on to the Baltimore roster for some six years despite a pathetic career OPS+ of 69.

Of course, Rip wasn't in charge of the club. His managers, *theoretically*, were always free to put the legendary Cal Ripken in his place and out of the lineup. His managers were also, theoretically, free to be attacked by an angry mob wielding pitchforks and torches. Even so, after a while, those who wanted to stay healthy and/or employed eventually figured out who was really calling the shots back in Bawlmer. As Johnny Oates once put it, "The Streak is bigger than Johnny Oates and even bigger than the game itself." Or so he said, anyway.*

---

* In 2001, during Ripken's last, undeserved All-Star Game appearance, the vastly superior Alex Rodriguez felt compelled to cede his place as starting shortstop to Ripken. Later in the game, NL pitcher Chan Ho Park served Ripken a slow fastball so he could finish with a (bogus) home run. No one said a word. By then, *everyone* was drinking the Kool-Aid. Many still are.

Ripken got away with it all, though, year after year, and even developed a ready array of rhetorical tricks. When Brooks Robinson and Joe Morgan had the guts to come out and say that the continuation of his streak was "detrimental" and "selfish and obsessive," Rip asked "Can you guarantee me that if I take a day off the next day will be any better?"(Well, other than the fact that fresher legs and a clear mind tend to help in playing ball…) At other times No. 8 would say, "If you could play baseball every day, wouldn't you?" Or he'd lean back and opine that, "Some people will never understand why I go about the things the way I do" (Buddy, we understood just fine).

Leaving aside the obvious artificiality and ego-tripping behind Ripken's streak, though, was the fact that the media actually managed to turn it around and make it a nauseating story of selflessness. It wasn't, not compared to the story Lou Gehrig authored.

Gehrig obviously didn't need his consecutive games streak to establish himself as one of the best sluggers who ever lived, and he never continued it for any reason other than the work's crystal-clear benefit to his Yankees. It wasn't widely mentioned in the national press until 1933, when he passed the previous (1,307-game) consecutive game record, and, as far as we know, it was never tied to any financial bonuses or endorsements. Fame and fortune were never high on the modest man's personal agenda.

Those who knew Gehrig best believed he took pride in his resilience, to be sure, but saw a deep-seated sense of insecurity as a motivating force. He seemed to live with a real, if completely unfounded, fear that he might lose his job if he took off a single day—a fear heightened by the fact that he married during a time when millions of hungry men were standing in the Great Depression's breadlines. To the extent that we can understand Lou Gehrig's true motivations, his streak was a testament to nothing but his urge to compete and to provide for his family.

Ripken, though? Not so much. The streak was, for all his claims to the contrary, his obsession and his meal ticket. Cal Ripken Jr. has a lower career batting average than Richie Hebner, a lower OBP than Aubrey Huff, a lower adjusted OPS than Solly Hemus, and fewer Gold Gloves than Roy McMillan. But he did have a first-ballot Hall of Fame induction. He has three books, his own computer game, a satellite radio show, and his own namesake section on Interstate 395. He's done commercials for pickup trucks, sugar water, shoes, theme parks, insurance...you name it, he sells it. He bought a minor league franchise and named it "the IronBirds." On Hall of Fame weekend, his marketing firm set up its own trailer in Cooperstown to peddle IronClad Authentics, a line of sports-related apparel, tchotchkes, and memorabilia. Heroism has been very, very good for business.

To believe that Cal Ripken didn't notice all he's gained from passing Gehrig's record is to believe he didn't notice that a baseball is round and the grass is green. Unfortunately, the Iron Man and the Iron Horse will always be linked, despite their differences.

CHAPTER 9

What Really Happened on Lou Gehrig Day

In the early 1900s in Morningside Heights, German immigrants Christina and Heinrich Gehrig hoped that their only child would grow up to be an architect or engineer. If he hadn't taken time out of his studies at Columbia University to hit screaming home runs off the steps of Low Library, surely that's what Lou Gehrig would have become. Great physical blessings ensured that he'd enjoy a career with the New York Yankees instead.

Sadly, a great physical misfortune ensured his career would all end long before its time. It was called amyotrophic lateral sclerosis. In the 1930s, as today, doctors knew that the condition struck about 5,000 Americans per year and caused a slow but persistent degeneration of the neurons of the brain and the spinal cord. They knew that the condition was painless, that it left the mind unaffected, and that it did not transmit to others. What they didn't know was what caused it or how to slow its paralyzing effect on the muscles, and, most important, how to stop it before it killed.

Gehrig may have suffered symptoms of the disease as early as 1937, when he was 34 years old; by 1938, he knew something was terribly wrong. Throughout the year, he had experienced clumsiness and trouble with his balance. His body became prone to periods of drastic slowing and weakness, especially around the hands and feet. There were strange moments when he could hardly handle a cocktail shaker or walk up a

Lou Gehrig, speaking from the heart

flight of stairs. At first, Gehrig responded in the only way he knew, by working. His already-rigorous exercise sessions increased in frequency and intensity. He began using lighter and thinner bats and somehow learned to overcome his faltering body through a combination of playing smarts and mechanical adjustments.

Incredibly enough, even as he was becoming more debilitated and terrified by the changes to his body, Gehrig still played every game on the 1938 schedule *and* put up a .295 batting average, .410 on-base percentage, and .523 slugging percentage. At age 35 and in, at best, a semi-healthy state, he still produced an on-base-plus-slugging number (OPS) superior to the career levels of Hall of Famers such as Billy Williams, Tony Gwynn, and Rod Carew.

By the spring of 1939, however, not even Gehrig could deny the undeniable. His symptoms and performance only grew worse and worse, to the point where teammates feared for his safety on the field. When a well-meaning teammate congratulated him for making a routine play, Lou knew that he couldn't go on. Finally, after playing the Tigers on April 30, the most resilient baseball player of his era asked manager Joe McCarthy to pull him from the Yankee lineup. He'd played his 2,164th and last game in a Yankee uniform.

On June 13, the still-active Gehrig and his wife, Eleanor, traveled to Rochester, Minnesota, to undergo observation at the country's most respected medical research center, the Mayo Clinic. His attending physician, Dr. Henry Woltman, ran every possible test to eliminate the worst-case scenario. On Gehrig's 36th birthday, he gave the official ALS diagnosis. The staff members later said that their celebrity patient seemed relieved, more than anything, to have an end to the unknowns.

Days later, when the clinic issued a statement referring to ALS as "chronic poliomyelitis, or infantile paralysis," most columnists and reporters mistook the import of the news. They assumed that Gehrig's condition was akin to polio, a serious condition that had crippled President Roosevelt but one that rarely proved fatal. One of the New York dailies reported "that Gehrig ultimately will win out in his fight for complete health," and Joe DiMaggio was quoted saying, "Don't count out Lou just because he's taking the first rest he's had in years." Virtually no one realized that it wasn't just Gehrig's career but his life that was slowly ending. Whether because he shunned the extra sympathy or attention, Lou never explained otherwise.

The Yankee organization responded to the Mayo press release by immediately scheduling a Lou Gehrig Appreciation Day. From the start, the event was destined to be special. Most such commemorations were scheduled for weekdays to provide the team with an extra attendance boost, but this time the front office bypassed that kind of ploy, instead holding the captain's day on the most visible possible occasion, the Fourth of July. Gehrig was the last active player from the World Champion 1927 Yankees, and the front office arranged for nearly a dozen of his former teammates to reunite for the first time. Out of respect for the player he first signed 16 years before, General Manager Ed Barrow would walk on the Yankee Stadium diamond for the first time in nearly 20 years.

Gehrig dreaded it.

He may have worked in the most public of careers, but by instinct he was a painfully soft-spoken and shy person who preferred to communicate through actions. He could go through entire days or weeks with hardly more than perfunctory chatter. One opponent, Charlie Gehringer, once said that, apart from a hearty handshake and a hello, Gehrig hardly spoke a word to him in 13 full seasons. He wasn't the type to get up and expound before friends in a living room, much less a stadium full of strangers.

Nonetheless, Independence Day arrived with a hot and sticky afternoon. Ceremonial red, white, and blue bunting, otherwise seen only during the World Series, was hung from Yankee Stadium's white frieze and upper decks. A capacity crowd of more than 61,000 rushed through the turnstiles. In the clubhouse before the game, most of the '27 Yankees traded reminiscences.

After the Yankees lost the first game of their scheduled doubleheader against the Washington Senators, attendants began setting up microphones and chairs in the area around home plate. Soon enough, the 1939 and 1927 Yankees, still the two greatest clubs in the franchise's history, found themselves arrayed behind the setup, the former in home pinstripes and the latter in dark business suits—except Ruth, who was incapable of doing anything somberly. The late-arriving Bambino was dressed in an impossible-to-miss all-white outfit.

The Lou Gehrig who slowly walked out to the ballplayers was fast becoming unrecognizable. His wavy brown hair had grayed, his handsome face was drawn, his once-bulging muscles had already begun to wither away. Lou self-consciously avoided eye contact with the players and fans alike, instead twisting a cap in his hands, shuffling his cleats, and occasionally dabbing his eyes with a handkerchief.

As the ceremony began, the man of the hour was presented with various gifts, including silver platters, a fishing rod and tackle, a silver cup, and a scroll from the Old Timers' Association. The Senators presented him a ceremonial scroll with the words "**DON'T QUIT**," and the Yanks' crosstown rivals, the Giants, donated candlesticks. Gehrig accepted the gifts and praise without a word of his own. After dignitaries such as Mayor Fiorello LaGuardia expressed their respects, McCarthy stood up to say, "It was a sad day in my life when you told me you were quitting because you felt you were a hindrance to the team.... My God, you were never that!"

It wasn't long before the master of ceremonies, Sid Mercer, called on Gehrig to address the crowd. After a long moment, he shook his head and stepped back. Mercer nodded and said, "Lou has asked me to thank all of you. He is too moved to speak," but the fans responded, chanting, "We want Gehrig! We want Gehrig!" For a moment, no one knew what to do.

McCarthy whispered in Gehrig's ear, most likely urging him to speak, so Gehrig, who always did what he was told, slowly raised his hand, as if to silence the noise. As he stepped up to the microphone, McCarthy quietly told Lou's replacement, Babe Dahlgren, to stand next to him, just in case he collapsed from the strain.

There was no ghostwriting for the words that came next. In fact, there was no writing at all. Gehrig simply spoke from the heart:

> *Fans, for the past two weeks you have been reading about the bad break I got. Yet today I consider myself the luckiest man on the face of the earth.*
>
> *I've been in ballparks for 17 years and have never received anything but kindness and encouragement from you fans. Look at these grand men. Which of you wouldn't consider it the highlight of his career just to associate with them for even one day?*
>
> *Sure I'm lucky. Who wouldn't consider it an honor to have known Jacob Ruppert? Also, the builder of baseball's greatest empire, Ed Barrow? To have spent six*

*years with that wonderful little fellow, Miller Huggins?
Then to have spent the next nine years with that
outstanding leader, that smart student of psychology, the
best manager in baseball today, Joe McCarthy?*

*Sure I'm lucky. When the New York Giants, a
team you would give your right arm to beat, and vice
versa, sends you a gift, that's something. When everybody
down to the groundskeepers and those boys in white coats
remember you with trophies, that's something. When
you have a wonderful mother-in-law who takes sides
with you in squabbles with her own daughter, that's
something.*

That last line prompted some muted laughter. Almost in spite
himself, Gehrig grinned, too, before continuing:

*When you have a father and a mother who work all
their lives so you can have an education and build your
body, it's a blessing. When you have a wife who has been
a tower of strength and shown more courage than you
dreamed existed, that's the finest I know.*

*So I close in saying that I may have had a tough
break, but I have an awful lot to live for.*

The response was immediate. As the visibly shaken Gehrig stepped
from the mic, the crowd gave him a deafening ovation that lasted several
minutes. Sportswriter Shirley Povich later recounted, "I saw strong men
weep this afternoon." For the first time in his adult life, DiMaggio was
among them.

Just as the honoree began to walk away, Ruth stepped up to
embrace him, speaking to him for the first time in nearly five years.
The applause and music of the Seventh Regiment Band covered the
conversation, but whatever was said, it made the two of them laugh.

The Picture

Just seconds after Lou Gehrig completed his "luckiest man" remarks on July 4, 1939, Babe Ruth rushed to embrace him as the house band struck up a tune called "I Love You Truly" as the crowd chanted, "We love you, Lou!" The photograph that captured the moment may be the most famous, and misunderstood, image in Yankee history.

In the picture, Ruth has his beefy arms around Gehrig, who is smiling but keeping his own hand at his side. Because the two had had a falling out some years before, many observers, Bill Dickey among them, took Gehrig's nonresponse to mean that he didn't reconcile with Ruth. That wasn't it. The fact is, Gehrig didn't embrace Ruth because he was physically incapable of doing so. The disease that was killing him made it impossible for him to hold the gifts he'd received minutes before. Immediately upon receiving them, he set them down on the ground. Summoning the strength to return Ruth's bear hug was out of the question.

What that Gehrig-Ruth picture represented, instead, was the two great ones' reconciliation, the beginning of their final peace. In the last months of Gehrig's life,

Ruth and his wife visited the Gehrigs' home frequently, most often to recollect their off-season barnstorming days or raucous championship celebrations. When his teammate died, the Babe came before his coffin and broke down in tears. He'd lost a dear, dear friend.

The image from that moment was captured in perhaps the most iconic photograph in Yankee history.

The months after Lou Gehrig Day were a blur. The team's former captain stayed in uniform and still carried the lineup card out to home plate, invariably drawing a huge round of applause, but as his coordination further deteriorated it became harder to maintain any kind of active role. More and more frequently, he would retreat to a side supply room, alone, later emerging with bloodshot eyes.

At the end of the '39 season, Gehrig's teammates voted him a full share in their World Series victory, the front office announced that No. 4 would be the organization's first retired number, and Cooperstown inducted him by acclamation. All the honors were bittersweet; Gehrig knew it was impossible for him to continue as a baseball man. After the season ended, he left Yankee Stadium, never to return.

The courage displayed on Lou Gehrig Day never left him, however. He worked for the city government's parole board for as long as he could still function, answered some of the more than 30,000 fan letters he received, and welcomed dozens of old players, writers, and old friends at his home on Delafield Avenue in the Bronx. Visitors invariably found him cheerful and accommodating, ever willing to discuss his memories, take in Mel Allen's radio broadcasts, and talk up the Yanks' chances for the upcoming seasons. Gehrig thought the Yanks had a good chance to take it all in '41 and, as it turned out, he was right.

He was, most remarkably, without a trace of self-pity in his last days. When surrounded by barely composed, incredibly saddened friends, he constantly claimed that he would, as countless times before, manage to come back and rally one last time. He'd say that it would get bad, that he'd hobble around with a cane, but he'd live. It's unclear that Gehrig even discussed his true diagnosis with Eleanor, presumably hoping to spare her the grief. Perhaps the outward acknowledgment of the fate was impossible because Lou was so used to enduring and winning.

At the very end, the man who was once the strongest slugger in the major leagues, whose line drives could smash bleacher seats to splinters and tear gloves from infielders' hands, became weaker and weaker. Eleanor later compared it to a radio signal fading into the distance or a mighty clock winding down into stillness. Finally, after becoming unable to walk, talk, swallow, or breathe, Henry Louis Gehrig's struggle ended. Not yet 38 years old, on June 2, 1941, the youngest Hall of Famer became the youngest to pass away.

In the next days Gehrig's body was visited by thousands of mourners at the Church of the Divine Paternity at Central Park West & 76th Street. Many more stood in the pouring rain during services at the Christ Episcopal Church in Riverdale, but by then there were no more words. Rather than deliver a eulogy, the pastor said, "You all knew him."

CHAPTER 10

Mickey Myths

Baseball abounds in stories. There are screwball stories, cheating stories, media stories, carouser stories, drinking stories, gambling stories, firing stories, groupie stories, and on and on. But as far as I know, there's only one story about a spring training debut.

The way it's told, Mickey Charles Mantle arrived at the Yankee camp in Phoenix in February 1951 and he absolutely dazzled. Without exception, teammates and eyewitnesses reported seeing someone who could hit 400-foot home runs right-handed, who could hit 400-foot home runs left-handed, who could outrun a thoroughbred and had a cannon for an arm. No one claimed that the fresh-from-the-minors prospect was faster than a speeding bullet, more powerful than a locomotive, or able to leap tall buildings at a single bound, but from then on, just about everything else seemed possible.

Recently, Walt Dropo, who had played against the Yankees during that spring-training season, said the 19-year-old Mick had Rickey Henderson's kind of speed and Mark McGwire's kind of power. Frank Crosetti, who was around major league baseball for more than 60 years, said No. 7 had more raw talent than any player he'd ever seen. Fellow prospect Tom Sturdivant said the kid with the storybook name was "probably the greatest athlete who ever lived."

Here was a figure ripe for some media mythmaking, and mythmake the media did.

Three To First

The first story, repeated in books such as Peter Golenbock's *Dynasty*, related to Mantle's speed. It was said that the teenage Mickey could make it from home plate to first base in 3.1 seconds while batting from the right side, 3.0 from the left. Always, it is those same 3.1/3.0 numbers. Averaging them at 3.05 seconds, Mantle would have traveled the 90 feet from home plate to first at the blistering pace of 29.5 feet per second.

Just how fast is that, exactly? Well, in 1951, the 100-yard dash record was held by Mel Patton, whose 10.3-second time translates into a pace of 29.1 feet per second. The 3.1/3.0 story is, therefore, a claim that Mickey Mantle was, in his day…the fastest man in the world.

Actually, the young Mantle would have to be even faster than those times would indicate at first glance, because his speed didn't come in anything close to an equivalent condition. Remember, Mantle had to take a big home-run hack immediately before running, wore a flapping flannel uniform, ran in clunky baseball spikes, and churned

The Rookie Card That Wasn't

When is a second-year player considered a rookie? When he's Mickey Mantle. The Mick's debut baseball card has long been among the most precious of all sports collectibles, but most who refer to the rookie card aren't talking about the first mass-produced card to feature Mantle's likeness, the Bowman Company's #253 card from 1951. Instead, they're usually making a mistaken reference to the card put out for his second playing year, the #311 card produced by the Topps Company in 1952.

The confusion basically comes down to the fact that Bowman's version isn't highly valued in terms of its artwork, size, and the statistical info printed on the back. Topps' card, on the other hand, is respected by collectors for its superior quality plus the fact that '52 represents the venerable outfit's very first year in business. Mantle's Topps debut can snare six figures at auction. The '51 Bowman card is worth less than half as much and, very often, it's forgotten altogether.

up diamond dirt. Patton and his fellow Olympians of the late 1940s and 1950s would, on the other hand, have the benefits that came from a jump start, running blocks, more aerodynamic outfits, lighter running shoes, and special surface tracks, not to mention the kind of nutrition and conditioning program followed by dedicated runners. These factors alone would have cost Mantle precious tenths of a second. In any kind of fair race—if the Mick's numbers are to be believed—the Mantle of '51 would have been not only the fastest man alive, but also, much faster than any other possible contender for the title.

I'm willing to suppose that Mantle was the fastest power hitter of all time and/or the fastest Yankee of all time, no problemo. I'm slightly less willing to suppose that he was one of the quickest baseball players who has ever lived and even less inclined to believe he was one of the fastest Americans who has ever dashed from here to there. The notion that he was, at one time, among the fastest *human beings* who've ever lived, though, that one raises some eyebrows. The three-seconds-to-first story *must* be a myth.

THE 565-FOOT, TAPE MEASURE HOME RUN

Another memorable young Mantle story relates to his power. It is said that on April 17, 1953, in Washington's old Griffith Stadium, he hit a home run blast that landed a full 565 feet from home plate. Yankee publicity director Red Patterson supposedly found the exact spot where the ball landed outside of the park, and it went down in the *Guinness Book of World Records* as the longest major league round-tripper and down in history as the first official "tape measure home run."

565 feet. Sounds like a big number. It's not. It's much bigger than big.

Consider that, from 1998 to 2001, when the 60-homer level was reached six times, only Mark McGwire, Sammy Sosa, Jim Thome, and Adam Dunn hit confirmed 500-foot home runs and that the two longest homers ever measured, two '98 shots by McGwire, came in at an official 535 feet. In more than 20 years of recorded, computer-measured homers, no one has come anywhere close to 565 feet, not even when aided by strong tailwinds and mile-high elevations.*

The fact that the pumped-up hitters of the late '90s couldn't come close to 565-foot home runs is the first reason to doubt the measurement, but it's hardly the last. Beyond the sheer, improbable length of the Mantle homer is the fact that the two people who knew the most about it both provide ample reason for doubt.

Mantle, for his part, always said that the '53 homer wasn't the hardest-hit ball among his 536 career blasts. Instead, that distinction belonged to a May 1963 drive off the Athletics' Bill Fischer, a homer that hit the Yankee Stadium frieze about 370 to 380 feet from home plate and ricocheted another 110 to 120 feet before landing, making for a combined 480 to 500 feet traveled through the air. If Mantle was telling the truth about the '63 job—and why would he lie?—then we know the '53 homer didn't come anywhere close to its official distance.

Even the final, "tape measure" part of the tape measure home run story doesn't hold up under any kind of serious examination. Harold Rosenthal, a sportswriter who worked with Patterson on a daily basis, acknowledged that the Yankees' PR director left the press box after Mantle's blast but said he was sure that was *all* he did. "He wasn't about to walk down the entire length of the ballpark, leaving the field, chase a kid down a street, and measure a home run. Where the hell would he get a tape measure? It was all a promotion," he asserted.

When Patterson was interviewed about the incident by author Bill Jenkinson in the 1980s, he still insisted that he did go out to the front lawn of 434 Oakdale Street, where Mantle's home run ball supposedly ended up, but conceded that, aside from 10-year-old Donald Dunaway, he had no independent witnesses to place the landing spot at anywhere close to 565 feet.

---

*And, possibly, ahem, some extra pharmacological help.

With that in mind, here's an educated guess about the events of April 17, 1953: Mickey Mantle definitely hit a home run that traveled beyond Griffith Stadium's outer wall, 460 feet from home plate, and, given the witness accounts of its downward trajectory, the ball probably traveled somewhere close to 500 feet before hitting terra firma. It may have hopped, skipped, and rolled a good distance further before coming to a stop, maybe somewhere close to 565 feet, but that last part doesn't count. They're called tape measure home runs, not tape measure grounders.

CHAPTER 11

DiMaggio 24, Mantle 0

"Your call is important to us." "It's not you, it's me." "We'll take it under consideration." There are some things that everyone says and no one believes.

They're lies. They may be well-intentioned, feelings-sparing little white lies, but they're lies. Despite the usual lines, everyone knows that your call couldn't be less important to them; yup, it's her; and, fellas, they ain't considerin' bubkes.

It was much the same thing when authors Ray Robinson and Christopher Jennison asked a panel of Yankee experts to select their all-time Yankee roster in 2002. As recounted in the *Pennants & Pinstripes* franchise retrospective, the 24 experts were unanimous on the best Yankee center fielder of them all, choosing Joseph Paul DiMaggio. None of them selected Mickey Mantle at center field, instead naming him as their all-time left fielder.

It was a nice try, that little move out to left field, but it didn't fool anyone who knew a pinstripe from a highway stripe. Mantle was a prototypical center fielder, playing more than three-quarters of his 2,000+ career games in the position (and fewer than 130 in left). What the commentators were *really* saying is that, given the either/or choice between Di Mag and Mantle, they'd have Mickey sitting on their all-time bench.

The selection was, on some level, more than understandable. Joe D. was a 13-time All-Star who won multiple league titles in batting average, slugging, and home runs. Tommy Henrich once said that the Yankee Clipper "does everything better than everyone else." Those judges who

1963: DiMaggio and the next DiMaggio

knew both center fielders—Casey Stengel, Yogi Berra, Whitey Ford, Bobby Brown, Jerry Coleman, Joe Collins, and Gene Woodling, among them—all said that DiMaggio was the best player they'd ever seen. Mickey Mantle himself often said Joe DiMaggio was better than he was. But if you look at the hard facts, it just wasn't the case.

To see Mantle's superiority to DiMaggio as a hitter, let's begin with the big-picture stats on their respective careers:

	DiMaggio	Mantle
	(1936–42, '46-51)	(1951–68)
Batting Average	.325	.298
On-Base Percentage	.398	.421
Slugging	.579	.557

Although DiMaggio had a higher batting average than Mantle, he didn't walk at the same rate, averaging 74 bases on balls per 162 games to Mantle's 117 and leading to a lesser on-base factor that largely neutralizes Joltin' Joe's edge in slugging. Accounting for a batter's two most important abilities, reaching base and hitting for power, the players end up in a dead heat in terms of on-base-plus-slugging (DiMaggio's .977 OPS mirrors Mantle's .978).

From that nearly identical starting point, though, the kid they called "the next DiMaggio" begins to look significantly better than the first one. The league context, for starters, strongly favors Mantle. DiMaggio put up his undeniably strong batting/OBP/slugging numbers in eras when the respective American League average mostly hovered around .270–.285/.340–.355/.405–.420 (the years before World War II) and .255–.270/.335–.350/.365–.380 (postwar to '51). Mantle toiled in times when the same numbers mostly ranged from .250–.265/.325–.340/.375–.390 (1950s to '61) and .235–.250/.305–.320/.355–.370 (post-expansion to '68). By the time of the Mick's last campaign, 1968's Year of the Pitcher, there was a single .300 hitter left in the entire American League.

To make a long story short, Mantle's performances came in times when hitting was a lot harder to come by, and as such, was a lot more impressive. The authoritative Baseball-Reference.com site has a statistic called OPS+, which normalizes the league context to a single baseline, and that stat has Mantle's 172 mark way, way ahead of DiMaggio's 155. You can easily add about .010 to .020 points to Mickey's numbers across the board, relative to the AL at large, and those rates would have added more than 130 hits and 60 homers to his career totals.

In addition to his more impressive standing relative to the league, Mantle was a more impressive star among his teammates. Like DiMaggio before him, the Mick played alongside more than his share of hitting stars, but his batting, on-base, slugging, and on-base-plus slugging performances stood out even more in the seasons with at least 100 games played:

	J.D.	M.M.
Led team in BA	7 of 12 years	5 of 16 years
Led in OBP	3	14
Led in SLG	8	11
Led in OPS	6	5

If Joe DiMaggio was, rightly, seen as the heart of the Bronx Bomber lineups of his time, then call Mickey Mantle the heart, arteries, and maybe a vital organ or two. Not for nothing did some of his teammates personally thank him whenever they received their paychecks.

Also, for those who talk about big years, let it be said that Mantle had a career full of big years. He finished with three of the 14 best adjusted OPS seasons in franchise history, behind only Babe Ruth and Lou Gehrig. DiMaggio's best efforts, on the other hand, don't register in the team's top 16 hitting seasons.

Mantle's advantage over DiMaggio, finally, extends into October. Check out the stars' career numbers in the World Series:

	Yankee Clipper	Commerce Comet
Batting Average	.271	.257
On-base Percentage	.338	.374
Slugging	.422	.535
OPS	.760	.909

He may have led his team to 10 American League pennants, but DiMaggio was seldom a primary contributor in the World Series itself, as his 199 postseason at-bats produced an overall OPS more than 200 points lower than his regular-season performance. To provide some context, DiMag's postseason on-base-plus-slugging was lower than the career regular-season marks of guys like Jim Hickman and Eddie Taubensee.*

On the other hand, Mantle's playoff numbers, while off his sterling standards from the regular season, were still far superior to DiMaggio's

---

*That's right, Jim Hickman and Eddie Taubensee.

in terms of on-base percentage and slugging. His home run/at-bat ratio actually improved (from 1/15.1 to 1/12.8) in World Series play, a major reason why he's still the all-time leader in World Series long balls and RBI. The fact that Mantle's pennant winners weren't *quite* as successful in October (only seven titles in 12 World Series), obviously, had a lot more to do with his weaker supporting casts than it did with Mantle's own work.

DiMaggio's defenders may not like these numbers, but they do offer counterarguments in the Yankee Clipper's favor. Most often, they point out that DiMag was a league-leading RBI producer, he almost never struck out, and he was robbed of his proper due by vast outfield dimensions at Yankee Stadium and his loss of career years during military service.

They're all important points, but they have ready answers that ultimately tilt in Mantle's favor.

On the RBI matter, there can't be any dispute that DiMaggio was a far more prolific run producer than Mantle. Joe D. averaged an astounding 143 runs batted in for every 162 games played, thereby producing 14 percent of team runs over the course of his 13-season career. Mantle, in comparison, averaged a relatively trifling 102 runs batted in for every 162 games, good for 12 percent of his teams' total runs.

However, the DiMaggio/Mantle RBI numbers, impressive as they may be, reflect not a difference in hitting ability but on the strength of their supporting casts. As it happened, DiMaggio was fortunate enough to play beside much better hitters than Mantle, and that applied to all phases of the offensive game. Here's how many of DiMaggio and Mantle's starting teammates broke through for seasons with a .300 or better batting average, .400 or better on-base percentage, and .500 or better slugging percentage* barriers:

---

*Why set the bar at .400 OBP and .500 slugging? Because, historically, major leaguers reach those levels at roughly the same rate as milestones such as a .320 batting average and a 47-homer season. The .400 and .500 marks are nice round numbers that say, "Hey, this is something very special."

	Joe D. Teammates	Mickey M. Teammates
Total w/ .300+ batting average	22	16
Average per year	1.7	.90
Total w/ .400+ on-base percentage	19	2
Average per year	1.5	.10
Total w/ .500+ slugging percentage	22	10
Average per year	1.7	.60

No one has the play-by-play information needed to derive DiMaggio's statistics with runners in scoring position, so there's a faint possibility that he simply hit better in RBI-type situations. At the same time, we know that Mantle, like almost all hitters, had overall/career offensive stats (.298 batting/.421 on-base/.557 slugging) that track with his hitting with runners in scoring position (.296/.466/.571),* so it's highly likely that most, if not all, the difference in the DiMaggio/Mantle RBI math was related to the fact that Joe D.'s clubs simply had more teammates getting on base and slugging their way into abundant RBI opportunities. That is to say, the Yankee Clipper probably knocked so many in primarily because, well, he had so many chances to knock them in.

On to the strikeout point, again, the DiMaggio defenders can point to one of their favorite player's most extraordinary qualities: Joe DiMaggio had such extraordinary bat control that he amassed barely more strikeouts (369) than career homers (361), achieving a nearly unheard-of ratio of 1:1. In contrast, Hall of Famers such as Tony Perez and Reggie Jackson produced strikeout-to-homer ratios close to 5:1. Mantle wasn't quite that bad, but the fact that he struck out 3.2 times for every career homer proves that he wasn't in DiMaggio's league for bat control.

That may be true, but when it comes down to it, strikeouts are relatively unimportant in discussing the relative merits of the Next DiMaggio and the Previous DiMaggio.

---

*Runners in scoring position data from 1956–1968

Sure, no one likes to strike out—it makes anyone look stupid—but sluggers from Babe Ruth on have known that whiffs are the inevitable byproduct of the long swings needed to power balls over the fence. Repeated statistical studies have determined that strikeouts aren't necessarily more harmful than other kinds of outs, whether a pop out, ground-out, or whatever-out.

If anything, DiMaggio's brand of contact hitting may have been a net detriment, seeing as how he grounded into far more career double plays than the power-swinging Mantle. (He hit into a double play once for every 38.2 career at-bats while Mantle did it once for every 71.7.) A double-play ball is a pitcher's best friend. As Earl Weaver once advised, "If you think you're going to hit into a double play, do the right thing and strike out."

It's also been said that DiMaggio was an even better hitter than his numbers indicate because he had the misfortune of playing in Yankee Stadium, where distant outfield fences swallowed up what would have undoubtedly been any number of righty hitters' home runs. If Joe hit at home like he did on the more neutral, fair fields to be found on the road, he would probably have another 65 or more homers, bringing his career total to around 425. Stat pioneer Bill James went so far as to claim that Joltin' Joe probably lost out on the most home-field homers ever.

To this, again, the proper answer is, "So what?"

Mantle was also born right-handed and played with virtually the same outfield dimensions as DiMaggio, so he lost plenty of would-be homers, too. His only additional advantage as a hitter was the one he earned by learning how to switch-hit as a child, the same hard-work/ ambidexterity advantage he used to eventually establish himself as the most complete ballplayer of all time.

Finally, in assessing DiMaggio the hitter, there's the war issue to contend with. As world historians and baseball fans know, DiMaggio traded in his pinstripes for khakis. We can only speculate what DiMaggio would have done if the war hadn't taken three years' worth of playing opportunities, but if we go by the two seasons immediately before and after his military service, Joe would have added another 500 or so hits and about another 70 home runs to his career totals. Those numbers are, as usual, absolutely outstanding, but they hardly erase Mantle's overall superiority. Although the increased hit totals would have put DiMag ahead of Mickey in overall hits (2,700+ to 2,415), Mantle would still have the yawning advantage in terms of four-bag hits (536 to 430 or so).

Add all the above together and it's clear that Mantle comes out the better hitter. When it comes to the final two areas, fielding and baserunning, it's more of a split decision.

The numbers tell us, for instance, that DiMaggio was every inch the phenomenal defender recounted in all the right history books. He exceeded the league average for outfielders' fielding percentage in nine of his 13 seasons and went a near perfect 12 for 13 when it came to range (combined assist and putout) numbers, ending his career with a 2.71 figure that exceeded the AL's average (2.31) by a staggering 0.40 points. To put that into context, consider that Ken Griffey Jr. and Torii Hunter, who won 17 Gold Gloves between them, are expected to end their center field careers with range factors exceeding their leagues' averages by 0.12 and 0.25 points respectively.*

Mantle, for his part, was very good with the glove, maybe B+ good, but he wasn't DiMaggio-level, A+ good. Of all the areas where his many injuries took their toll, defense may have been one of the most costly, as Mantle's outstanding fielding percentage and range factor both fell off after 1960, when he was just 28 years old. By the time all was said and done, he finished his career with neither DiMaggio's sure hands (exceeding the average league fielding percentage in seven of 16 outfield

---

*There's folklore that says that, at the crack of the bat, DiMaggio could call a ball's final landing spot to within five feet. Teammates swore that he never had to make an impressive-looking catch, only because he had already anticipated exactly where a line drive would end up. They said he never, ever made a mental mistake in throwing back to the infield.

Based on those fielding numbers, I believe them.

years) nor his range (finishing with a 2.26 range factor that exceeded the AL average by 0.26 points).

When it comes to base running, however, Mantle's advantage once again asserts itself. Here are the duo's respective numbers in the main speed categories, normalizing for 162 games played:

	DiMaggio	Mantle
Stolen Bases	3	10
SB Success Rate	77%	80%
Ground Into Double Plays	12	8

DiMaggio has a mysterious reputation for being one of the most proficient base runners of all time. Allie Reynolds and Joe McCarthy, among others, always believed it, maybe because he could leg out singles into doubles and doubles into triples. If so, that's already accounted for in his power numbers, which are largely built on those extra-base hits.

DiMaggio's strict base-running stats, however, certainly don't bear out any overwhelming skill level. The stats say that he couldn't steal like Mantle, he got caught more often, and, as already mentioned, grounded into more double plays. He was good at breaking up double plays at second base and going from first to third base on singles, without a doubt, but how could he have been better than a man who was, by all accounts, much faster and stronger? Because DiMaggio couldn't drop a bunt down at any time or smash line drives from foul line to foul line. He wasn't as disruptive to defenses, either.

Again, DiMag was an outstanding base runner. Again, you-know-who was even better.

Mickey Mantle was a first-ballot Hall of Famer. His No. 7 will never be worn by another Yankee. He was considered the very best player in the world for long stretches of his career. His many records won him MVP trophies, All-Star honors, world championships, and the usual accolades.

He's not the first person you think of when it comes to a great lack of recognition, but, based on all the above, he may have deserved even more than he received. Relative to Joe DiMaggio, Mantle was the greater hitter, the one who displayed a greater domination of his league and era, had more monster years, made many more contributions to his teams' effort, and had a greater impact on the World Series. Factors such as DiMaggio's RBI totals, strikeout rate, and home field disadvantage, while interesting, explain only the ways Mantle was a different and, ultimately, better offensive force. True, Mickey wasn't nearly the same fielder as DiMaggio, but, then again, Joltin' Joe wasn't nearly the same base runner as Mantle.

Maybe, with all that in mind, some historic reassessment is in order. Maybe historians should note that the post-DiMaggio Yankees never skipped a beat because they found an even greater player in center field. Maybe critics should talk less about what Mickey Mantle could have been and talk more about what he was. Maybe he was the one who should've taken the bows as "America's Greatest Living Ballplayer" and been introduced last at Old Timers' Day. And it wouldn't have killed Paul Simon to mention the Mick in a song or two.

At the very minimum, maybe Mickey deserved an all-time Yankee lineup spot that amounted to more than a thinly veiled consolation prize. To my mind, the center-field selection should've been unanimous, all right, but with a different result: Mantle 24, DiMaggio 0.

CHAPTER 12

"Yogi-isms" (Part One)

Yogi Berra was one of the best bad-ball hitters of them all, but he wouldn't swing at just any pitch between his nose and toes. He was one of the greatest slugging catchers of all time, too, but he finished with 358 homers, not 716. He may have been one of the most effective celebrity pitchmen Yoo-Hoo ever had, but at no point did he serve as CEO of PepsiCo.

And he did author a lot of funny, memorable quotations, but not nearly as many as the general public has been led to believe. In other words: he said a lot, but a lot of what the media said he said, he didn't really say.

Lawrence Peter Berra stood apart virtually from the moment he arrived on the Yankee roster in 1946. It wasn't hard to do.

The very young Yogi came to the Yankees with one of the most unusual baseball nicknames of them all, a tag inspired by the fact that his squat looked like that of an Indian yoga master. Co-owner Larry MacPhail said that his short, stout look called to mind "the bottom man on an unemployed acrobatic team." Berra even looked funny, with the distinctive, rubbery facial features that were, if not necessarily unattractive, unusual enough to stand out in a crowd, much as latter-day guys such as Randy Johnson or David Ortiz stand out in a crowd. Bill Veeck once called Yogi "an ugly duckling who made it big in a world of swans."

What really set Berra apart was a persistent habit of tripping over words and phrases, a habit that traced back to his earliest childhood. His parents, Pietro and Paulina, were first-generation immigrants who

Yogi Berra: he said a lot, but a lot of what the media said he said, he didn't really say.

spoke only Italian in their St. Louis household. The teenage Berra was never inclined to master proper English in school, either; he dropped out at age 14.

Yogi wouldn't say that a Hall of Fame catcher was tutoring him from his own background; he'd say Bill Dickey was "learning me all his experiences." He wouldn't say that his batting mechanics were fine despite some bad luck; he'd say, "Slump? I ain't in no slump, I just ain't hitting." And he wouldn't say that the 1960 Yanks made too many mental errors in the World Series; he'd say, "We made too many wrong mistakes." Whatever the cliché, Berra could be counted on to trip over it. Berra's funny name and looks, combined with his unusual linguistic style, gave rise to his popularity.

The mixed-up, off-kilter quotations stemmed from a certain lack of book learning, to be sure, but, Berra didn't care to straighten out his grammatical imperfections. He figured he'd get his message across well enough, one way or another. When a reporter would ask him, as manager, whether he'd made up his mind about a particular move, Yogi didn't have any qualms in answering, "Not that I know of." Or, when asked about the '69 Mets' bench strength, he'd say, "We had deep depth." At another time, he ruefully remarked on his team's lack of up-and-coming prospects by noting "the future ain't what it used to be."

It's fairly certain that Berra's combination of unschooled phrasing and his whatever-works attitude did produce those memorable lines and several others besides, but there is a whole set of questionable phrases and/or fabricated ones that have been attributed to him.

That was because reporters and friends collectively decided to take Yogi's verifiable quotability a little farther, coming up with ever-more outlandish, comical sayings. With Berra's lack of education as a given, for instance, they'd say that when a woman once asked him if Yoo-Hoo was hyphenated, Yogi responded, "Lady, it ain't even carbonated." They said he said, "It's déjà vu all over again" and "It's tough to make predictions, especially the future."

None of those quotations, and several others still attached to Yogi's name, were true, however, and we can be fairly certain of it. He has repeatedly denied that he never said them, for one thing, and few, if any, outside observers were in the room when Berra supposedly uttered them, either.

All those quotations, and others concerning pizza slices or Dr. Zhivago or whatnot, were apocryphal, which is a 50-cent word for "made up." Much like a team of comedy writers worked behind the scenes to craft Bob Hope's one-liners, an informal circle of Yankee reporters worked to link their own words to the one and only Yogi Berra. It served their purpose to manufacture a cuddly folk hero, a brand-name quotemeister who could be used to add some life to the day-to-day humdrum of the baseball season or some color to an off-season speech.

The highly unofficial creation that became known as "Yogi-isms," it should be said, was initially unwelcomed and unwanted.

Berra had an affable enough demeanor and could share the occasional clubhouse wisecrack with the best of them, but he didn't ask anyone to portray him as something he wasn't—particularly when that something was an over-the-top stereotype of a dumb jock. He disliked that strangers would constantly walk up to him and try to bait him into reciting some of the more tired old lines, many of which he had never uttered to begin with. And there was something undeniably weird in the fact that later generations knew Berra less as an absolutely phenomenal catcher/slugger/pennant-winning manager and more as the forerunner to Yogi Bear, the Hanna-Barbera cartoon who swiped picnic baskets at Jellystone Park.

Quasi-Yogi

If Yogi-isms can be defined as English phrases just twisted enough to provide a laugh, there are any number of other authentic Yogi Berra gems that convey an unfiltered wisdom in their own right.

When he was asked what he remembered best about catching Don Larsen's perfect game, for instance, Yogi responded, "Everything," then added that the perfecto was "the best it ever got. How could you ever beat perfect?" After the '63 World Series, he said, "I see how Koufax won 25 games. What I don't see is how he lost five." On another occasion, when Berra was asked what makes a good manager, he answered, "good players." And, of course, there was the inevitable "It ain't over 'til it's over."

If it's possible to possess a very perceptive grasp of the obvious, let it be said that Mr. Lawrence Peter Berra possessed a very perceptive grasp of the obvious.

That being said, though, Berra eventually gave up on trying to set the record straight and began to use his own exaggerated, faux-quotability in his own favor. He knew that the quotations could translate to cash, for instance, and he authored half a dozen autobiographies/quotation collections and ultimately founded a thriving, well-funded Berra Museum at Montclair State University. Surely he didn't mind how his name, if not his exact words, was invoked in speeches enough to make him "the most quoted American since Abraham Lincoln," according to biographer Allen Barra. In addition, the man sportswriter Dan Daniel once called "the most sociable, best-liked player in the American League" surely appreciated the fact that so many people enjoyed a laugh out of the Yogi-isms, at least.

More than anything else, Yogi Berra may have learned to ignore the falseness around him because he was comfortable with himself. As it happened, the high school dropout still had enough common sense to marry well and raise three college graduates, and the kid who shrugged off the jokes still displayed the personal pride needed to become a remarkably successful business investor and community ambassador. About that, he was deadly serious. As Casey Stengel once said, "They say he's funny, but he has a lovely wife and family, a beautiful home, money in the bank, and he plays golf with millionaires. What's funny about that?"

CHAPTER 13

"Yogi-isms" (Part Two)

Just how many of those supposed Yogi-isms belonged to Yogi?

Well, Mickey Mantle once estimated that about one-third were legitimate, with the balance crafted by guys like Len Koppett of the *New York Times*, Leonard Schecter of the *Post*, Jackie Farrell of the Yankee PR staff, and childhood friend and professional "character" Joe Garagiola. That percentage may have dipped even lower over the years, as Berra eventually learned to cash in on the malaprop reputation though quotation collections and the completely canned lines used in the Miller Lite commercials of the 1980s and the Aflac spots of more recent times.

It's impossible to know the exact provenance of the most-mentioned quotations, of course, but it is possible to make some educated guesses. Their believability quotient is set on a scale of 0 to 10, with a 10 representing the credibility of God-fearing Bobby Richardson and 0 for accuracy-challenged Joe Pepitone:

The quotation: I want to thank everyone for making this night necessary.

The believability quotient: 10. Tens of thousand witnesses heard this, one of the very first Yogi-isms, uttered on "Yogi Berra Night" in 1947. Yogi repeated it during his Hall of Fame induction in 1972.

Quotation: It gets late early out there.

Quotient: 10. Again, this one was widely confirmed. It referenced the deep shadows in Yankee Stadium's sun field. Berra played more than 130 games out in left.

Quotation: In baseball, you don't know nothin'.

Quotient: 10. This was Yogi at his best: humble, to the point, and exactly right.

Quotation: I've got nothing to say, and I'm only going to say it once.

Quotient: 9. This one was connected to his firing as the Mets manager in 1975.

Quotation: If you see a fork in the road, take it.

Quotient: 9. Berra's fairly certain he said this at some point, probably while giving directions to his home in New Jersey. Both streets at the fork lead to the house, you see.

Quotation: It isn't too far; it just seems that way.

Quotient: 9. Bill Madden claimed this was uttered while Yogi was providing him with driving directions.

Quotation: When you get to the house, you'll see it.

Quotient: 9. Ditto.

Quotation: He must've made that picture before he died.

Quotient: 9. Mrs. Carmen Berra confirmed this one; it was a reference to the late Steve McQueen.

Quotation: How can you think and hit at the same time?

Quotient: 8. It's unverified, but it's comparable to a bona fide gem such as, "I ain't in no slump—I just ain't hitting," so let's give it to him. Yogi supposedly said this in response to batting tips.

Quotation: If you can't imitate him, don't copy him.
   Quotient: 8. This was a reference to a young player's attempts to emulate Frank Robinson. Everybody knew what he meant.

Quotation: Nobody goes there anymore; it's too crowded.
   Quotient: 8. Cute enough to be suspicious, but Berra believes he did say it. He may have been referring to a restaurant in St. Louis, Minneapolis, or maybe New York.

Quotation: It's never happened in World Series competition, and it still hasn't.
   Quotient: 8. A reference to Don Larsen's perfect game. It's close enough to the considerably more boring thought he was getting at: it hadn't happened before and hasn't happened since.

Quotation. I didn't care what people said. That's for them to say.
   Quotient; 7. Again, this isn't too far from making sense. Yogi *tried* to provide bland quotes, plenty of times, but it just didn't come out right.

Quotation: I'd say he's done more than that.
   Quotient: 6. A supposed response to a question about a young Don Mattingly exceeding expectations. To me, it's a bit too out there.

Quotation: You mean now?
   Quotient: 6. Supposedly his answer to either Tom Seaver or Mickey Mantle asking for the time. This one is debatable.

Yogi didn't necessarily stop to think before talking, but this one could just as easily come from a cutesy sportswriter.

Quotation: If people don't want to come out to the park, nobody's going to stop them.

Quotient: 5. A reference to low attendance, but it sounds less like a catcher and more like a sportswriter.

Quotation: I think it's wonderful. It keeps the kids out of the house.

Quotient: 4. Berra's supposed comment on Little League, of course, is more questionable than credible. As much as he tripped over language, he rarely, if ever, said something opposite to his intention.

Quotation: Baseball is 90 percent mental, and the other half is physical.

Quotient: 4. Yogi's said he isn't sure about this one, but I'm playing the percentages.

Quotation: You can observe a lot by watching.

Quotient: 3. He wouldn't say, "It's tough to make predictions, especially the future" or something like this. He'd consider it pontificating.

Quotation: I would rather be the Yankees' catcher than the president, and that makes me pretty lucky, I guess, because I could never be the president.

Quotient: 3. Doesn't sound like him at all. Putting Mr. Catcher in the same sentence as the President of the United States was almost certainly someone's lame attempt to make Berra look ridiculous.

Quotation: Why buy good luggage? You only use it when you travel.

Quotient: 2. Berra could be tight with a dollar, but only a genuine F-O-O-L would come out with this one.

Quotation: Even Napoleon had his Watergate.

Quotient: 1. This one's been linked to the Phillies' Danny Ozark, among others.

Quotation: Good pitching beats good hitting and vice-versa.

Quotient: 0. How true. But this gem belongs to former Pirate pitcher Bob Veale.

Quotation: If the world was perfect, it wouldn't be. Wherever you go, there you are.

Quotient: 0. Maharishi Mahesh Yogi, maybe. Yogi Berra, definitely not.

Quotation: You should always go to other people's funerals or they won't come to yours.

Quotient: 0. No way. If someone walked up to you and said this with a straight face, you'd think he was an idiot. Yogi was nobody's fool.

CHAPTER 14

The Copa Fight and Billy Martin's Exile

> *"We all think that [general manager] George Weiss made Billy the scapegoat because he never really liked him and was looking for an excuse to get rid of him."*
> —Whitey Ford, from *The Illustrated History of Mickey Mantle*

> *"Several Yankees, including Billy Martin, were celebrating a birthday at the Copa when a drunken brawl ensued...Weiss, who always wanted his Yankees to behave like Boy Scouts, seized on the opportunity to get rid of Martin."*
> —Ray Robinson and Christopher Jennison, *Pennants and Pinstripes*

It is possible to frame a guilty man. Take Billy Martin, for instance.

In the early morning hours of May 16, 1957, Martin, the Yankees' second baseman, was out with teammates Mickey Mantle, Whitey Ford, Yogi Berra, Hank Bauer, Johnny Kucks, and their wives. The occasion was Martin's 29th birthday, and the group was celebrating at the Copacabana Club on West 51st Street.

Soon after the Yankees and their better halves arrived at the Copa, however, a group at a nearby table began to heckle performer Sammy

After the grand jury, Mantle, Martin, and Hank Bauer. "Hit him? I haven't hit anybody all year," Bauer said about the Copa incident.

Davis Jr. with some racist language. Bauer told the bigots to shut up, to which he was told, "Don't test your luck tonight, Yankee." Bauer decided otherwise, immediately challenging the others to a fight, but was pulled away before any blows landed. Soon afterward, one of the hecklers went into a nearby bathroom, where he presumably had a close encounter with a fist, staggering out with a bloody nose, and, I'm guessing, some hurt feelings.

It's almost certain that none of the Yankees were involved in the bathroom brawl. The ballplayers all denied it, with Bauer wryly commenting, "Hit him? I haven't hit anybody all year."* Several witnesses blamed a club bouncer for the fight, and when the Manhattan District Attorney's office investigated the case, it didn't find any evidence of involvement from the boys in pinstripes.

---

*Hank was dragging around a .203 batting average at the time.

As Yogi later said, "Nobody did nothin' to nobody," including Martin, who, by all accounts, was nowhere in the vicinity of the bathroom. When he was nonetheless traded to Kansas City exactly one month later, Martin spent the rest of his life claiming to be the scapegoat for others' offenses ("I got the rap even though it isn't fair, dammit!").

It all *sounds* above board, but is it true? Not exactly.

The biggest part of the myth was the supposition that the Kansas City trade was intended as a punishment, as if Billy's mere presence in the ZIP code of someone else's dustup was enough for the front office to cut him loose. Martin's *Yankeeography* suggested that the Yankee brass was scared by one bad headline, while author Peter Golenbock accused them of snobbery: "Billy didn't have enough class [for them]."

Please. Like the rest of George Weiss' deals, the Martin trade was a team-building move, one intended to clear more middle-infield playing time for up-and-coming prospects named Bobby Richardson and Tony Kubek. Both of them were younger (21 and 22, respectively) than Martin, even better fielders, and were tearing up Triple A Denver with .300+ batting averages in the earlier part of the year. As it happened, Weiss was more than right to believe he had a ready upgrade at hand; Richardson was named as a first-year All-Star, Kubek as Rookie of the Year, and both were big contributors to the Yankees' surge from a trade-time second place standing up to first place and the '57 pennant.

Still, baseball matters aside, there's no denying that Martin's exile had a personal side to it. Weiss hated him.

He grew up a hot-tempered street punk in Berkeley, California, and from the moment he arrived on the Yankees scene in 1950, he was a magnet for trouble. He was given to frequent fistfighting and the kind of profane language that would make a longshoreman blush, which might have been excused in the name of competitive spirit, but what couldn't be excused was his influence as Mickey Mantle's little sidekick.

Martin freely admitted that he encouraged Mantle to abandon his wife and toddler sons for serial extramarital affairs, days-long alcoholic benders,* and also much worse. Mantle, who couldn't swim, nearly drowned when Martin talked him into a Hawaiian surfing expedition. At least three separate incidents involved gunplay. Oh, and shortly before the Copa incident, Martin took Mantle out for a little stroll around the Book Cadillac Hotel in Detroit, which wouldn't have been too newsworthy except for the fact that the two were on the building's ledge at the time and staying on the 22nd floor.

Martin never tried to deny guilt for those dire distractions, only excusing it by noting that Mantle never particularly needed his encouragement to act out. The Mick brought all sorts of personal imperfections with him from Commerce, Oklahoma, and those imperfections carried on long after Martin's dismissal. But as far as the front office was concerned, the last thing the Mick needed was a little devil on his shoulder, a bad influence to egg on his worst instincts—battling the press, blowing off the fans, and ignoring physical rehab assignments, not to mention the screwing around and boozing. Martin may not have created Mantle's personal problems, but he could only push them from bad to worse. Mantle later admitted as much, saying that his father, had he lived, would never have allowed him to hang out with someone like Martin. "He would have taken one look at Billy and told him to get back in his friggin' car to go back to California."

George Weiss was the winningest baseball executive of all time because he knew every detail of his club's operations, from Single A Binghamton to last night's box score. Of course he knew about the Martin and Mantle connection and its effects. Understandably, Weiss was concerned that the star's antics might get him hurt, or just maybe, killed.

---

*Mantle once said that their typical night out was dinner and drinks, with dinner optional.

In that light, what's remarkable isn't the fact that Weiss traded Martin away, but that the Yankees spent eight long seasons tolerating an unstable, belligerent, and highly replaceable (career .262) infielder. It was a minor miracle best explained by the fact that Weiss didn't want to tick off either Martin's superstar pal or Stengel. The Copa fight was merely the occassion where more than enough got to be enough, where no amount of cronyism could save Brawlin' Billy's hide.

After the Copa fight, Billy Martin was traded to the Athletics in exchange for rifle-armed Ryne Duren, among others. He may have been not guilty in the Copa fight, but he was guilty of far worse offenses against common sense and teamwork. Me, I'd have shipped him out for an old rosin bag and a slightly-used fungo bat.

CHAPTER 15

"Casey Stengel Screwed Up the 1960 World Series"

"Both Pirates and Yankees believe the most pivotal act of the Series might have been Yankees manager Casey Stengel's decision not to start [Whitey] Ford in Game 1, which kept Ford from starting three Series games, including Game 7. 'He was a money pitcher,' said Vernon Law."
—Sean D. Hamill, in "1960, a Series to Remember (or Forget)," *New York Times*, June 24, 2008

"Lord, we all wanted to kill him."
—Jim Coates

When Casey Stengel decided to bypass his #1 starter, Whitey Ford, for Game 1 of the 1960 World Series, it wasn't a leap to criticize the move. The 70-year-old skipper had visibly been slowing down that year, sometimes falling asleep on the bench and calling in bullpen pitchers and pinch hitters that had left the ballclub several seasons before. In skipping over Ford in favor of Art Ditmar, Stengel was showing a lack of confidence in a veteran star who was already well on his way to compiling the most World Series wins in major league history.

However unconventional the move may have seemed, it was far from crazy. Stengel had based his decision on cold, hard facts.

First off, Stengel was sharp enough to realize that the Pirates were a much better ballclub than most casual observers realized. In spite of playing in the considerably tougher National League, Pittsburgh's lineup had a higher regular-season team batting average than the Yankees (.276 vs. .260) and its staff had a lower ERA (3.49 vs. 3.52). Pittsburgh's biggest disadvantage was a lack of pitching depth (beyond starters Vern Law and Bob Friend and reliever Elroy Face), but that could be neutralized in a short series. The Yankees' biggest advantage, in home-run power, was diminished by the relatively cavernous dimensions back at Forbes Field. Add in the Pirates' incredible comeback ability (40 of their 95 regular-season wins came through late-inning rallies), their loosey-goosey, nothing-to-lose attitude, and their home-field advantage, and you had all the makings of a potential upset.

Into that dangerous situation, Stengel knew that his starting assignments had to be based on the present, not the past, and that meant starting Art Ditmar in Game 1. After all, it was Ditmar who notched an (ever-so-slightly) lower earned-run average in 1960 (3.06 vs. Ford's 3.08) while pitching more innings (200 vs. 192⅔) on the year. From September 1 on, Ditmar also had a significantly lower ERA (3.11 vs. 4.41) despite tossing more innings (37⅔ vs. 34⅔).

Whitey Ford's overall pitching career ranks as the single greatest in Yankee history, true, but that didn't mean he was the single best Yankee starter as of October 1, 1960. On that day, the best the team had going, arguably, was Art Ditmar. Still, it's been said that Stengel should have overlooked those numbers and gone with Ford as a proven postseason performer. Here, again, the facts didn't favor that assignment.

Ford was indeed a terrific playoff pitcher in Yankee Stadium, where he could more easily overmatch lefty hitters, but his road performances were another story. In five road postseason starts prior to 1960, playing against the Dodgers and Braves, he'd gone 0–3, averaging fewer than four innings pitched per start and a 6.53 ERA. Sure, a few of those road runs came in Ebbets Field, which was a bandbox, but I don't care if you're in a sandbox, 6.53 is no one's idea of a good ERA. Again, Ditmar was more than a match for that track record, as he gave up zero earned runs in nine-plus innings pitched during the 1957 and 1958 World Series.

In holding Ford back until Game 3 in the Bronx, Stengel did limit Whitey to two starts against the Pirates, rather than three, but in the process he also ensured that, if the Series went seven games, Ford would have to work in unfriendly Forbes for only one start, not two.

Finally, let's address the real basis of the second-guessing, which was the fact that Ford absolutely cruised through his two starts while Ditmar struggled. From that starting point, many still assume that Ford would have delivered a third straight gem in a third Series start, but Stengel had two solid reasons not to assume any such thing.

It would have been hard for any pitcher to win three Series games against a lineup featuring Roberto Clemente (121 OPS+ on the year); Don Hoak (120 OPS+); and that year's NL MVP, Dick Groat (110 OPS+); not to mention a Dick Stuart/Rocky Nelson platoon that chipped in 30 homers and 118 RBIs. Two wins against those guys was hard enough. Three straight Ws in the space of eight days would have been pushing it; both the level of competition and fatigue would probably have been too much for any pitcher.

Stengel could have fought that ominous history and given Ford a third Series start, but he'd already tried that move. Casey had Whitey go three times in the '58 Series and, after solid performances in his first two starts (five total earned runs in 14 innings), Ford completely fell apart in the third go-around, coughing up five hits, a walk, and two earned runs in lasting just 1⅓ innings. His overreliance on a single ace backfired in '58. Stengel, quite reasonably, decided to go in a different direction in '60, setting up matchups with fresher pitchers who were less familiar to the opposing team.

Casey Stengel made a smart bet, on balance, but even the smartest bet doesn't always pay off. As it turned out, Ditmar's struggles were matched by Bob Turley, Ralph Terry, and Jim Coates, all of whom put up 4.00+ ERAs against Pittsburgh. People were too busy raking Casey over the coals to notice those flops, but, if you want to assign blame for the '60 World Series' outcome, you might start with those culprits.

CHAPTER 16

"Casey Stengel Was a Clown"

When Casey Stengel was hired as manager in 1949, Red Smith wrote of "a comedian running the Yankees," and one of the club's co-owners, Del Webb, was heard to mutter, "My God, we've hired a clown." It was a false impression, but Ol' Case may have said and done a few things to encourage it.

Charles Dillon Stengel was simply blessed with a God-given gift for fun and games. It was evident from his earliest days, when the teenage Casey bypassed schools, churches, and business offices in favor of pool halls, bars, amusement parks, or any other place where he could do more than his fair share of drinking, dancing, and socializing. He never changed, either. Even in the mid-1960s, up until his retirement at age 75, Stengel was known to saddle up to the nearest bar and regale all comers with monologues that would last well into the early morning, hours after men half his age had dozed off.

What distinguished Stengel from other party guys was his knack for constantly authoring one-of-a-kind, flamboyant gestures. Within a few years of coming up to the majors in 1912, he was linked to a couple nutty pranks involving a hidden sparrow and errant grapefruit, and, remarkably, he never lost a taste for those types of original, attention-grabbing sight gags. When he was in his forties, after more than 20 years in the game, he once mocked umpires' refusal to call a rain delay by carrying an umbrella out to the third base coach's box. Pushing 70

Casey Stengel: an overgrown boy graced by genius

years of age, he lit a sparkler and danced a little jig in front of Comiskey Park's new exploding scoreboard. And when the guy was nearly 80 years old, a publicity event had him riding around Shea Stadium in a Ben Hur–style chariot, whip in hand.

The temptation, in his time and ours, was to read Stengel's style as a lack of substance or an absence of a certain intellectual gravitas. And, it must be said, the type of individual who would willingly decide to wrestle a greased pig might not strike observers as a deep thinker. In Stengel's particular case, however, there's every reason to believe the man was even more intelligent than he was funny.

As many contemporaries could attest, Stengel always displayed an absolutely astonishing, near-photographic recall of the literally tens of thousands of at-bats he'd witnessed over the decades. Even more important, the Ole Perfesser could apply those memories to piece together a brand of highly unconventional lineups, skill-based platoons, pinch-hitting assignments, and rotation/bullpen roles that few other managers could ponder, much less execute. Although the Yankee powerhouses of the '50s enjoyed an undeniable advantage in terms of on-field talent, they also had an advantage in their leader's abilities. Long before number-crunchers were employing massive databases to optimize their teams' competitive edges, Stengel was using his own supercomputer: the one between his ears.

In addition, there was something else that made Casey Stengel an especially gifted baseball humorist. Call it a certain flinty wisdom, an innate insight into how the world of baseball worked. One way or the other, Casey never seemed to lose sight of the ways that what some might consider fluff could actually be used for very practical purposes, including public relations.

Stengel started off as a skipper for basement-dwelling ballclubs in Boston and Brooklyn in the 1930s and '40s. He was well aware that the beat reporters, not to mention the fans, were disappointed by the dismal doings on the field, so often he chose to make *himself* the lead story. His tactics helped take the heat off the losing clubs but still kept the public's attention on the dismal Dodgers and the bumbling Braves. He was skilled in providing "my writers" with another beauty of a one-liner, mugging for the cameras, talking up a bevy of spectators, and popping up at sandlots to give kids an impromptu clinic on the finer points of the game. No matter how monotonous his other clubs were in their constant losing—or, for that matter, the Yankees were in their constant *winning*—Casey's promotional tactics never failed to entertain.

At other times, Stengel's comedy had a more pointed intention. He'd often mispronounce players' names—Henrich as "Handricks," Kuzava as "Gazzara," Pepitone as "Pepperone"—to emphasize that individuals were, ultimately, less important than the whole. The Ole Perfesser's joking could keep everyone bright and loose during any losing streak, of course, but when the skipper saw mental errors, his public remarks could become so cutting that the targets would've preferred he'd scream at them instead. Even the most off-the-cuff jokes always had serious messages behind them.

Without a doubt, the very peak of Stengel's fusion of fun and purpose came in his invention of a mangled form of English dubbed "Stengelese," which gained its fullest popularity as the Yankees won championship after championship in the '50s. Most Yankee fans know it well: the long-winded, screwball responses that mixed grammar with endless, word-tripping digressions that sounded interesting but didn't commit him to anything in particular.

What Casey Said: "It's possible a college education doesn't always help you if you can't hit a left-handed change-up as far as the shortstop, but I'm not bragging, you understand, as I don't have a clear notion about atomics or physics or a clear idea where China is in relation to Mobile."

What Casey Meant: "Book smarts aren't baseball smarts."

What Casey Said: "They say you can never do that, but he is, and it's a good idea, but sometimes it doesn't always work."

What Casey Meant: "I'm not going to answer your question."

What Casey Said: "I'm outta baseball and I was in it for a long time and it don't have to be forever."

What Casey Meant: "I haven't decided if I want to stay retired."

What Casey Said: "Sometimes I get a little hard-of-speaking."

What Casey Meant: (Wink)

What Casey Said: "Everybody line up alphabetically by height."

What Casey Meant: (Nudge)

Stengelese, like legalese, could be difficult to understand at times, but there was always a very careful sense behind the nonsense. He was more than capable of communicating in crystal-clear, succinct sentences, but he chose to do otherwise when confronted with serious topics—stuff like benchings, injuries, clubhouse feuds, losing streaks, and on. He knew that every minute he kept beat reporters chuckling was another minute he didn't address them head on. At minimum, the linguistic somersaults helped keep the media pressure off ballplayers who had quite enough New York pressure on them already.

The most memorable example of Stengel's humor-as-distraction occurred when he was called to testify before Congress in 1958. The issue was federal regulation over baseball, a popular initiative that might have cost the Yankees dearly, but with the canny Stengel on hand, attention soon shifted from the pending legislation to an impossibly disjointed 45-minute ramble through the old-timer's life and times from Shelbyville, Kentucky to New York City, from night games to the minors, from pensions to payrolls. Stengel just rollicked on and on, making just enough sense to string his listeners along but never quite enough to fully answer their queries.* By the time the witness finished up the performance, sure enough, the Senate subcommittee on antitrust and monopoly was in stitches, having long forgotten its initial question—just as he'd intended all along.

It was a moment that could have been authored by only one character. Casey Stengel was an overgrown boy graced by fully formed genius, a practitioner of serious fun, a kidder who truly mastered the game. This was one of the Yankees' greatest winners—and in more ways than one. At his funeral in 1975, Richie Ashburn bestowed a eulogy anyone would envy: "Casey loved life, and he loved laughter. He loved people, and above all he loved baseball. He was the happiest man I've ever seen."

---

* Stengel's Senate testimony is part of the public record and a hilarious read. You can find it at www.baseball-almanac.com/quotes/casey_stengel_senate_testimony.shtml

CHAPTER 17

Reel Life vs. Real Life—the Maris of "61*" vs. the Maris of '61

Sure, it was a movie, not a documentary. When Billy Crystal debuted *61** on HBO back in 2001, he just wanted to give the audience a diverting way to spend a couple hours. In recounting the Roger Maris and Mickey Mantle race to eclipse Babe Ruth's single-season home-run record of 60, sure, the director wasn't aiming to preserve the exact facts exactly but taking some artistic liberties while sticking to the essentials. He just wanted to craft an entertaining little drama. The usual Hollywood thing.

Still, although Crystal always had a right to his own interpretations of the 61 in '61 record, his docudrama was a whole lot more drama than docu-. To see how that's so, consider how *61**'s reel life differed from '61's real life:

The issue: The Babe

The 61* version: Fans harp on Babe Ruth for no apparent reason. One fatso* dresses up as the Babe and tosses a folding chair at Maris from the upper deck.

The '61 version: Both Ruth and Maris donned the same Yankee uniform, hit from the same left side, batted in the same number three

---

*Again with the fat thing?

Maris: "I was born surly, and I'm going to stay that way."

slot in the lineup, challenged the same short porch, and played the same right field. It would have been impossible *not* to compare the two, but that was no real comparison whatsoever. My favorite line on the issue came from best-selling author Bill James, who wrote, "Anyone who thinks Roger Maris is in a class with Ruth and Gehrig probably thinks Tony Orlando was in a class with Beethoven and Mozart."

Why *wouldn't* people bring up the record-holder when they talk about a would-be record breaker? And why wouldn't everyone dread a vastly inferior player's wiping out the record of a vastly superior player?

The issue: The Bad Babe People

The 61* version: Claire Hodgson Ruth and Commissioner Ford Frick, a former Ruth ghostwriter, both treated Maris and his wife obnoxiously. A jealous Mrs. Ruth tells Pat Maris that "the Babe loved his record"; Frick generally regards Roger Maris as something he just found on the bottom of his shoe.

The '61 version: It's true that both Mrs. Ruth and Frick were kind of untoward to the Marises, but that was on them, not on the Babe, who had little-to-no vanity when it came to his many, many records. Ruth didn't bat an eye when Hank Greenberg threatened the 60 mark by swatting 58 in 1938, for instance, and when Ralph Kiner hit 51 home runs at age 24 in 1947, the Bambino volunteered the opinion, "The kid in Pittsburgh might break my homer record."

The Babe was beloved, in large part, because he was about as unpretentious as they come. There's every reason to believe that, if he had been alive in 1961, the Bambino would have encouraged Maris to take his best shots.

The issue: The Below-Average Batting Average

The 61* version: No big deal; Yankee owner Dan Topping pulled Roger over to the side early in the '61 season and told him not to worry about hitting for average, so Maris' .269 basically came on orders.

The '61 version: That meeting never happened.

Topping may not have been a Joe McCarthy when it came to baseball acumen, but, like anyone else who's ever graduated from Little League, Maris knew that it was more than possible to combine a high batting average and a high homer total. Mickey did it all the time, with the back of his baseball card noting several years with a .300+ batting average and 35 or more home runs; in 1956, at his peak, he hit .353 on the way to 52 round-trippers.

Maris, on the hand, never came close to batting .300 for a full year. He didn't hit for a decent average in the '61 season because he couldn't hit for a decent average in any season.

The issue: The Lineup

The 61* *version:* New York fans come up with the fantastical notion that Maris' record was the result of Mantle hitting behind him in the cleanup spot. One lout screams, "You're nothing without Mantle!" Another jerk chimes in, "If I hit in front of Mickey, I'd have hit 50 home runs, too!"

The '61 version: In his five full seasons without Mantle (ages 22 to 24, then 32 and 33), Maris averaged 14 round-trippers in a season. In his first five full seasons with the Magnificent Yankee, though, he averaged more than than 36 per year. According to the Elias Sports Bureau, Maris had a dismal .365 slugging percentage in nine games played without Mantle in '61, but a .682 slugging percentage (and zero intentional walks!) in the 152 games when guess-who was waiting in the on-deck circle.

Maybe the fans got the idea that Maris' record was Mantle's creation...because Maris' record *was* (in large part) Mantle's creation.

The issue: The Expansion Thing

The 61* *version:* What expansion? The issue's barely mentioned in the movie.

The '61 version: The eight American League teams of 1960 were joined by new franchises in Washington and Los Angeles in 1961. This introduced dozens of unready rookies, over-the-hill veterans, and career minor leaguers onto Major League staffs. Babe Ruth faced experienced, authentic major leaguers in 1927; in 1961, Maris could feast on two full rosters' worth of scrubs.

Expansion caused a power surge throughout the AL, as non-expansion teams' average home run production jumped from 132 up to 153 (16 percent) in a single year. Mediocre guys such as Diamond Jim Gentile (46 homers, 141 RBIs) and Norm Cash (.361 batting average, 132 RBIs) had career years, but Maris was the single biggest beneficiary of the league-wide hitting bonanza. In the year before expansion diluted pitching staffs, he had 39 homers. When things settled down a year later, he had 33.

The issue: The Media Done Him Wrong

The 61* *version:* The New York beat reporters and columnists taunt Maris, calling him a "zombie" and "Most Vacant Personality" while trying to misquote him and put words in his mouth. Then they have the nerve to ask, "How come Maris never smiles?" In response, Maris gets annoyed and mumbles, "I'm getting tired of all these questions."

The '61 version: It couldn't have been fun for a player to be grilled by the press for hours on end—especially because the atmosphere was so poisonous to begin with. At one point, famously, Maris' hair started to fall out in clumps.

Let's remember, though, this was 1961. The reporters of the day were more lap dogs than watchdogs. They might well have peddled the obvious, feel-good storyline about an underdog homering his way into America's hearts, but their would-be cover boy wouldn't play along. Unfortunately for everyone concerned, Maris wasn't interested in doing anything but making a bad situation infinitely worse.

He routinely referred to beat reporters as "shit-stirrers," and when one of them wrote an unfavorable piece, Maris described the writer with a word that sounds like "rock sucker." On good days he'd be blah and bland, on bad days he'd snap off a "how the f—— do I know?" a "none of your f——ing business," a "don't ask me about that f——ing record," or a "you've got to be a f——ing idiot." Later, sportswriters, straining to put a positive spin on the matter, tried to describe the Maris approach as no-nonsense truth-telling.

The issue: The People vs. Roger Maris

The 61* *version:* Spurred by reporter enemies who buy their ink by the barrel, the New York fans send Maris stacks of hate mail, viciously booed him, and, oh yeah, one Babe impersonator throws a chair at him. Maris is mildly rude once, but it was a misunderstanding.

The '61 version: Was the real Roger Maris reviled? Well, there's every reason to believe that he was a solid family man. And many of

Roger's teammates, including Mantle, respected him enough to attend his funeral nearly 20 years after his last game in pinstripes.

However, as with the media, he did plenty to sabotage his relationship with the fans of New York. "I was born surly," No. 9 once said, "and I'm going to stay that way." Contrary to the movie's depiction, he didn't answer fan mail ("I got enough work to do without writing letters"), avoided autographs ("I don't want to get one of their pencils in my eye"), and didn't contribute to charity work ("The club shouldn't expect you to go to hospitals. They don't ask, and I don't go").

All that was just a warm-up to his main act, however—the one where Maris refused to tip his cap to cheers but gave the one-finger salute to jeers. He called the Yankee followers front-runners and, when he was told they paid for his salary, Rog responded by saying, "I didn't ask them to come [to the ballpark]." He made no secret of his preference for Kansas City over New York City and once announced that he didn't give a damn about the fans. Given all that, it's no wonder he didn't have them on his side.

The issue: The Fargo Kid in the Big City

The 61* version: Maris is a voice of sanity for insane times. He says, "I don't think [respect is] something you earn on a ballfield" and dismisses commercial endorsement possibilities with the comment, "I just wanna play ball."

The '61 version: Fans are willing to forgive just about anything but a player's disrespect for the game and, more than any other Yankee, Roger Maris had an unforgivable disrespect for the game. He was all about money.

He once said, "I'd have played college football if I'd been smart enough to get into school," and "If I could make more money down in the zinc mines, I'd be mining zinc." He was mercenary enough to stage annual contract holdouts and constantly gripe about his salary. He shilled cigarettes. When spectators booed him, Maris responded by shouting, "How much are you making?" and, in contrast to all the players who find a way to stick around until the jerseys are about ripped off their backs, Maris quit the game at his first opportunity, despite his team's entreaties to stay on for another pennant-winning season.

How about this one? Years after the fact, he said he didn't particularly care about his homer record, seeing as he expected more money out of it. "You can't eat glamour," he explained. "All it ever brought me was trouble."

The issue: The Mantle Majority

The 61* version: Everyone's against Maris because they're all sort of dim-witted. Teammate Bob Cerv believes the masses favor Mantle simply because he's been on the ballclub longer, while the fans' voices explain that "Mantle is a dreamboat" but "Maris is always frowning" and "leaves me flat."

The '61 version: If ever there was such a thing as a True Yankee, Mickey Mantle was obviously a True Yankee. By 1961, he was in his second decade in the Bronx, playing in the only major league uniform he would ever wear and well on his way to playing in the most games anyone would ever play in pinstripes. He'd already won five World Series, and his name was all over the Bombers' record book, as it still is.

Maris, in contrast, played in Cleveland and Kansas City before arriving in the Bronx via an inside-fix trade with the Athletics. He ended up playing 1,500 fewer regular-season games and fewer than half as many postseason games for the Yankees than Mantle. He is nowhere to be found on the team's career leader boards.

Leaving aside the fact that Mantle was, yeah, significantly more handsome and charismatic than Maris, everything the Mick did on the field merited support for him in taking the Yankees' ultimate home-run record. Those who knew the M&M boys best, their teammates, may not have minded Maris, but they didn't make any pretense about favoring their cleanup hitter in the home-run race.

The issue: Mickey Mantle, Nervous Wreck

The 61* version: The very mention of Joe DiMaggio's name sends the Mick into a psychological tailspin; he binges and womanizes his way through the evening before a visit from the Great Man.

The '61 version: It's impossible to know how Mantle felt about DiMaggio in his heart of hearts. If he didn't particularly like his predecessor in center field, it might have been understandable, as the veteran DiMaggio did absolutely nothing to encourage the 19-year-old Mickey during his rookie year, and Joe's late call on an outfield fly ball may have contributed to the Mick's devastating knee injury during the '51 World Series. It seems safe to assume that, like most everyone else, Mickey thought Joltin' Joe could be secretive and cold to the nth degree.

However, there's little or no reason to believe that Mantle had some kind of deep-seated resentment of DiMag. In fact, the ever-humble Mantle said that Joe D. was his idol when he was growing up, called him "the greatest player ever," and, when his No. 7 was retired in 1969, Mantle suggested that his plaque at Monument Park be placed just a little lower than that of No. 5.

The issue: Roger Maris, Savior of Lost Sluggers

The 61* version: After Mantle's literal and figurative car wreck, the kindly Roger Maris, among others, is there to pick up the pieces, providing him with an apartment and support as Mantle's bestest friend in the whole world.

The '61 version: It's true that Mantle lived with Maris and Cerv during the '61 season. He got along well with them. He got along well with everybody.

There was a soft heart beneath those rippling muscles. For a good portion of his glorious career the Mick acted as an unofficial team captain, the first to welcome rookies aboard, round up a dinner party, pick up the check, crack a joke, and generally bring everyone together. Most of his teammates flat-out idolized his generosity and good humor;

more than a dozen named their sons after him. Mantle, for his part, surely appreciated the chance to live life as one half of the M&M Boys, but he wasn't nearly as close to Maris as he was to, say, Whitey Ford, Hank Bower, Moose Skowron, Johnny Blanchard, and a lot of others besides.

Also, according to Cerv, it was *Mantle* who initiated that apartment arrangement so that he could be around to diffuse some of the off-hours pressure on Maris. Mantle did that kind of thing all the time. Once, Mick moved out of his house to a hotel just so that newly promoted Jerry Lumpe would have a place to stay with his family.

CHAPTER 18

*

*"Commissioner Ford Frick...suggested that since Maris
had not accomplished his record in a Ruthian 154 games,
there should be a pesky asterisk next to his name in the
record book."*
> —Ray Robinson and Christopher Jennison,
> *Pennants & Pinstripes*

*"Roger Maris, complete with asterisk, became the Home
Run King of baseball."*
> —Peter Golenbock, *Dynasty*

One of my favorite scenes in *61** is when it's become clear that either
Roger Maris or Mickey Mantle could end up breaking Babe Ruth's
home run record.

Commissioner Ford Frick decides to convene a Politburo-like
gathering of New York sports columnists to chat over a poker game,
and, through a thick blue haze of cigar smoke, one of those good old
boys notes that the 162-game season's record would have to be compared
to a total compiled in 154 games. Did it seem fair for the new guys to
get an extra eight games to reach the 61-homer level?

One of the other sportswriters suggests that the commissioner
print an asterisk in the record books, one designed to differentiate how
the new homer record came in the new, longer schedule. Frick raises his
eyebrows. Eureka! In the very next shot, he's before a press conference,
pompously intoning, "If a player does not hit more than 60 until after

his club has played 154 games, there would have to be some distinctive mark in the record books to show that Babe Ruth's record was set under a 154-game schedule."

From those dramatics, film viewers and fans assumed that an infamous asterisk was slapped onto Maris' eventual home-run record. Or maybe it was something suggested by the film's title. Either way, the commissioner of Major League Baseball has never enjoyed an imperial dominion over sports records or a monopoly over printing presses. Frick's statement about a "distinctive mark" wasn't a proclamation but an unsolicited suggestion, one that the rest of the world was perfectly free to ignore.

As it happened, they did. No major publication ever printed an asterisk on the Maris record, though many did choose to list separate home run records for the 154- and 162-game seasons, just as they'd list separate track and field records for the 1,000- and 1,500-meter footraces. Even those separate listings eventually disappeared so that, by the 1990s, every respectable publisher was running a single record for homers in a season. They all listed Roger Maris in the #1 slot.

CHAPTER 19

"The Most Hallowed Record in Sports"

> "Babe Ruth's home-run mark...sports' most hallowed record."
>
> —Jim Reisler, *The Best Game Ever*

> "Baseball's most cherished record."
>
> —Phil Pepe, *Magic Moments Yankees*

Baseball commentators long defined Babe Ruth's single-season home-run record of 60 as being "the most hallowed record in sports." Many continued to do so after it was broken by Roger Maris back in '61. It should be said that the man behind the mark, Ruth, was usually far too busy having fun to particularly hallow anything, but, to the extent that he valued any one of his 50-plus major league records, he was most proud of having pitched 29⅔ consecutive shutout innings in World Series play. Maybe it was because the streak highlighted his oft-overlooked pitching ability, maybe because all the blanks contributed to his status as a perennial winner. He surely knew that he was the winningest player of his generation, in fact, compiling 10 pennants and seven championships in 19 full seasons while playing on Red Sox and Yankee teams that averaged 99 wins per 162 games.

If it's true that success is, in the end, the most hallowed achievement of them all, some other Yankee marks deserve some pretty serious

Breakable

Bill Veeck once wrote that, before Roger Maris, Ruth's 60 homers stood out as *the* baseball record in the same way that Everest was *the* mountain. The movie *61** strongly implies that the popular animosity toward Maris was largely built on his having the nerve to break what was widely regarded as an "unbreakable" record.

As the cliché would have it, records are made to be broken, and Ruth's record was no exception. In the 1930s, everyone knew that guys like Jimmie Foxx and Hank Greenberg had hit 58 homers in a 154-game season, a pace that worked out to more than 60.9 homers for a 162-game stretch. With eight extra games and expansion teams flooding the league with more than two dozen new pitchers, the 1961 season was primed for someone to finally break through. No one expected that Maris would be the one to break it—that, no one argues, was a big surprise—but everyone knew that the record could be broken.

consideration as the most respected records in sports. Maybe Joe DiMaggio's .900 winning percentage on World Series teams. Or Yogi Berra's 14 pennants and 10 championship rings. Or Whitey Ford's .690 winning percentage, the best among 20th-century starters with at least 200 decisions. Or Joe McCarthy's .615 winning percentage as a manager. Or George Weiss' 15 championships and 19 pennants as an executive. Or Mariano Rivera's 34 postseason saves. Or, just maybe, George Steinbrenner's 18 titles, six championships, and more than 3,100 regular-season wins as an owner.

As far as single-season hitting records go, Babe Ruth's 60-homer season *was* hallowed. Of course it was. But no one in his right mind would trade any single season for a lifetime of Yankee wins.

CHAPTER 20

"Steinbrenner Made His Money the Old-Fashioned Way: He Inherited It"

"Steinbrenner's peers—and some of his employees— thought at least part of his success was due to luck: he was born wealthy and struck gold with his investment in the team, but lorded over others as if he was the model businessman."

—Buster Olney,
The Last Night of the Yankee Dynasty

"Born on third base; thinks he hit a triple."

—Jim Bouton

Much has been written about George M. Steinbrenner III, a good portion of it unprintable in a family book. One label rarely, if ever, comes up, though it should: *businessman.* Steinbrenner, as the unprintables might describe, has never been much of a baseball expert, but, for all his faults and foibles, he's always been a more than able capitalist. That's how he had both the resources and the foresight to buy the Yankees in 1973.

George M. Steinbrenner III, shown here in 1977, started off with a nearly bankrupt shipping company.

Contrary to popular belief, Steinbrenner's early life story wasn't a riches-to–greater riches tale. His father, Henry, owned a Cleveland-based shipping company called Kinsman Marine Transit and did use an upper–middle class income to finance young George's military school education, but the elder Steinbrenner was also a strict taskmaster who believed in his only son earning his way up. George labored on the Lake Erie docks as a teenager, and when he joined Kinsman in 1957 at age 27, he was given an entry-level position.

He was expected to work just as hard as anyone else, and work he did. The late 1950s were tough times for Great Lakes shipping as several major steel mills started building ships of their own, but Steinbrenner managed to secure an iron transport commitment that rescued Kinsman from bankruptcy in 1960. Three years later, at age 33, he arranged the financing to buy out (not inherit) his father's share of the company, then used the older business as a vehicle for a takeover of the much larger American Shipbuilding Company in 1967. Within six years of the merger, in 1973, it had braved a serious recession to grow from a regional company into a national one, tripling its premerger revenue to more than $100 million per year in the process.

With its enviable relationships with steel plants and unions alike, ASC was considered one of the best shipping companies in the world. His commitment to work, including 100-hour workweeks, no vacations, and an uncompromising drive for perfection, made Steinbrenner one of the most respected leaders in the industry. *Fortune Magazine* named him one of the top young executives in the nation.

Of course, 1973 was about the time that Steinbrenner was preparing his most important business move of all, the one to buy the New York Yankees.

In retrospect, the team purchase now seems obvious. The Yanks had the most illustrious past possible, after all, and were playing in the largest city in the country. Who wouldn't want them? Well, as it happened, almost no one wanted them—and for very good reason. Like the near-bankrupt ship company Steinbrenner once knew, the circa-1973 Bombers were no great prize.

The club's corporate owners, CBS, had the franchise in shambles. It had averaged a fifth-place finish (and zero playoff appearances) over the previous eight years, particularly bad news to a fan base spoiled rotten by decades of championships. The Yanks finished the 1972 season with less than a million in attendance for the first time since World War II while receiving a meager $200,000 per year for its TV rights. About the only lively aspect to the Bronx of 1973 was its rapid descent toward urban decay.

The entire atmosphere seemed ruinous. After you got past reliable contributors like Thurman Munson and Bobby Murcer, the talent base consisted of the one-dimensional likes of Ron Blomberg and Stick Michael and the no-dimensional likes of Horace Clarke and Celerino Sanchez. Someone once said that, in those days, it was like the bona fide starters had missed the bus to the stadium.

Hard as it might be to remember, the Yankees were once so hard up that they couldn't even compete in their own town. After the

Mets moved from the old Polo Grounds to a brand-spanking-new Shea Stadium in 1964, they bested the Yankees as a gate attraction without fail until 1976, outdrawing the big club by about one-half million paying customers per year. By 1973, the Amazin's were earning more than six times as much as the Yankees in media revenues, largely because they were poised to win their second pennant in four years behind ever-popular manager Yogi Berra and superstar Tom Seaver. An entire generation was growing up with the Mets as the city's hipper, more successful team.

Few would-be owners were running into the arms of an unpopular, talent-deficient, second-rate franchise. The fact that a Tampa-based shipbuilder had any kind of shot at the team purchase was a testament to the fact that no New York–based millionaires were seriously interested. The fact that Steinbrenner actually succeeded with his offer was a testament to the fact that no major bidders anywhere were seriously interested.

Today, more than 35 years and $1.3 billion or so later, George Steinbrenner's businesses have paid off in such spectacular fashion that it's tempting to imagine that he somehow lucked his way onto Easy Street. Like him or loathe him, the Boss inherited nothing but small opportunities and big challenges. He had to work plenty hard to buy his team and make it into something.

CHAPTER 21

"And Then Steinbrenner Fired..."

You've been there. I've been there. We've all been there. Maybe you're just not cutting it at work. Maybe you are cutting it, but due to some economic downturn, it's just not good enough. Or maybe it is good enough, but the boss doesn't like you. Whatever the reason, things just don't work out. You're gone. Canned. Downsized. Laid off. Streamlined. Let go. Dismissed. Ousted. "You're terminated," as Sarah Connor once put it.

Although the experience is nearly-universal, the Yankee managers of the George Steinbrenner epoch had a special appreciation for that out-the-door feeling; they were fired on an almost yearly basis for more than 20 years. There were 20 skipper tenures in the 23 seasons from 1973 to 1995.

Oh, where have you gone, Ralph Houk, Bill Virdon, and Billy Martin?

And Bob Lemon, Billy Martin (second time around), Dick Howser, and Gene Michael?

And also Bob Lemon (take two), Gene Michael (once more), Clyde King, Billy Martin (yet again), Yogi Berra, and Billy Martin (number four)?

And you, too, Lou Piniella, Billy Martin (for the fifth time), and Lou Piniella one more time?

And let's not forget you either, Dallas Green, Bucky Dent, Stump Merrill, and Buck Showalter.

Before they were fired: Billy Martin (left) and Lou Piniella (right) with Steinbrenner

Steinbrenner did make his club a virtual laughingstock by effectively placing a revolving door inside the manager's office. But unlike a typical firing, a Yankeeland termination wasn't necessarily bad news for the firee, who was guaranteed his salary for the term of his contract.

Neither were those ex-Yankee skippers sent packing. All of them were welcome to stay on as organization employees, and the majority chose to do so for years after they left the dugout. King worked as a scout, for instance; Michael as a superscout and general manager; and Dent and Merrill settled into long-term roles as minor league instructors and managers. Of course, Martin, Lemon, and Piniella were all given encore shots as managers, too. Houk, Virdon, Berra, Green, and Showalter—and, eventually, Piniella—all departed for greener pastures but did so of their own will.

Remarkably enough, most of those who stayed on with the Yanks were effectively promoted to better jobs—new roles that called for just as much money but far less scrutiny. Having survived the trauma of termination, they were seen as battle-tested, and, most often, given a slot as an inner-circle adviser among the "baseball people" in Tampa. King and Lemon in particular seemed to enjoy the transition from second-guessed manager to second-guessing exec.

Even those who opted out or moved on were taken care of. After Michael left to join the Cubs for a few years in the 1980s and resigned as Yankee general manager in the 1990s, he still had open invitations to return as a superscout. After his 1985 dismissal, Berra went into a self-imposed exile, but when he did decide to return, he was immediately employed as a spring-training instructor and community liaison. Mostly he instructed old baseball buddies and liaised with golf courses, but like the rest, he had about as much responsibility and money as he could have wanted.

Why the plush treatment for Steinbrenner's many former managers? No one knows for sure, but, without straying too far into armchair psychology, it's possible to make some guesses. The cushy jobs and comfy paychecks may have been implicit acknowledgments that everyone, including Steinbrenner, believed that the terminations weren't a good idea in the first place. Behind all his bluster and bullying, Big Stein has always been one of the most generous philanthropists in baseball history, so it's not hard to imagine that the golden parachutes were a means of providing the down-and-out with some comfort. Yeah, it would have been better if he wasn't the one making them down-and-out in the first place...in a perfect world...but at least the old softie didn't want them to go through additional bad times on his account.

Another reason for Steinbrenner's brand of "un-firings" may be that, in the words of another overzealous boss, the firings were "not personal, just business."

Steinbrenner actually seemed to believe what other team owners gave lip service to—the notion that his franchise deserved to win a championship every year, and for the sake of that sky-high goal, he also bought into the notion, "No ship sails on a calm sea." To all appearances, the managerial moves were his means of stirring up some sort of organization-wide sense of creative tension, urgency, and accountability. The ready-*fire*-aim approach was wrong in its extremes—at minimum, it betrayed a fundamental overestimate of a manager's impact on team results—but at least Steinbrenner took out his underlings in a sincere, if misbegotten, desire to prove "winning is essential" and all that.

With that unpleasantness behind him, however, Steinbrenner didn't want to completely jettison men he still respected. He seemed to believe in a "Yankee family," however dysfunctional it might have been; even when he bruised his family members' feelings, he didn't want to lose their friendship and counsel.

CHAPTER 22

"Mr. October" (Part One)

REGINALD MARTINEZ JACKSON
"MR. OCTOBER"
—plaque inscription, Baseball Hall of Fame

"Reggie Jackson, a former Yankee who belted 563 career home runs in a Hall of Fame career, led New York to three World Series. His five homers in the 1977 Fall Classic earned him the nickname 'Mr. October.'"
—Les Krantz's *Yankee Stadium: A Tribute*

No cow anywhere has been milked more than the heifer branded "Mr. October." Good luck finding a mention of a sentence or more about Reggie Jackson that doesn't include the most grandiose nickname of all time. Or a baseball playoff that doesn't feature his grinning mug. Or a playoff hitter rating that doesn't have Jax at or among the very top.

"No matter what, I'll always be October," the ever-unassuming Reginald M. Jackson has declared.

To be fair, the Mr. October tag has a validity to it. He was an absolutely ridiculous World Series performer, hitting for a .357 batting average, .457 on-base percentage, and .755 slugging percentage in five career Fall Classics from 1973 to 1981. He put up better slugging and on-base-plus-slugging numbers than Babe Ruth (not to mention every

Reggie Jackson in mid-yawn—or mid-sentence?

other ballplayer with more than 30 plate appearances) and knocked 10 homers in 98 at-bats, a pace that would have yielded more than 60 dingers in a full regular season.

If that wasn't enough, many commentators believe that Jackson's finale to the '77 Series, featuring three straight home runs on three straight swings of the bat, is the most impressive single-game playoff performance of all time. I'm one of the commentators.

All things considered, if someone were to claim that Reggie Jackson should be dubbed "Mr. World Series," I'd have no problem with that. Then again, the World Series story isn't the whole *October* story, is it?

Let's remember, Jackson played his entire postseason career after the leagues instituted a League Championship Series in 1969, and for would-be champions, those contests were just as vital as World Series games. If anything, the LCS contests of the Jacksonian era were even more vital. Not only did they represent a crucial stepping-stone in the road to the World Series, but also all but one of them consisted of five-game elimination rounds (as opposed to the World Series' seven-game rounds), making each game that much more crucial.

Not only was there less margin for error in the League Championship Series, but also there was the psychological pressure in the fact that a World Series team is, by definition, a pennant winner. Even if a club ultimately loses in the Fall Classic, it has already had a successful season in making it to the biggest stage in baseball. Losing in the LCS, on the other hand, often leaves a team contemplating the playoff series it lost rather than the division it won.

You'd expect someone proclaimed as Mr. October to excel in those vital, pressure-packed situations. But as good as Reggie Jackson was in the World Series, he was almost as bad in the LCS. He was, again, ridiculous, only not in a good way.

The man some consider to be the greatest postseason performer of all time couldn't hit his way out of a paper bag in League Championship Series, putting up a puny .227 batting average, .298 on-base percentage, and .380 slugging mark in 45 games and 163 at-bats in action. In six of his 11 LCS, he didn't even reach the Mendoza Line's .200 batting average. I'll put it this way: if he'd improved (by a lot), Jackson might have batted almost as well as guys such as a regular-season Jake Gibbs, gotten on base almost as often as Matt Nokes, or slugged almost as well as Danny Cater. Jackson's paltry numbers were a major reason his powerhouse teams failed to advance so often, going a lackluster 6–5 in LCS play.*

Reggie Jackson's World Series performances were, often, stunning enough to make up for his failings in the League Championship series, so much so that, on balance, he can be rightfully considered a very good playoff performer. But to say that he had a lock on the entire month would be a step too far. I'd call him "Mr. *Late* October."

---

*Believe it or not, it was Jackson's woeful 2-for-16 stretch in the '77 ALCS that gave birth to the "Mr. October" nickname in the first place. Thurman Munson gave it to Jax in the same sarcastic tone one would use to call Steve Balboni "Slim" and Goose Gossage "Mr. Slow-Pitch."

CHAPTER 23

"Mr. October"
(Part Two)

If the search for the real Mr. October is a quest for the one Major Leaguer who could best be counted on to deliver in every outing, there is only one answer: Mariano Rivera.

No pitcher who's ever registered 26 or more postseason innings has ever posted a lower earned-run average than Mariano's 0.77. Not even superlative playoff performers such as Christy Mathewson and Bob Gibson could match that kind of ERA, despite the fact that they threw significantly fewer October innings than Mo's 117. His only "problem," if that's the right word, has been that he is so dependable that the few missteps he has had (in the 1997 ALDS, 2001 World Series, and 2004 ALCS, chiefly) have been rare enough to stand out. Other than those isolated spots, Rivera has been a *major* major leaguer.

On the other side of the roster, Babe Ruth and Lou Gehrig have to run neck-and-neck as two of the greatest playoff hitters of all time. Both are still among the MLB leaders in World Series on-base, slugging, and associated power numbers such as homers, extra-base hits, and total bases, meaning that their all-time performances from April through September easily stretched into the 10th month of the year.

Confining the Mr. October sweepstakes to hitters in and, let's say, the last 40 years, we have a larger field of contenders. Guys such as Carlos Beltran, Troy Glaus, Willie Aikens, Carlos Delgado, Kevin Youkilis, Billy Hatcher, and Kirk Gibson have all had monster years in the postseason, but they can't be rightfully included in the Mr. O conversation because none of them proved themselves through as many postgame series. Without a sufficiently large basis of comparison, they have to be disqualified from the running.

Going with those modern-day hitters who have had the opportunity to play at least five full series with at least 150 at-bats, we have a field of five contenders. Through 2007, here are their career playoff stats in terms of at-bats, batting averages, on-base percentages, slugging percentage, and on-base-plus-slugging:

	AB	BA	OBP	SLG	OPS
George Brett	166	.337	.397	.627	1.024
David Ortiz	189	.317	.418	.587	1.005
Manny Ramirez	353	.269	.376	.513	.889
Reggie Jackson	281	.278	.358	.527	.885
Bernie Williams	465	.275	.371	.480	.851

As the numbers might shout, Reggie Jackson hasn't been the greatest playoff hitter in living memory. Manny Ramirez edges him by a small margin in the all-important OPS category, David Ortiz by a larger one. And Jackson's contemporary, the Royals' George Brett, wipes him out.

The Brett/Jackson comparison tells the same story across the board. Brett had a higher batting average, got on base more often, and hit for more extra-base power while driving in more runs per game (1.87 vs. 1.60). What's more, Brett was far more consistent, putting in a .300 or better batting average and .500+ slugging percentage in six of his nine career postseason series while Jackson reached those levels in just eight of 17 series.*

The irony in the Yankees' perpetuation of the Mr. October label is the fact that they, of all teams, should know better. After all, Brett did

---

*I could also compare Brett and Jackson in base running and fielding, but Jax has already been embarrassed enough for one chapter.

some of his worst damage when he was facing the Bombers in the four ALCS series from 1976 to 1980, alternating between oft-spectacular glove work and devastating extra-base hits. In Game 3 of the 1978 series, for instance, Brett hit three homers off Catfish Hunter, and the rip he hit off Goose Gossage in Game 3 of the 1980 ALCS very nearly bounced off a passing 747.

Why does Jackson, rather than Brett, enjoy such a strong association with the 10th month of the year, then? Well, the New York media brigade and Jackson's Trump-like instinct for self-promotion may have had something to do with it. There never was a Midwestern answer to the Reggie! candy bar.* Apart from that, the Mr. October thing probably comes down to Jackson's starring status on some extremely strong ballclubs.

The teams' first, greatest benefit was in the fact that Jax had so many chances to shine in the postseason. He played for clubs that made it to almost twice as many playoff series as Brett's Royals (17 vs. 9), had almost 70 percent more postseason at-bats (281 vs. 166) and the chance to compile significant leads over Brett in everything from doubles (14 vs. 8) and homers (18 vs. 10) to RBIs (48 vs. 23). Those raw totals had everything to do with the number of opportunities, but it also bolstered the popular impression that wow, Reggie was always doing something in October.

Jackson also benefited from better team results. His clubs went 11–6 in playoff series en route to six pennants and five championships while Brett's Royals put up a 3–6 series mark and earned just two pennants and a single World Series. Again, Reggie had higher- quality teammates, but that didn't seem to prevent the winner label from being affixed to Jax.

Still, if Reggie Jackson had better teams, George Brett still had a better game. If I couldn't have Mo's pitching or the Babe's or Lou's swinging, I'd take Mr. George Howard Brett as my Mr. October.

---

* When the Reggie! candy bar was announced in 1977, word went around that Jax already had a candy bar—Butterfinger—named after him.

CHAPTER 24

Jax Facts

THE 160 IQ

There were different theories on why Reggie Jackson was so disliked in the Yankees' clubhouse. It could have been his tendency toward low batting averages, lackadaisical fielding* and base running, troubles with lefty pitchers, or weeks-long batting slumps. Or maybe it was because he showed up to spring training in a Rolls Royce or his habit of peeling hundreds off a thick billfold in his locker. Some of the more sensitive souls may have been annoyed when he asked, "What the hell would [the team] be if Reggie Jackson wasn't there?" Or maybe his Billy Martin feud/psychodrama was too much to bear. No one wanted to deal with it, not even the amiable Willie Randolph.

It could have been any of those things, but Reggie, being Reggie, had his very own theory. He said, "Some people simply can't deal with a black man with a 160 IQ." You see, it was simple, small-minded jealousy over his huge…intellect.

Hmm…let's think that over. Intelligence quotient scales are bound by extremes at both the lower and higher ends. Some of the most unfortunate individuals among us, those with IQs ranging from 30 to 50, are capable only of performing household chores. Those with above-average IQs of 110 to 120 typically have jobs as teachers or upper-level managers, while the truly select few, at around 125 to 135,

---

* In all but two of the nine seasons before he came to New York, Jackson either led or tied all American Leaguers in outfield errors.

Reggie and the Reggie! One was sweet and nutty, and the other was a candy bar.

might become high-level doctors and astrophysicists. Brain surgeons and rocket scientists, in other words.

And those with IQs of 160? They're way, way above those elites. They're in the top tenth of the top one percent of all human beings, those who have virtually no mental limitations. Dr. Arthur Jensen of the University of California estimated that guys such as Thomas Jefferson and Albert Einstein had IQs of about 160.

Now, I'm not saying that Reggie Jackson is a liar in claiming a 160 IQ, but...perhaps...umm...there might have been...a bit of hyperbole...in a moment of ill-considered haste...when he could have gotten a bit carried away.... Oh, forget it. I'm saying Reggie Jackson is a liar.

ℐ𝒬 𝒬&𝒜

Jackson's IQ claim led to some of the best quotations to come out of the eminently quotable Bronx Zoo years.

When Mickey Rivers first heard about Reggie's 160, he asked, "Out of what? 1,000?" Shortly afterward, when Mick the Quick was giving Reggie a hard time, Jackson said, "I must be crazy. I've got an IQ of 160 and I'm arguing with a man who can't even read or write," to which Rivers replied, "Well, you better stop readin' and writin' and start hittin.'"

Mickey must have been thinking of those exchanges not long afterward. He once told Rudy May, "I'll bet you a hundred bucks I have a higher IQ than you." May answered, "Man, you don't even know how to spell IQ."

"FOR FOUR F——IN' PAGES?!"

In spring training in 1977, before he played a single official game in pinstripes, Reggie Jackson decided to conduct the magazine interview destined to introduce him to his new teammates.

Sitting with sportswriter Robert Ward, Jax rambled through an unforgettable monologue:

You know, this team…it all flows from me. I'm the straw that stirs the drink. It all comes back to me. Maybe I should say me and Munson…but really he doesn't enter it…I'm a leader and I can't lie down…but "leader" isn't the right word…it's a matter of presence…. Munson can't intimidate me. Nobody can…. There is nobody who can put meat in the seats the way I can. That's just the way it is…. Munson thinks he can be the straw that stirs the drink, but he can only stir it bad.

When Reggie's target, Munson, read the story, he walked up to Jackson's one designated friend on the roster, backup catcher Fran Healy. Fran was so diplomatic that they called him "Kissinger."

Munson waved the magazine around, asking, incredulously, "Have you read this?" Healy, ever the gentleman, said no.

129

Munson jabbed at the print and read a few choice selections out loud while muttering, "He ripped me here, he ripped me there…."

Healy nodded and listened quietly until the team captain stopped. "Gee, Thurm," he ventured, "maybe it was taken out of context."

Munson shouted "*For four f——in' pages?!*"

"THREE SWINGS, THREE HOME RUNS"

In the 1977 World Series, Reggie Jackson hit three straight home runs on three swings against three different pitchers. He did. But it wasn't nearly the whole story.

It's seldom mentioned anymore, but Jackson hit a home run in his last at-bat in Game 5 of the '77 Series, off the Dodgers' Don Sutton. Back at home in Yankee Stadium for Game 6, he walked in his first plate appearance and then proceeded to blast three straight first-pitch homers (off L.A.'s Burt Hooton, Elias Sosa, and Charlie Hough). If you count the last at-bat in Game 5 and ignore the four-pitch walk to start off Game 6, Reggie Jackson hit four straight home runs on *four* swings against *four* different pitchers.

He sort of did it a couple times over, actually.

The '78 Yankees started the season on the road, and then came home for an April 6 home opener. As a capacity crowd chomped on their free Reggie! bars, the man of the hour came up to the plate for his first at-bat, took a 2–0 count off Wilbur Wood of the White Sox, then blasted yet another homer. If you connect the home opener's dinger to the three in the '77 Series finale, Reggie Jackson hit *four* straight homers in *four* straight Yankee Stadium swings.

"WINNING TEAMS TEND TO FOLLOW ME AROUND"

Within a few years of Reggie Jackson's debut for the Oakland Athletics, he was surrounded by teammates such as Sal Bando, Vida Blue, Bert Campaneris, Rollie Fingers, Ken Holtzman, Catfish Hunter, and Joe Rudi, all of whom made multiple All-Star appearances while playing alongside Jax. When he signed with the Yankees, he walked into a clubhouse with talents such as Goose Gossage, Ron Guidry, Tommy John, Thurman Munson, Graig Nettles, and Willie Randolph. When he signed with California, it was the same story, as Reggie found himself teamed with Rod Carew and Fred Lynn, not to mention the still-potent Bobby Grich, Bob Boone, and Doug DeCinces.

But here's the question: did winning teams follow Reggie Jackson around or did Reggie Jackson follow winning teams around?

"ONE OF MY BIGGEST MISTAKES"

In 1981, after Reggie Jackson played out the five-year free-agent contract he signed in 1977, the Yankees elected not to re-sign him. George Steinbrenner later called it "one of my biggest mistakes," surprising words for a man who had so many to choose from. Even so, Steinbrenner was mistaken about the "mistake." Reggie averaged .239 batting, 25 home runs, and 75 RBIs per year over his five-year contract with the California Angels. Heading into the wrong side of age 35, he was no longer a big-time slugger, and his always-bad fielding became so unforgivable that he served as a full-time DH. Jax did have a big year immediately after leaving New York, in 1982, but after that he was basically circling the drain. About his only memorable moment as a California Angel was the occasion of his 500th career home run.

REGGIE JACKSON, MR. YANKEE

The visage of Reggie Jackson smiles down from underneath a Yankee cap in his Hall of Fame plaque. His No. 44 has been permanently retired in Monument Park. His *Yankeeography* is in heavy rotation on the YES Network. To this day, more than a quarter-century after his last game as a Yankee, his memorabilia still outsells most active players.

I dare you to spend more than a blissful few days in Yankeeland without seeing him hanging around the batting cage, being quoted somewhere, or throwing out a ceremonial first pitch. Mr. October is now, in effect, Mr. Yankee, and that's pretty strange.

It's certainly not because Jackson devoted most of his career or homers or much-heralded playoff appearances in the Bronx. Excluding a single season in Baltimore in 1976, his 1967 to 1987 playing career breaks down this way:

Team	Years	Games	HR	Years w/ Playoffs	WS Titles	OPS+ 150+
Athletics	10	1,346	269	5	3	3
Yankees	5	653	144	4	2	2
Angels	5	687	123	2	0	0

Not only did he begin and end his career in Oakland, he also left behind more than twice as many A's games, nearly twice as many homers, and more playoff wins. He also won his only MVP, in 1973, back in Oak-Town. Yet the fans, media, and others have cast him as a Yankee *par excellence.*

What's more, Jackson is particularly miscast when compared to the other players and managers honored in Monument Park. Excluding Roger Maris, who was, for all his faults, responsible for one of the most memorable records in Yankee history, none of the other 14 honorees spent fewer than 11 years in pinstripes, and that one was Thurman Munson, who died in a plane crash at age 32.

Reggie spent just five years in the Bronx, however memorable, and he's gotten a lifetime of mileage out of them. But when it comes to the all-time Yankees, he's never belonged.

CHAPTER 25

"Bucky Dent's Homer Was a Big Deal"

"The history between [the Yankees and Red Sox] goes back to the sale of Babe Ruth, and surely it reached a climax of sorts when Bucky Dent hit his storied home run in a 1978 playoff game."
—Tony Massarotti and John Harper,
A Tale of Two Cities

"Dent hit his famous home run that was a dagger to the hearts of Red Sox fans."
—Phil Pepe, *Magic Moments Yankees*

When the Pirates' Bill Mazeroski hit the home run that won Game 7 of the 1960 World Series, Yogi Berra was so crushed that, for the only time in his career, he couldn't bring himself to congratulate the winners in the other clubhouse.

When Scott Brosius hit a ninth inning, game-tying home run off Byung-Hyun Kim in the 2001 World Series, the reliever slouched off the mound with the kind of traumatized expression you'd expect after a man's favorite dog had just died. In front of 60,000 screaming fans.

But when Bucky Dent hit his "historic" home run in the 1978 AL East's tie-breaking game against the Red Sox, Boston's Jerry Remy thought to himself, "Big deal."

133

No big deal?

Consider the situation as it happened. The 1978 Yankees mounted a furious second-half comeback to surge ahead of Boston in the regular season's division race, but the Red Sox staged their own late season run to finish in a 99–63 first-place tie with New York. The contest set aside to finally settle matters, played at Fenway, produced a 2–0 Red Sox lead after six innings.

Enter Dent.

In the top of the seventh inning, with two men on and two outs, Red Sox starter Mike Torrez got ahead on the count to Dent but tossed an inside slider that didn't quite slide, and one three-run homer later, the Yankees went from a two-run deficit to the one-run lead that they would never give up. To this day, Mr. Russell Earl Dent is "Bucky F——ing Dent" throughout the wide swaths of the Red Sox Nation. To this day, it's supposed that he hit "the home run that broke New England's back."

Without question, that's the way the homer is remembered, but it certainly wasn't the way it was taken at the time. Even after the Dent homer, the Red Sox still had three innings to score the single run they needed to tie the 3–2 score. They were playing at Fenway, in the ballpark that practically trademarked the term "home field advantage." The Sox had stormed to a 59–22 record in Boston that season, averaging 5.44 runs per game. Both figures led the Majors by a mile, so, if ever there was a team that didn't have to worry about scoring a single, game-tying run over three innings, the 1978 Red Sox, playing at home, were the guys.

If that wasn't enough to hearten the Red Sox, very recent history would have provided plenty of morale boosts. After all, it, was Boston who had found a way to erase New York's 3½-game lead with 14 games to play in September, going 12–2 to end the year even as the Yankees finished 8–5. Maybe the Red Sox weren't especially flustered by the Dent homer because they'd already won an elimination game just the day before; when either a Yankee win or a Sox loss would have eliminated Boston, it was the Yankees who lost and the Red Sox who had won.

Which One of These Is Not Like the Others?

The more you look at it, the more insignificant Bucky Dent's homer looks in comparison to baseball's most historic plays. Take ESPN's recent listing of "The 100 Greatest Home Runs of All Time." No really, please take ESPN's recent listing of "The 100 Greatest Home Runs of All Time."

Bucky is listed all the way up at #10 and, leaving aside record-breaking blasts, all the homers ahead of Dent were shots that ended their games. When Bobby Thomson, Bill Mazeroski, Carlton Fisk, Kirk Gibson, and Joe Carter had their star turns, they delivered irreversible coup d'grace, leaving no possible hope for an opponent comeback. They closed the books on their game stories. But that wasn't the case in the Dent situation. What made the '78 playoff game so unforgettable was in the way that the Red Sox could (and did) come back.

Some might say that the Dent home run was, nonetheless, pretty important because it allowed New York to replace a tiring Ron Guidry with their star reliever. Again, not true.

The Red Sox knew that the Goose Gossage who came into the ballgame that afternoon wasn't the same pitcher who later fireballed his way into the Hall of Fame. They also knew that the Goose had never pitched in a de facto playoff game before, let alone a win-or-go-home elimination game—and this, in front of the most hostile possible road crowd. Gossage later conceded that, in the moment, he was about as nervous as he'd ever been, and he sure showed it—he gave up five hits, a base on balls, and two earned runs in 2⅔ innings. He got shelled, in other words, and the damage would have been even worse if not for Lou Piniella's key defensive play on Remy in the bottom of the ninth inning.

As it was, the Red Sox did reach Goose to score the two runs they needed to overcome Dent's three RBIs. The Yankees' lead held up in a 5–4 final not because of Dent's three-run dinger, but because of an RBI double by Thurman Munson later in the seventh inning and a solo homer by Reggie Jackson in the top of the eighth.* It was those two Dent-free plays that provided what turned out to be the deciding runs for the Yankees.

Why, then, is the Dent homer still described and depicted as some kind of epic deathblow? Primarily it was because there wasn't anything particularly compelling in telling the strict, narrow truth: *there was a big game where a banjo hitter popped one out, but the other team had plenty of life left in it until they were victimized by later hits from proven run-producers.* Inflating the importance of the Dent homer, on the other hand, played into the undeniable emotions involved on the afternoon of October 2, 1978. If it's true that baseball is most fascinating in the way it serves as unscripted drama, the Dent homer was easily woven into one of the most dramatic stories the national pastime had ever seen.

The entire prelude to the 1978 tiebreaker called out for something stirring. It featured the game's two flagship franchises, its premier rivalry, and one of its oldest and most picturesque ballparks. The game capped a season that saw absolutely unprecedented comebacks from both New York and Boston, teams battling to decide win number 100 and the best record in the majors. It was only the second time the Yankees and Red Sox had ever fought to the very last contest of the year, and the first time it had happened in nearly 30 years. There was an unforgettable cast of stars—and characters—in both dugouts.

The stage was set for something epic. Lou Piniella took a look at the perfect New England weather and said, "I could imagine Harvard and Yale playing on a crisp fall Saturday afternoon like this." Scribe Jonathan Schwartz later wrote, "It was the afternoon of my very imagination, the handpicked sunlit hours during which my perpetual baseball game had always been played."

---

*Afterward, he said, "It was an insurance homer—that's why I hit it halfway to the Prudential Building."

In a scenario that fairly cried out for a memorable leading man, Bucky Dent was a memorably unlikely fit for the part. His 5'9" height made shortstop a very appropriate position, he choked up on the bat in grade-schooler fashion, and he hit just .243 with four homers in 1978; all in all, it was a fairly typical year in an undistinguished career. Going into the infamous seventh inning, he was mired in an 0-for-13 skid. Bucky F——ing Dent was batting in the nine-spot in the lineup that day, and the Yankees likely would have batted him 10th if they could have.

Even the Dent drive itself, somehow, seemed to come out of nowhere. Mike Torrez had a four-hit, six-inning shutout going with two outs in the seventh and had worked an 0–2 count against Dent. On the pitches immediately before the fateful homer, he'd dominated Dent, even forcing him into a painful foul ball off his own leg, meaning that the most harmless hitter in the Yankees lineup was, effectively, crippled. When the fateful ball came off the bat, it was so soft and shallow that Boston's nearest outfielder, Carl Yastrzemski, immediately patted his glove in anticipation of an easy flyout; only a late arriving, strong gust of wind pushed the ball over the shortest fence in the majors—and by no more than a couple feet.

Add that moment and that man and that magic all together and you had a once-in-a-lifetime confluence of elements, something that made for a vivid storyline. The media members did their part. They painted a scenario in which one swing decided the one game that decided it all. They made an otherwise undistinguished slap hitter a symbol of the Yankees' triumph. They found an angle that highlighted a long tradition of Yankee celebrations and Red Sox frustrations. They forgot the stats and went for the story.

CHAPTER 26

"The '79 Yankees Collapsed After Thurman Died"

"On August 2, Thurman Munson died in a plane crash. In a real sense that was the end of the season for the Yankees. There could be no recovery from such an event."
—David Falkner, *The Last Yankee*

"Munson's death in early August removed what little fight the 1979 Yankees had left. We went through the motions in the final seven weeks of the season."
—Goose Gossage, *The Goose is Loose*

Some years are for parties; some years are for hangovers. Any Yankee fan who went through 1978 and 1979 knows as much.

The '78 campaign was eventful even by Yankee standards. It started with the Bombers hoisting their first championship banner in 15 years and proceeded through months of Bronx Zoo melodrama, complete with feuds between the star slugger, his manager, and many others—all of it lovingly chronicled day by day in dozens of newspapers. It was a year the ace pitched himself to a peerless 25–3 record; the year a soon-to-be–ex-manager said, "One of them's a born liar and the other's convicted"; the year of diva turns from Sweet Lou, Gator, Dirt, Catfish,

The Yankees after Munson's death in 1979. "Our endeavors will reflect our love and admiration for him," wrote Steinbrenner.

Sparky, Goose, Chicken, Reggie, Mick the Quick, Bucky, Lem, Puff, and the Boss.

When the ballclub actually got around to playing some ball, it somehow found a way to storm back from a 14.5 game deficit in July and swept its way through a "Boston Massacre" series in September to end the season with 99 games won, thus setting up a win-or-go-home contest against the Red Sox. The Yankees won that contest by the slimmest of margins, took yet another League Championship Series from their old rivals from Kansas City, and then triumphed in a World Series rematch against the Dodgers. In more than a century of Yankee baseball, never had winning been so crazy and colorful.

1979, though, was the yearlong morning after. Even before the season started, things took a somber turn as manager Bob Lemon's son Jerry died in a car accident and coach Elston Howard learned that he'd contracted the heart ailment that would soon take his life. Fan favorites

Mickey Rivers and Sparky Lyle were traded away, Catfish Hunter was finished at age 33, and mainstays such as Goose Gossage and Reggie Jackson lost significant playing time with injuries. Wild and wondrous became tense and tired. Through mid-June, the team was sputtering along with a .500 record, well below the Orioles' runaway lead in the American League East.

The 1979 campaign had all of the makings of a disappointment well before a far, far more grievous blow struck the Yankees on August 2, when their beloved teammate, Thurman Munson, died in an off-day plane accident. Times that were disappointing became tragic, hitting the entire roster with a shock and grief that was almost beyond description.

When Ron Guidry said, "I had the feeling that it would never be the same" without his friend and catcher, he was right, without question. Thurman was the team captain because he was universally regarded as the toughest competitor on a roster full of tough competitors, the one person who could always be counted on to work hard, bear down, and play through pain. Gossage once said that he'd never seen a teammate display more enthusiasm or joy. That kind of thing couldn't be replaced, not by a young Jerry Narron, not by anyone.

But when Glenn Stout's *Yankee Century* writes that Thurman's death "gave the team an unspoken excuse for underachieving," that goes too far. Although the Yankees could have been forgiven for mailing in the remainder of the season, they didn't. They still played very hard and very well.

After Billy Martin replaced Lemon as manager on June 18, the team's .579 winning percentage (55–40 record) pace would have translated to 94 wins in a full 162-game season and was third only to the Orioles (.632) and Brewers (.621) among the 14 AL teams in that stretch. They finished up with a relatively middling 89–71 record only because they'd dug themselves into a big hole in the beginning of the season.

Far from having the bottom fall out after Munson's death, the ballclub went 31–23 (.574) in August and September, continuing the outstanding pace from midseason. They "collapsed" into their two best months of the season, second only to the Brewers among AL teams in those two months—and they did it all despite playing 45 of their last 54 ballgames against winning teams. If they hadn't had to make do with Narron's limp bat (.171) and rookie game-calling behind the plate, they'd have been even better.

The Yankees' single proudest victory in the final, grief-marred months of the '79 season may have occurred on the evening of August 6. Immediately after attending Thurman's funeral, the team flew from Ohio back to New York, then rushed from the airport for a game that was to be broadcast from coast to coast. The first-place Orioles struck first, setting up a four-run lead through six innings, but the Yankees rallied and prevailed with a 5–4 win.

Even on that day of all days, when they had every reason to give up, the Yankees kept persevering, kept fighting, kept winning. The team did live up to the commemoration from that night, the one that said, "Our captain and leader has not left us today, tomorrow, this year, next. Our endeavors will reflect our love and admiration for him."

Surely, somewhere, Thurman must have approved.

CHAPTER 27

The Yankees Were Pedro's Daddy

"I tip my hat and call the Yankees my daddy."
—Pedro Martinez, Sepember 24, 2004

You wouldn't know it from their fierce game faces, but a lot of ballplayers are remarkably quiet. Get them away from the heat of the moment, and they can be pretty low-key. Almost as if to retreat from the pressure, the majority learn to relax and take it easy.

Pedro Martinez is not one of those players.

During his brilliant tenure with the Red Sox, Petey was never afraid to fire verbal brushbacks. He talked trash and taunted batters. He goaded them. During Game 3 of the 2003 ALCS, his harangue against Jorge Posada sparked a brawl, during which he knocked a charging, 72-year-old Don Zimmer onto the Fenway infield dirt. Once, in May 2001, he said, "I don't believe in damn curses. Wake up the damn Bambino and have me face him. Maybe I'll drill him in the ass."

Then, on September 24, 2004, Pedro underwent a complete personality overhaul—or so it seemed. After Boston's 6–4 loss to New York, he appeared before a packed press conference and muttered the most meek, widely circulated soundbyte to ever cross his lips: "They beat me. They're that good right now. They're that hot. *I tip my hat and call the Yankees my daddy.*"

Was Mr. Defiant really saying "the Yankees own me?"

Of course it was a media circus. Of course, Pedro's "daddy issue" made headlines for weeks on end, provided heavy artillery to sports jockeys, and launched a thousand fan T-shirts, cartoons, banners, and signs.* The quotation was colorful. It was memorable. It isn't true.

In fact, no pitcher has ever had a seven-year run to match Pedro Martinez's Red Sox campaigns from 1998 to 2004. He may have been the first pitcher in history to display four dominant pitches and throw any of them on any possible count. In '99, for example, Martinez displayed the greatest combination of power and control of all time, putting up a 8.46 ratio between strikeouts and bases on balls in the course of striking out a record 13.2 batters per nine innings. In 2000, he may have been just as otherworldly when he set the MLB record for fewest hits and walks allowed per nine innings.

Martinez never finished lower than fourth in the Cy Young voting in his six full seasons. By the time he returned to the National League in 2005, his .705 career winning percentage (182–76) was the greatest of any pitcher with at least 200 decisions. Sources such as *Baseball Prospectus* have labeled him "the best pitcher ever."

It's the highest possible baseline for comparisons, and, predictably, Martinez's unprecedented numbers fell off when he was facing the Yankees, who were on quite a tear of their own in the 1998 to 2004 era, averaging a third-place finish among the 30 major league teams in terms of runs scored per game.

Here's how El Duro did in regular season walks-plus-hits-per-innings-pitched, strikeouts-per-bases-on-balls and earned-run average against the league as a whole, as well as his numbers against the Bronx Bombers:

---

*My favorite, in keeping with the Yankees' Evil Empire image, had a Darth Vader wearing an NY insignia and the inscription "I AM YOUR FATHER."

	WHIP	K/BB	ERA
Against All Opponents	.978	5.45	2.52
Against the Yankees	1.100	4.34	3.30

When facing the Yankees he allowed more base runners than normal, had a higher WHIP, showed less dominion over the strike zone, and put up a higher ERA in five of his seven seasons with the Sox.

Still, by any standard other than his own, Martinez was still pretty darned awesome against the Yankees. In fact, Martinez's Yankees-specific WHIP would have finished no lower than fourth in the AL in six of the seven years involved and would have been the very best in the league for three of the seasons. His Yankee-specific strikeout-to-walk ratio, similarly, would have finished no lower than fifth in the AL. Working with a "quality start" definition of six or more innings pitched with three or fewer earned runs, he put together quality starts in 21 of 27 contests.

A better illustration of Martinez's dominance over the Yankees can be found in New York's numbers against him as compared to the rest of the league. Consider:

	WHIP	K/BB	ERA
Martinez versus Yankees	1.10	4.34	3.30
All Opponents versus Yankees	1.50	1.62	5.41

Quite clearly, the Martinez–Yankee matchups were pretty tough on both sides. Just as Pedro fell from his own heights when matching up against the pinstripes, the Yankees also failed to live up to their usual standards. The Yankees suffered more severe drop-offs in base runners (WHIP), control over the strike zone (strikeouts-to-walks), and overall results (runs per game). There wasn't a single year when they reached their averages against Martinez and, in most years, they weren't within shouting range.

It bears repeating that Martinez would still be among the best pitchers alive if he always pitched like he did against New York. Had the Yankees played at their Martinez levels always, they would have been, by far, *the worst offense in baseball.*

So, why all the "daddy" talk, then? Because Pedro was playing a team game, and as it turned out, his efforts weren't doing the team a whole lot of good. Consider Martinez's outstanding won/loss percentage against the AL compared to his record against the Yankees for the 1998 to 2004 time period:

	W	L	W percentage
Against All Opponents	117	37	.760
Against the Yankees	9	10	.473

Martinez's win totals fell through the floor when he saw the Yanks, but the Red Sox's team results were even more pitiful, as they went 10–17 over his 27 Yankee starts. In Martinez-pitched games from June 2000 to the infamous contest in September 2004, they hit rock bottom, putting up a woeful 6–15 mark.

The won/lost situation can be easily explained by the fact that Pedro's on-field performance simply wasn't being matched by his teammates on the Red Sox, not in any dimension. For the 27 New York–Boston games in question, for example, the Sox offense averaged an anemic 3.22 runs per game. In their 17 losses, it shrunk to a mere 2.06 runs. The Bosox bullpen was even worse. The likes of Curtis Leskanic and Pete Schourek torched Pedro leads in eight of the 17 losses. The Sox's defense, mediocre in the best of times, chipped in to the losing effort by averaging nearly an error per game.

Pedro Martinez had a de facto Ph.D. in pitching, so of course he knew what was going on. The Yankees weren't *his* daddy. The Red Sox were losing because his teammates couldn't hit, relieve, or defend with the other side. The Yankees were *their* daddy.

My theory goes in a completely different direction. By the end of September 2004, after Pedro had made his last regular-season start against his team's biggest rival, he'd seen more than enough. He'd seen at least a dozen wins slip away through no fault of his own. He'd seen Grady Little blow Game 7 of the 2003 ALCS when he was kept in the game long past exhaustion. In 2004 he saw his last, best chance to win a championship before his contract expired at the end of the year.

After seeing all that, he shrewdly delivered a quotation guaranteed to shake the baseball world. He might have been calling himself out, on the surface, but by doing so he shone a spotlight on the Red Sox–Yankees issue in a way that showed his teammates' shortcomings. It was a challenge to his teammates. In effect, he was telling them that he was paying attention, that he wanted them to turn things around, and that they needed to beat the Yankees.

A few weeks later, in the 2004 ALCS, they did.

CHAPTER 28

Derek Jeter: Clutch Superstar (Part One)

I have a confession to make: I've never understood clutch hitting.

Sure, I know how the notion's defined. It's based on the belief that some moments are more important than others in deciding a baseball game. The exact parameters vary, but the general consensus says:

- The late innings of a ballgame are more important than the early ones;
- At-bats with runners in scoring position are more important than those when the bases are empty;
- At-bats in close or tied ballgames are more important than at-bats during a blowout; and
- Late-season ballgames are more important than early-season contests.

A "clutch" hitter is one who rises to the occasion, coming up with big hits in the later innings, with guys on base, in close games, and during September playoff runs.

I hear it, but I don't buy it. To me, one of the unique things about baseball games is the possibility that any point might be a turning point. Virtually any play, in any inning, might lead to a game-changing hit, walk, or error. The implication that many innings and situations are less important makes the clutch notion ring hollow.

147

The specifics of the clutch concept seem inherently flawed and in fairly obvious ways:

- As it turns out, early-inning leads are absolutely crucial to winning baseball games, and are at least as important as late ones, because they buck up the team's starting pitcher. They also put pressure on opposing pitchers and hitters and force managers to call in weak middle relievers. Managers have always sought to take control of games before the late innings arrive. Recent studies have only confirmed that fact of baseball life: the team that scores first wins more than two-thirds of all games.
- Because the deciding margin in most ballgames comes in one big inning, at-bats with the bases empty can be at least as important as at-bats with the bases occupied. After all, the ability to get on base provides teammates with multiple-RBI

Derek Jeter: always cool, sometimes ice cold

opportunities, and no one can clear the bases if no one's on the bases to begin with.

- At-bats during games with big run differentials can be just as important as those with close games, and that's especially true in these high-scoring times, when any new run might make the difference in the final victory margin. This is Baseball 101. A championship-caliber team is largely defined by its constant commitment, no matter how far ahead or behind it might be.

- Like early inning scores, early season wins are absolutely crucial in the way that they bolster a leader's confidence and cloud a trailing team's outlook. As the old cliché goes, pennants can be won and lost in April. In fact, one of the reasons that late-inning rallies are so memorable is the fact that they are so rare—90 percent of the time, the team with a significant advantage in the last stages of a game or a season will win out.

I suspect that the resiliency of the clutch concept has much to do with people who might confuse drama with effectiveness. It's impossible to deny that certain baseball moments are inherently more emotional and, therefore, more memorable. It's very tempting to take a further, far shakier step and believe those moments deliver an impact beyond their actual effect.

Think of the way fans tend to overlook very worthy contributions while focusing on other, supposedly more clutch spots:

- A two-run home run in the first inning may make the all-important difference in a 3–2 victory, but its importance can be obscured by the hard-fought eight innings that followed it. It's much more likely that a run-scoring clutch single in the eighth inning will be noted, if only because its impact was obvious in the moment.

- The runners who get on base in front of a home-run hitter may represent the tying or winning runs in a ballgame, but their scores can be easily lost in the luster of the later shot. In the Giants and Dodgers' landmark playoff finale in 1951, for example, few remember how Alvin Dark, Don Mueller, and Whitey Lockman got on base with the tying runs in the ninth inning, but everyone remembers how Bobby Thomson later plated them with the "Shot Heard 'Round the World." Without those runs, the game could have easily been lost, but instead Thomson's homer took the clutch label.

• In Game 7 of the 1960 World Series, Bill Virdon, Dick Groat, Roberto Clemente, and Hal Smith all drove in runs that the Pirates needed to battle back against the Yankees' lead, but only Bill Mazeroski's walk-off homer has been singled out as the defining moment.

Clutch successes will always be part of the emotions and memories that make baseball the sport that it is, but the athletes who know the game best know enough to treat *every* situation as clutch. They understand that the difference between a .330 batting champion and an ordinary .280 hitter is an additional hit or so per week. That the difference between a 3.00 ERA champion and a mediocre 4.50 might come down to a single (home run) mistake for every nine innings (or 140 or so pitches). That the difference between a very good, sure-handed outfielder (.980 fielding percentage) and a mediocre defender (.970) can come down to one measly error for every 100 chances.

With those tissue-thin margins separating stars from mediocrity and mediocrity from unemployment, major leaguers can't afford to hold back until clutch moments. For them, every moment is essential, whether it's the fourth inning or the fourteenth, whether the bases are empty or loaded, whether the score is 10–0 or 0–0, whether they're battling for first place or last.

Of course there are "un-clutch" players who lack in mental or physical capability to perform consistently, but they're weeded out before they reach the highest levels. What defines successful major leaguers is

One More Tiny Problem with the Clutch Concept

Quintessential clutch situations are more dramatic than ordinary situations because they're so rare. But it's also their relative rarity that makes them so relatively unimportant.

Everyone knows that, by the time a supposed "clutch" situation has come up, there's an excellent chance a ballgame or season has already been decided. About two-thirds of all at-bats come in the first six innings of a ballgame and, depending on his place in the lineup and his teammates' offensive stats, about three-quarters of a hitter's at-bats can come without men on base. As many as 525 of every 600 at-bats in a season come up in situations where a ballgame isn't close in the late innings. Of course, by the time September rolls around, about five-sixths of the season is already in the books.

Even if a player has the proven, special ability to step up in those crunch times, they're rare enough that the contributions wouldn't be particularly useful because the truly great players will probably have decided the ballgame or season already, based on their consistent performance throughout the season.

their ability to give high but sustainable efforts in their game—which is why they do everything but chant the word "consistency" like a mantra.

Dozens of major statistical studies, starting with Dick Cramer's groundbreaking 1977 research, have backed the view that major leaguers generally try to succeed as well in ordinary situations as they do in those involving late innings, men on base, close games, or September contests. The extra edge that's supposedly found among a clutch breed either doesn't exist or is so rare that it's negligible.

Why the persistent belief in special clutch hitting, then? That's what makes players great—their ability to constantly grind it out, to perform any time and all of the time.

To say that individual players can't perform better in certain key moments by sheer willpower is not to say that all players are alike. In the ninth inning or in the playoff stretch run, a team will always prefer to bat a veteran slugger over a nervous slap hitter. Why? Because the power hitter has already proven that he knows how to produce more offense. He'll be a better hitter in the ninth inning, it's true, almost entirely because he's a better hitter in innings one through eight.

In addition, the clutch concept has lingered because it's easy for observers to draw hasty conclusions from small data samples. For as long as stats have been compiled in baseball, they've been subdivided, and we've now reached the point where we know how every hitter in the game performs in different ballparks, in day games and night games, versus different pitchers, in different strike counts, against different pitchers...the list goes on. Those countless little data slices can reveal all sorts of exceptions and aberrations. Any statistician worth his salt will tell you that a data sample taken at random will tell you nothing about the predictability of a system.

Be that as it may, mainstream commentators seem to believe in the clutch, and do they ever believe in Derek Jeter. *Newsday* has hailed him as "one of the greatest clutch players ever." SI.com's "Mr. Clutch" piece states, "Some baseball fans say there is no such thing as a clutch hitter. Have they ever seen Derek Jeter play?" Jayson Stark of ESPN thinks he's "one of those rare people who understands everything there is to understand about the Big Moment."

Of course, the notion that Jeter is a terrific hitter is perfectly reasonable. He is, in fact, in the company of Honus Wagner and Arky Vaughan as one of the best-hitting shortstops who ever played the game. At the end of the 2007 season, after 12 full seasons in the major leagues, he boasted a .317 career batting average, .388 on-base percentage, and .462 slugging percentage. Barring catastrophe, it's probable that he'll finish his career with more than 3,000 hits and 2,000 runs scored. When the time comes, he'll undoubtedly be named as a first-ballot Hall of Famer.

Those are stellar numbers, but the clutch claim insists that he's *even better than usual* in those select scenarios involving the late innings, runners in scoring position, close or tied ballgames, and late-season ballgames. Except for one small detail: he isn't.

First, consider Jeter's late-inning performance. Thanks to the superlative efforts of Sean Forman and his colleagues at Baseball-Reference.com, we have all the data needed to contrast Jeter's overall batting average, on-base percentage, slugging, and on-base-plus-slugging in all situations to his numbers in innings seven through nine. Jeter's numbers are still good, but he's not nearly as good as he is in innings one through six.

	BA	OBP	SLG	OPS
Innings 1–3	.325	.385	.482	.867
Innings 4–6	.332	.402	.477	.879
Innings 7–9	.283	.368	.410	.778

Jeter's numbers in at-bats with runners in scoring position tell the same story:

	BA	OBP	SLG	OPS
All Situations	.317	.388	.461	.849
Runners in Scoring Position	.313	.407	.438	.845

Once again, Captain Clutch is very good in prime RBI opportunities, but his overall OPS isn't *quite* as good as it is in other times.

For at-bats in which the ballgame is either tied or within two runs:

	BA	OBP	SLG	OPS
All Situations	.317	.388	.461	.849
Tied	.320	.387	.473	.860
Late and Close	.286	.384	.419	.803

To be as generous as possible, let's call this a wash. Jeet puts up higher totals in tie ballgames—by the equivalent of a few extra bases for every full (650 at-bat) season—but his numbers drop off in the late and close slots.

Finally, Jeter's season numbers in contrast to his performance in late-season, playoff race games:

	BA	OBP	SLG	OPS
All Situations	.317	.388	.461	.849
September and October	.326	.400	.480	.882

Well, give him that one. Jeet *does* pick it up when the leaves start turning and the margins start shrinking in September.

Jeter may not flop in the clutch situation scoreboard, but his late-season hitting success doesn't make up for hitting declines in late innings, with runners in scoring position, and in tight ballgames.

CHAPTER 29

Derek Jeter: Clutch Superstar (Part Two)

I have another confession to make: when I said I didn't really understand what clutch hitting was, I wasn't telling the complete truth. Oh, I still believe that one of the beauties of the game is in the fact that any particular play or contest can be the one that makes all the difference. I also believe that ballplayers' emphasis on consistency is a direct contradiction to "clutchiness." I believe that some of baseball's lazier columnists use the clutch as a crutch and do so because they mistake the game's most dramatic situations with its most important ones.

But analysts are exactly right to define playoff games as inherently more important (or clutch) than those during the regular season. The scarcity of the contests—no more than seven in a do or die series—means that every individual failure has a bigger impact on the team's fate, just as individual successes have a bigger impact on the team's championship march. In that respect, a playoff hero can be described as coming through in the clutch while a playoff zero can't.

Then again, the very thing that makes a playoff game so clutch—its scarcity—is what makes clutch play irrelevant when assessing a player's overall skill level.

Strange things can happen over a few days or weeks in baseball. In any given period, a Mickey Morandini could hit like Mickey Mantle. Maybe Morandini was playing over his head for a few glorious days because he was physically healthy and unusually focused, and maybe

155

Mantle was *choking* for a little while due to tired legs or trouble at home. Stuff happens. Over a handful of October days, guys such as Dusty Rhodes, Mickey Hatcher, and Pat Borders have played like World Series MVPs while guys such as Ty Cobb and Willie Mays have performed like scrubs. Short-term variables eventually even themselves out, and when they do, Morandini and Mantle, like all players, put up numbers that reflect their true skill levels, the ones they can repeat time and again.

But let's put it all to the test with our main man, Derek Sanderson Jeter.

On the one side are those who believe that certain athletes have the personal fortitude to put up special performances in the most important games of the year. This is the official *Yankeeography* view, that no one thrives on the big stage more than DJ. Included in that crowd is Joe Morgan, who has told national television audiences that "the stage gets too big—it overwhelms some people. It doesn't overwhelm DJ."

On the other side is me, your trusty author, who believes that Captain Clutch is just like any other player. I don't believe that he is the Fonzie of the ballfields. I do believe that, like everybody else, he'll have his postseason ups and downs before returning to the norms established over the longer term.

Which side wins the case study?

Maybe you already guessed: I win. Jeter is good in the postseason, but he isn't good enough to be called clutch.

Here's how DJ's regular-season numbers compared to his postseason stats in batting average, on-base percentage, slugging, and combined on-base-plus slugging (through 2007):

	BA	OBP	SLG	OPS
Regular	.317	.388	.461	.849
Playoffs	.309	.377	.469	.846

Keeping up his usual pattern, Jeter has been very good in postseason situations, but not quite as good as he is every day. On average, his overall OPS comes in just a hair under what you'd expect at all other times.

On the positive side, there have been many times that Jeter has been just as good as advertised. Using the generally accepted benchmarks of a .400 on-base percentage and .500 slugging percentage to add up to a combined .900 on-base-plus-slugging (OPS), he's put up awesome numbers in 11 of 25 career postseason series from 1996 to 2007. During the 1996 American League Championship Series against the Orioles (1.042 OPS) and 2000 ALCS against the Mariners (1.055), for instance, Jeter made his case as the best hitter on the field, and he had every right to win the MVP trophy for his terrific (9-for-22, two doubles, one triple, two homers) play in the 2000 World Series, too.

On the negative side, however, there have been times when Jeter's gone from cool to ice cold. Going with the generally accepted benchmarks of .300 OBP and .400 slugging to add up to a measly .700 OPS, he's had subpar series in nine of the 25 career postseasons, and when he's been bad, he's been very bad. His résumé includes the 1998 American League Division Series against the Rangers (.384 OPS), the 2001 ALCS against the Mariners (.318), and the 2007 ALDS against the Indians (.352), times when Jeter was building a case as the single worst player in *either* lineup. Those were the kind of 1-for-9/2-for-17/3-for-17 lines that would embarrass Bobby Meacham or anyone else who's ever managed to hold down a major league job for any length of time.

The only constant in Jeter's numbers is the fact that there hasn't been any particular constant. He's had multiple years (1996, 2000, 2001) when a stepping-up series alternated with a stepping-down series, plus multiple occasions (1997 and 1998, 1999 and 2000) when a good year's been followed a bad one. The Yankees went 7–4 in playoff series when he was at his best, but then again, they went 6–3 when he was at his worst.

The more you look at Jeter's playoff performances, the more you realize that they don't surpass his regular-season norms, haven't been especially consistent, and haven't dramatically affected game outcomes, either. The only real question left is why so many still seem so intent on hanging on to the ever-familiar "big stage" notion.

Perhaps it's just that it fits so nicely with his image. There's no denying that Jeter has an unflappable, wholesome way about him. He loves his family. He's always polite. He's never shown up on the police blotter. His Turn Two Foundation is among the most generous charities in sports, many of its good deeds being done in anonymity. Women everywhere consider him attractive. He's the kind of guy you want to root for, the type of positive person you'd like to believe can consistently deliver when needed.

He picked the perfect moment to show up in the Bronx. He played his first full season just when the Yankees had finally assembled their first championship roster in 18 years in 1996, then enjoyed an unprecedented 14–2 playoff series run over the next six years. After that 1996–2001 period, Jeter became the unshakable symbol of success—when he did well, the Yankees won, and when he didn't do well, heck, the Yankees still won. It didn't take a huge leap to assume that he was 6'3" worth of good luck at shortstop.

By now, everyone's so familiar with that storyline that no one remembers to blame him for his part in its downside, like the fact that Yankees put up a 3–6 playoff series record from 2002 to 2007, including a 1–6 mark in series elimination games. Still comfy with the winner tag, no one's especially eager to point out that Jeter has also played in the most losing playoff games and series in Yankee history. Derek's lead in career postseason hits is a well-known achievement; not so his lead in October strikeouts.

CHAPTER 30

Jeter Leader

"There are things he brings to the table—as far as his leadership and things like that—that set him apart."
—Joe Torre, ESPN interview, March 2008.

"Is it possible to be any cooler than Derek Jeter? Smart, single, good-looking, on the cover of GQ, *Saturday Night Live.... You couldn't ask for a better man to serve as leader than Derek."*
—*Yankeeography*: Derek Jeter

On every team, there are certain key individuals who lead the way. They're the ones who make sure everyone comes to play every day. They buck up morale during the slumps and calm down everyone during the streaks. They volunteer tips on improving performance. They carry themselves properly, providing an example for the players to aspire to. They tell everyone to check their egos at the door, to give all without trying to do too much. They know all the clichés. These individuals are so important, in fact, that they have a special title: we call them *coaches*.

Beyond the coaches, there always seems to be one special guy in the clubhouse. He's the hub of the wheel, the one who takes charge. The one who sets the tone. He demands 100 percent effort from everyone. He always lends support but constantly expects accountability. He knows the percentages but also knows when to go with his gut. He knows the clichés, too, and may coin a few new ones to boot.

A-Rod and Jeter in 2004. At shortstop, No. 2 was looking out for No. 1.

This individual is so important that he, too, has a title: *manager.*

After the coaches and managers, individuals who are *paid to lead*, there's not a lot more to clubhouse leadership. Active players, in particular, can do little to nothing to influence their fellow athletes.

To be sure, catchers have to work closely with pitchers, and middle infielders have to relate well enough to turn a mean double play. Veterans can give advice that the coaches don't get around to mentioning. Apart from that, though, good ballplayers are mostly defined by the fact that they know how to lead themselves. They realize that they'll be all alone in the batter's box or mound or field when the time comes, and they take that very individual responsibility to heart.

Just as Diana Ross once had the Supremes, Derek Jeter now has the Yankees. It's said that he plays the game the right way, and you know what, he does. It's also said that he helps teammates play well, and that he doesn't.

One might argue that the key attribute of a leader is one's ability to put the greater good of the team ahead of his own interests. In that vein, Jeter, as a leader, has failed.

In some ways, Alex Rodriguez and Derek Jeter led parallel lives through 2004. They were born less than a year apart and just 30 miles from each other, one in Washington Heights and the other in Pequannock, New Jersey. They both grew up rooting for New York teams, playing shortstop, and both turned down college to enter the amateur draft in 1992–93. When they first saw action in the 1995 season, they were two of the three youngest players in the majors, and from their rookie season on they were both mentioned in the debate over the best shortstop in the American League. By 2001, they were among the highest-played athletes in American sports.

Those surface similarities apart, though, A-Rod and Jeter were worlds apart where it mattered most: on the diamond. When it came to actual performance, Rodriguez dominated Jeter. After eight full seasons, 1996 through 2003, A-Rod was running almost neck-and-neck with Jeter in career batting average (.307 to .314) and on-base percentage (.385 to .386), but A-Rod topped Jeter's personal best in slugging (.552) and home runs (24) in seven of his eight seasons. By the end of the '03 season, at age 28, A-Rod was on track to finish with nearly 800 career homers, while DJ was at one-third of that pace.

Rodriguez's superiority over Jeter was even more pronounced when it came to defense. Through the 2003 season, he had a higher fielding percentage than the Yankee (.979 vs. .974) but, more important, far more range. A-Rod's putouts and assists per game exceeded the league average every year; Jeter went above average just once in eight years. While Rodriguez was his usual superstar self with the glove (a sparkling 4.47 range factor vs. the AL average of 4.15), Jeter significantly underperformed in his typical year (posting a lowly 3.99).

All of this A-Rod–Jeter stuff was of more than debating interest during the 2003–04 off-season, as it happened, because it was at that time that the Yankees' starting third baseman Aaron Boone's co-rec basketball career took a fairly catastrophic turn, resulting in a torn ACL in his knee.

With a new position suddenly open, the Yankees found the money and chips to trade Rodriguez from Texas to the Bronx, put him and his completely superior numbers into the shortstop position, then slide Jeet elsewhere, likely to center field, where an aging Bernie Williams was 35 going on 53. All Jeter had to do was follow the precedent of guys such as Robin Yount and Ernie Banks, inner-circle Hall of Famers who agreed to mid-career moves away from shortstop.

It's what any true leader would have done, putting his team's needs ahead of his own. One can imagine the gracious Lou Gehrig would have smiled and said, "Welcome aboard, kid." The gentlemanly Don Mattingly, in his day, might have given A-Rod a firm handshake and a "Good luck." Thurman Munson, depending on his mood, may have given him a kick in the behind or a pat on the back, followed by a "Don't f—— it up."

But Jeter had other plans. He decided to pull rank, making it clear that he intended to hold on to the shortstop position for the 2004 season, no matter what the Rodriguez numbers shouted, and politics being politics, that settled things for all intents and purposes. The front office forced A-Rod, the inarguably superior player, to learn a new team and a new position at the same time. As the numbers demonstrated, one of the worst defenders in the league would be starting over one of the best defenders in the league and at the most crucial position in the infield.

It wasn't a criminal offense, but Jeter's choice was disappointing. Given an opportunity to act for the greater good, No. 2 shouldn't have been looking out for No. 1. He should have been a team guy. He should have led.

CHAPTER 31

Joe Torre's "Insult"

*"I expressed my dissatisfaction with the length of con-
tract and the fact that the incentives, to me, I took as an
insult. If somebody wanted me to manage here, I'd be
managing here."*

—Joe Torre, October 18, 2007,
on his departure as Yankees manager

Joe Torre beat very long odds in being named Yankee manager and
even longer odds to last through an oft-spectacular 12-year tenure. His
"insult"-ing departure in 2007 may have been the unlikeliest outcome
of them all.

The first improbability for the Torre story was how he became
Yankee skipper in the first place. In the fall of 1995, Torre had no
reason to believe he'd have another chance to manage a major league
team. He had compiled a lifetime 894–1,003 record and just a single
playoff appearance over the previous 18 years with the Mets, Braves,
and Cardinals. His career winning percentage was .471, inferior to
that of Al Buckenberger, Lee Fohl, Gus Schmeltz, and nearly 100 other
managers with at least 1,000 games managed.

If "Clueless Joe" wasn't expecting job offers from anyone at all, the
New York Yankees seemed to be a particularly unlikely suitor. Apart
from growing up in Brooklyn—rooting against them as a kid—Torre
had no real connection to the Yankees or any other American League
ballclub, for that matter. It was a serious impediment. New York had
hired a single outsider (the failed Dallas Green) in the previous 16 years.

Joe Torre didn't want to be the highest-paid manager in baseball.

If the Bombers were to hire outside their own organization, they were expected to reach out to future Hall of Fame managers such as Sparky Anderson and Tony La Russa.

The Yankees chose Joe Torre instead. And things went very well, to put it mildly.

The Yankees' 1996–2001 run was historic even by their lofty standards, as the Torre-led clubs averaged 97 regular-season wins a year and compiled a 56–22 playoff game record en route to five pennants and four World Series Championships. Not bad for a guy who walked through the stadium door needing a 109-game winning streak to reach a career .500 managerial record.

Any skipper producing those kinds of results would have been a popular man, but Torre was beloved, partly because of the particulars of his personal story. Joe grew up with siblings who included a future major league ballplayer, a cop, and a nun. He overcame his own troubled childhood and established a foundation to children in abusive homes. He finally found love with his (darling) third wife. He fathered a child at age 56. He beat prostate cancer. His 1996 World Series title was the culmination of a quest that spanned nearly 40 years and 4,200+ games played or managed; his hospitalized brother, undergoing (successful) heart transplant surgery, witnessed the quest in a tearful bedside vigil.

That was special, but what made Torre even more popular was his personality. As successor to control-obsessed Buck Showalter, Torre seemed to present living proof that one could be a highly successful baseball leader without lapsing into La Russa's brand of neurotic intensity, Jim Leyland's chain-smoking, or Lou Piniella's rageoholism. Many a column was written about how he handled star egos, defused media pressures, limited power struggles, dealt with demands, and generally kept his team at an even keel. The words "calm," "laid back," "steady," "dignified" and "classy" were tossed around when Torre was described. Several players called him a second father.

Then things went sour. No one agrees exactly when it happened. Buster Olney believed that the 2001 World Series, lost in the last inning of the last game, signaled the eclipse of the Yankee dynasty. Others pointed to 2002, when the Angels battered the Yanks' creaky pitching staff with 31 runs in four games. Looking back, it might have been 2003, when the Yankees needed Grady Little's valuable assistance to escape the Red Sox in the ALCS, only to stumble against the overachieving Marlins, of all teams, in the World Series.*

Without a doubt, however, things had taken a decidedly southward turn for Joe Torre and the Yankees by 2004, when, against all odds, they blew a three-game lead in the ALCS versus the Red Sox, a series of unfortunate events that will forever be known to many as the Worst Playoff Collapse in Baseball History. Over the next three years, from

---

*The back pages read, "YANKS SLEEP WITH THE FISHES."

2005 to 2007, the Yankees' playoff opponents (Angels, Tigers, and Indians) changed, but not the (first-round exit) outcomes. In the fall of 2007, as the Yankees' playoff performances went from awe-inspiring to awful, serious questions began emerging.

Anyone can have a bad year in a short series, but it's another thing to have seven years without a championship, four years without a pennant, and three years without a Division Series success. That looked less like bad luck and more like bad work, didn't it? With the exception of the 2004 Red Sox, all the Yankees' opponents were being outspent two and three times over. Granted, money can't buy everything, but shouldn't it have bought more than a 4–9 stretch over three postseasons? With the possible exception of the 2004 Sox, anyone would have traded their rosters for the Yanks' roster. Why was New York losing to significantly less talented ballclubs?

By fall 2007, people were starting to make some new, unkind observations about Joe Torre. Analysts noticed that their old pal seemed to put in the shortest office hours in the game and that he didn't know much about the statistics in key player matchups. They didn't like the fact that the skipper was in love with relievers such as Paul Quantrill and Scott Proctor and stuck hurlers like Kyle Farnsworth into the bullpen equivalent of Siberia. They noted, with some concern, that their hitters never seemed to do well when facing a pitcher for the first time, indicating that they were unprepared. They also noted that Torre's teams, star-studded though they may have been, never seemed to do too well in the fundamentals, like fielding percentage and base-stealing conversion—and that they performed particularly poorly after bench coach Don Zimmer departed at the end of the '03 season. When matters got tight, as they often did against playoff-caliber pitching staffs, the team wasn't well-led enough to turn in crisp defense or execute on a key steal.

Analysts especially disliked the fact that the Yankees put up a 69–59 (.539 winning percentage) record in one-run games while putting up a 217–141 mark (.606) in all other contests. Those numbers indicated that in the games where manager moves mattered the most, the Yanks played more like a mediocre 87-win team than a more formidable 97-win team.

Most of all, a small but increasing band of critics was starting to notice that, year after year, Joe Torre had his fingerprints all over the Yankees' worst playoff disappointments.

- In 2001, against the Diamondbacks, Torre was caught napping while the fully awake opponents noticed Andy Pettitte tipping his pitches during Game 6.
- In 2002, against the Angels, it was in the Yankees' failure to maintain plate discipline when they were trailing in the late innings.
- In 2003, against the Marlins, it was in Torre's failure to monitor David Wells' back problem, decision to have Aaron Boone either sacrifice or work pitch counts with men on base, and his choice to bypass the immortal Mariano Rivera for the mortal Jeff Weaver in the late innings.
- In 2004, against the Red Sox, it was in his failure to order bunts against knuckleballer Tim Wakefield and the crippled Curt Schilling, to call for a pitchout during an obvious steal situation against Dave Roberts, to monitor (again!) Kevin Brown's back problem, or to instill any kind of confidence in the shaky-but-talented Javier Vazquez.
- In 2005, against the Angels, it was in his napping (again!) as the other guys noticed Randy Johnson tipping his pitches in Game 3.
- In 2006, against the Tigers, it was in his decision to start a hobbling Gary Sheffield at first base and bumping Alex Rodriguez down to eighth in the batting order.
- In 2007, against the Indians, it was in his skipping Andy Pettitte in favor of Chien–Ming Wang and his failure to halt play during a Cleveland bug swarm.

Some people defended a few of those failed moves, but nobody defended all of them, and that spurred still more questions. What good was it for the Yankees to make the playoffs every year if they couldn't get results any year? If the postseason was some kind of random crapshoot, why did it come up craps for the Yankees over and over? If Torre couldn't be blamed for the later failures, then why was he rewarded for the earlier successes? How would that you lose/we win philosophy square with the teamwork concept?

That question seemed to be on the mind of the Bombers' brass as they contemplated Joe Torre's contractual status in October 2007. His most recent contract, the one that made him the longest-serving manager in the American League, paid out an average of $6.4 million over the previous three seasons, but the Steinbrenner brothers and team president Randy Levine thought a modest pay cut was in order and offered $5 million in guaranteed annual salary plus $3 million in team performance bonuses. Another $8 million bonus was vested in a pennant win. It was still, by any interpretation, an extremely lucrative package. The base salary would ensure the once-obscure Torre a continued status as the highest-paid manager in baseball—and by several million dollars per year. If the bonuses and guarantee were also triggered, they'd allow him to earn *twice* as much as any other skipper in the game.

Many expected Torre to take it in a heartbeat. I personally harbored some hopes that, in the process, he'd also display some of his famed classiness. Maybe he'd reaffirm the fact that performance was more important than personality, express sincere disappointment over his team's many failures, and acknowledge the need for accountability. In a perfect world, Joe would give thanks for a second (third? fourth? fifth?) chance and note the Yankees' extreme generosity.

It didn't quite happen that way. That was the third surprise in Joe Torre's time with the Yankees. According to the Yankees' now-former manager, the Yankees didn't get back to him quite quickly enough ("If it takes them two weeks to figure out, 'Yeah, we want to do this,' you're a little suspicious"). He disliked the fact that he couldn't deal directly with his good buddy, the general manager ("I looked around and saw business people"). Accountability? Never heard of it ("I didn't think motivation was needed"). He wanted them to fork over even more cash (which he termed "commitment and trust"). He also hinted that the organization was letting everyone down with all the above ("I didn't think it was the right thing for my players").

On his way out the door, Joe Torre summed up the entire situation as "an insult." One might say that he was right about that one but wrong about just who was insulting whom.

CHAPTER 32

Yankee Stadium, 1923-2008

Ah, the old Yankee Stadium. I really miss it. At least, I'm sure I would, if I'd ever seen it.

You see, like most fans under the age of 40, I never had the chance to visit the old ballpark. It's been gone since 1973, when I was barely old enough to hold up a toy bat.

The interior look and feel of the place was completely transformed to start. The Ballantine Ale & Beer sign, Longines clock, "No Betting" notices, and billboards for Philip Morris cigarettes and Gem razors disappeared as new corporate signage appeared. The hand-operated scoreboard made way for something called a Jumbotron, and the vast, 64,000-plus seating capacity was trimmed down to just more than 54,000—every one of the old wooden seats supplanted by bigger, bluer plastic ones. Even the signature frieze encircling the perimeter of the park was torn down and cut up, though the team did retain a mini-replica on the center-field perimeter.

The playing field was out, too. The low, metallic outfield fences were replaced with padded blue walls and moved 60 feet or more closer to home plate. The monuments that once stood out in center-field grass were moved away from the field to a new area called Monument Park. The ground itself was, literally, shifted under the workers' feet. The dirt was hauled away, and the field was sunk to five feet below its original level.

Yankee Stadium (before and after): victimized by the Invirex Demolition Company

The clubhouses the Yankees had known since 1923 were gone, too. The lockers that once belonged to Hall of Famers were donated to Cooperstown and the Smithsonian while lesser memorabilia—tarps, duffel bags, foot lockers, and the like—were sold to collectors. Everything had to go. Claire Hodgson Ruth and Eleanor Gehrig were given the stadium's home plate and first base on the last day of the '73 season.

The interior support structure the fans once knew, that too was gutted. None of the old turnstiles, ticket booths, gate signs, or concession stands survived the mid-1970s renovation; all were replaced by newer versions. Luxury boxes, private dining rooms, and VIP clubs were constructed. The stadium was stripped to nearly everything but its structural beams. The Invirex Demolition Company tore out virtually everything but the core structural beams.

The exterior was replaced, too. Have you ever seen that famous picture of cars lined up outside Yankee Stadium on its first Opening Day back in 1923? The granite and limestone facing depicted in that image met a wrecking ball in 1973 and was then replaced by the battleship-grey concrete exterior familiar to fans of recent generations. The art deco windows depicted on the 2008 commemorative sleeve patch were also carted off and replaced, and the gold-leaf YANKEE STADIUM lettering and flanking eagle pendants disappeared, too, replaced by the boxy blue lettering that topped the all-new facade.

Of course, the 1973–76 demolition wasn't called a demolition but a "renovation."* Renovations involve a fresh coat of paint, some furniture, a thorough cleaning, maybe a bit more. They don't cost roughly $400 million in inflation-adjusted (2007) money, involve more than 20,000 tons of concrete, and take two and a half years to complete. That's the kind of money, material, and time it takes to completely destroy something and build something new in its place.

Many acknowledged as much, stating that the Yankee Stadium originally built in 1923 was, indeed, gone well before it reached its

*As if that term made the slightest bit of sense.

172

85th anniversary. Many sports reference sources, CBS Sportsline among them, call the building that stood from 1923 to 1973 "Yankee Stadium I" and the new one (1976–2008) "Yankee Stadium II." When *61** was filmed, the production crew used Tiger Stadium to serve as the Yankee Stadium of 1961; the Yankees' current building was not a suitable stand-in for its predecessor. Yogi Berra conceded, "I didn't play there."

Still, the obvious doesn't hold much of a chance against the majority of commentators who habitually insist that a singular Yankee Stadium survived from 1923 to 2008. The mythmaking might be partially explained by the fact that, if nothing else, at least the venue kept the same 161st Street address, the same name, the same pinstriped uniforms, the same stop on the Woodlawn–Jerome Avenue line. They brought the incomparable Bob Sheppard, "the Voice of God," to continue with the announcing duties he'd performed since 1951. Of course, the new place has also provided its own memories since '76— Guidry's 18-strikeout game, Thurman's memorial service, Righetti's Fourth of July no-hitter, Donnie Baseball's farewell, and the late '90s dynasty, just to name a very few.

The larger continuity, though, is in the fans' imagination. It is more fun and interesting to believe that a single Yankee Stadium existed from the days of Babe and the Iron Horse and the Yankee Clipper all the way to the days of Jeter and A Rod and Mariano. It taps into that sense that ongoing stories are being passed from grandfathers to fathers and to sons. It makes fans' associations all the more vivid, the building's aura all the more overwhelming, and its final, irrefutable demise all the more bittersweet.

CHAPTER 33

Yankee Imperialism

The New York Yankees are about winning. They're about beating all comers to become the most legendary franchise in American sports, the one with the trophies, the Hall of Famers, the mystique, the aura, the tradition. Many have tried to do the same, but no team has succeeded quite like the Yankees.

All that winning explains why the Yankees are the most admired team in baseball, and it helps explain why they're the most hated, too. Winning is taking. It's taking the victories and glory that would otherwise belong to the competition.

But how about another accurate, if unlikely, word to describe the New York Yankees? Giving. That's right, giving. If the on-field Yankees are baseball's greatest takers, the off-field Yanks are the game's greatest givers. They give, generously and repeatedly, something that rates a rare mention or two.

The Yankees give to their players through an extremely generous payroll. Three decades ago, George Steinbrenner was among the first owners to embrace free agency by paying market rates for player services. The Yankees' $200-plus million budgets of recent years carry on that more-is-more legacy. The Yanks' pockets have been so deep, in fact, that they've long been subject to the major league's so-called luxury tax. In 2007, the team was required to spend more than $26 million to promote youth leagues and player development in foreign countries. Worthy causes, without a doubt, but equally so for all 30 major league teams. As it happens, these particular causes are bankrolled almost entirely by the single team that doesn't treat the luxury tax like it's radioactive.

At least no one's ever accused the Boss of stiffing fans from their money's worth. Consider the recent Opening Day payrolls, in millions, coming from the Red Sox, who have the richest region in the country all to their lonesome, or the Mets, who also have a fairly large market area to work with:

	Average Payroll, 2003-08	Average Millions Behind
NY Yankees	$198.2 million	—
Boston Red Sox	$129.5	$68.7 million
NY Mets	$110.4	$87.8

Neither the Red Sox nor the Mets have ever been shy about charging fans ticket prices and cable fees equal to or greater than those of the Yankees, but when it comes to reinvesting the cash back into their on-field product, it's always been a different story.

Although Steinbrenner has been more than generous to his own players and with baseball's future, the game's economic system guarantees that he'll be generous with other major league teams, too. It's no secret that the 2002 Basic Agreement's revenue-sharing plan targeted one special franchise as a cash cow,* and the latest Basic Agreement, from 2006, was even more draconian, handing over no less than 39 percent of locally generated money into a pool for lower-revenue franchises. These deals stipulate that, in a typical year, the Yankees, who consistently lead the league in gate receipts, must hand over more than $75 million to smaller-market franchises in Milwaukee and Pittsburgh—with no real strings attached and no end in sight.

Of course, no one forced Steinbrenner's hand. With a penalty especially designed to curb payroll spending, most any businessman would have taken the hint, pocketed the additional $110 million or so per year, and fielded a less-expensive, less-talented roster. Any other businessman would forget about the innovative deals he could

---

* The owners' approval vote was a 29–0 squeaker.

cut on everything from training facilities and memorabilia licensing to regional cable networks and stadium sponsorship. Of course, that never happened because, for better and for worse, the Yankee owner isn't most any businessman; Steinbrenner wants to win so badly that he's been willing to fund the billionaire owners who rigged the system in their own favor.

Of course, even when they're on the road, the Yankees are still shoveling cash into their rivals' registers. The 2005 roster, for instance, complete with 16 former or current All-Stars, was one of the strongest road draws in the pastime's 130-year history, playing before more than 3.3 million fans when they were in enemy territory. Those road games drew an average of 13,000 extra fans per contest, earning millions in extra profit for their hosts in the routine course of business.

What's more, the Yankees' money has been spread around in still more ways. Just examine MLB merchandizing. Steinbrenner's Yankees, for all their interest in championships, have been just as interested in maintaining their status as a brand. The dean of baseball's owners was reinventing the business of baseball before A-Rod was in T-ball and, along the way, Yankee ingenuity introduced or popularized everything from big-money cable deals to in-stadium marketing and first-rate spring-training facilities, its lucrative merchandising income, in addition to the hats, T-shirts, mugs, and other apparel that earns, etc.

The Yankees' push to increase merchandizing has been a spectacular success, of course, helping to fuel more than a decade of ever-rising MLB attendance, along with ever-rising revenues and profits, but here again the Yankees' have been doing a lot of giving and very little taking. According to league rules, virtually all merchandizing profits are share and share alike, so the Yankees pick up 100 percent of the direct expenses while receiving about 3 percent (1/30th) of the pooled profits. That's right, 100 percent commitment, ~3 percent reward.

When it comes to the international pastime, it's much the same story. In recent years, the fans have seen the Yankees sign foreign-based stars such as Hideki Matsui of Japan, Chien–Ming Wang of Taiwan, and Orlando Hernandez of Cuba—moves that, once again, work to everyone's benefit by goosing excitement in overseas markets. New York's win was the major league's win; the signings ignited worldwide revenues.

Again, though, the gravy train ran on a one-way track. It was a handful of front offices, chiefly the Yankees, Dodgers, and Mariners, that took the initiative to invest in Japan starting in the '90s, but when it came to the resulting boom in baseball's international media rights, the Yankees and the other pioneers got back about the same share as the Tampa Bay Rays and San Diego Padres.

Think about that one every time you hear another jab at the Yankees' place in the major leagues. The real story is the one that's never mentioned. It's about an owner's insistence on investing in the fans' product, even to the point of spilling megafortunes into charities, smaller markets, and fellow American Leaguers. It's about one organization doing all the heavy lifting in area merchandizing and international outreach, despite disincentives that turn over the rewards to its competitors.

Not only do the Yankees win, but, more important, they give.

CHAPTER 34

Misc. Myths

THE FAÇADE

The white picket fence thing above the stands in center field at Yankee Stadium isn't, technically, a facade. A facade is the entire exterior face of a building. Architects and designers call the 560-foot-long accoutrement a "frieze."

GEHRIG IN THE SHADOWS

Lefty Gomez always supposed that Lou Gehrig felt overshadowed by Babe Ruth and Joe DiMaggio. If those two hadn't been around, it's likely Gehrig would have been mentioned as the single best slugger the game had ever known. Because they had been around, the Iron Horse wasn't often mentioned as the best slugger in his own clubhouse.

Funny, though, Gehrig's supposed jealousy has never been borne out by evidence of private or public complaints. Quite the opposite. Lou went out of his way to constantly praise both "headline guys," maybe because he knew that the Babe and Joe D. were taking public attention that he never wanted in the first place. He was all about winning, first and foremost—that's why he was the captain.

EVEN BETTER THAN THE REAL THING

Honest memorabilia collectors will tell you that their industry is flooded by fakes of all kinds, and that's particularly true when it comes to Yankee collectibles. About as soon as autographs came into overwhelming demand, stars from Babe Ruth on down secretly assigned their signing chores to the Yankees' clubhouse attendants. They got so good at it that even expert authenticators can't often tell a signature is an authentic Joe DiMaggio or a forged Pete Sheehy, a bona fide Mickey Mantle or a fake Pete Previte.

GORDON MANTLE

When he gave his Hall of Fame induction speech in 1974, Mickey Mantle noted that his father, Elvin, had named him after another Hall of Famer, Mickey Cochrane. A lot of people know that, but fewer remember that if the Mantle family members had gone by Cochrane's birth name, they would have named their oldest son Gordon.

MR. KEKICH & MRS. PETERSON AND MR. PETERSON & MRS. KEKICH

In the spring of 1973, Mike Kekich and Fritz Peterson announced their mutual intention to divorce and marry the other's wife. The news came as a thunderbolt. Reporters and legions of booing fans denounced what were altogether new definitions of "trade" and "teamwork." Fellow Yankee Lindy McDaniel, a devout Christian, hinted that both pitchers would be going to hell. The front office canceled Family Day.

However, what was always referred to as a wife swap wasn't *exactly* that. In reality, both Susanne Kekich and Marilyn Peterson stayed put, as did their children, pets, and households. It'd be more accurate to call the exchange the first *husband* swap in major league history.

DON'T CALL ME LIGHTNIN'

Phil Rizzuto started calling Ron Guidry "Louisiana Lightnin'" in the late 1970s, and the nickname has been in everyday parlance ever since, even making its way onto Gid's Monument Park plaque. Still, friends have never called him Lightnin'. They call him "Gator."

Mr. May

In September 1985, while the Yankees were in the process of losing the American League East by two games, George Steinbrenner made an impulsive decision in a career full of impulsive decisions. He ruefully reflected on the transition from Reggie Jackson to Dave Winfield by saying, "I got rid of Mr. October and got Mr. May."

Steinbrenner was right. Winfield's numbers in the regular season were solid, but in the '81 postseason he went 10 for 55 in 14 games (including 1 for 22 in the World Series). When he returned to the playoffs with the '92 Blue Jays, he again performed poorly (11 for 46, four extra-base hits). Big Dave closed his playoff career with a .208 batting average, a .304 on-base percentage, and .337 slugging in more than 100 October at-bats.

A Better Baseball Player

Peter Gammons spoke for legions of stat skeptics when he once wrote, "A-Rod has more power, he is a better fielder, has more speed, and can steal more bases, but Derek Jeter is a better *baseball* player."

His point was that the stats couldn't tell us everything, that they couldn't account for unquantifiable but real factors such as confidence, hustle, determination, fight, and passion. In assessing ballplayers, you can't cram a guy's intangibles into a box score. But baseball is the consummate numbers game because it's uniquely set up to measure most player contributions to winning. It's those simple, measurable acts that win most ballgames.

Don Zimmer, Metalhead

In July 1953, Don Zimmer was batting for St. Paul of the American Association when he was hit in the head by a fastball from Jim Kirk of Columbus. Coming in an era when ballplayers didn't wear helmets, the injury brought Zimmer close to death, and the resulting fracture left him unconscious for two weeks, hospitalized for a month, and dizzy for months afterward. At one point, a team of surgeons drilled four small metal/ceramic buttons into the left side of his skull in order to relieve swelling against his brain.

Rumor has it that he emerged from the experience with a metal plate in his head, but it's just not so. He didn't need it—like he didn't need (four extra) holes in the head.

"MR. NOVEMBER"

When the 9/11 tragedy delayed the 2001 season by two weeks, the Yankees–Diamondbacks World Series became the first Fall Classic to be pushed into the 11th month of the year. In a World Series Game 4 that began on the night of October 31 and ended on the morning of November 1, Derek Jeter's home run off Byung–Hyun Kim won a 4–3 contest in extra innings.

The homer was a very important hit in an important game, but it hardly distinguished DJ as Mr. Anything. Over the course of the seven-game series, he went 4 for 27 (.148) with one extra-base hit. In November itself, while playing Games 5 through 7, Jeet went 2 for 11 with one run scored. Sure, one of them won the game, but the Yankees went on to lose two straight clincher games (and the World Series).

The Over- / Under-

CHAPTER 35

The Most Overrated Yankees of All Time

As our friends in Brooklyn might say, I mean no disrespect. None at all.

All the players listed below were very good, sometimes outstanding performers in their prime. They were major league baseball players, which automatically makes them better than 99 percent of all would-be jocks to venture out between the white lines, and they were Yankees, which made them all contributors to a tradition second to none. The players listed here are the ones who've been a bit *too* respected and *too* appreciated.

DON MATTINGLY, 1B (1982–95)

The rep: The smooth-fielding, power-hitting MVP of the mid-1980s, the unquestioned heart of the order.

The reality: Half terrific, half terrible.

When Mattingly was himself, he was as good as anybody, supplementing Gold Gloves in fielding with enough line drives to average 114 RBIs per year from 1984 to 1989, but back problems ensured that No. 23 wouldn't touch those numbers in the second half of his career. Playing at the ultimate power position, the old Mattingly suddenly became the *old* Mattingly, averaging fewer than 10 homers per year in the six seasons from 1990 to 1995.

Why so overrated? Class.

For the fans coming of age in the 1980s and early 1990s, Donnie Baseball was a beacon of dignity in undignified times.

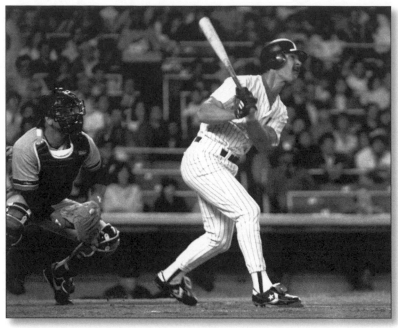

Don Mattingly: half terrific, half terrible

BOBBY RICHARDSON, 2B (1955–66)

The rep: The sparkplug to some championship lineups, Ralph Houk called him "the finest all-around player I ever managed."

The reality: Although Richardson was a durable Gold Glover, he was a complete liability as a leadoff man. He rarely walked (averaging just 30 bases on balls per 162-game season), couldn't run (eight stolen bases per 162), and didn't hit for power (34 homers in 12 years). His career OPS+ was a squishy-soft 77, the main reason why he sometimes batted behind pitchers in the lineup.

Despite more than 600 at-bats per year and the presence of power hitters such as Mickey Mantle, Moose Skowron, Elston Howard, and Yogi Berra behind him in the lineup, Richardson, unbelievably, never scored 100 runs in a season.

Why so overrated? God only knows.

In addition to the shine of his dynastic teams and 1960 World Series MVP trophy, Richardson founded the Baseball Chapel, became a lay preacher, and presided over the funerals of Roger Maris and Mickey Mantle, among others. Criticizing Bobby Richardson, the individual, might not square with the man upstairs.

DEREK JETER, SS (1995–)

The rep: The greatest Yankee of his generation.

The reality: Jeter's a very good-hitting shortstop, among the best ever, actually, but his defense is another story altogether.

In his first 12 full seasons, through 2007, Jeter's range factor (putouts and assists per game) numbers were below average eight times. With moves such as his patented jump and throw, he makes average plays look hard and hard plays look impossible, the main reason some scouts have long nicknamed him "pasta" (as in that ground ball's scooting *past-a* diving Jeter).

In all fairness, it should be said that Jeter has made his share of spectacular fielding plays, none more memorable than the flip play in the 2001 ALDS against the Athletics or the relay throw to gun down a Met runner in Game 1 of the 2000 World Series. Still, a handful of highlights can't begin to make up for his deficiencies over a full season, much less a career. DJ's day-to-day numbers confirm what most insiders already knew: he takes too long to react to batted balls, gets too many bad jumps, doesn't have sure hands, exhibits poor footwork, hesitates on throws to first base, and covers second base too slowly. Liabilities for a guy playing shortstop.

Serious analysts such as John Dewan rank Jeter as one of the worst American League defensive shortstops of his era. Bill James has suggested that, when all is said and done, *Jeter might be the single worst defensive shortstop of all time*, if only because his above-average hitting has allowed him to stay in the field for so long.

Why so overrated? Icons.

Every Yankee generation needs a face, someone to join the emblematic likes of Ruth, Gehrig, DiMaggio, Mantle, Jackson, and Mattingly. Jeter has spent his entire career in pinstripes. Combine his very impressive offense and durability with his "knack for PR" personality, and there you go.

GRAIG NETTLES, 3B (1973–83)

The rep: A slickster with the leather and a slugger with the lumber.

The reality: Nettles was always above-average in fielding and everyone seems to remember his flashy glove work in the '78 World Series, but he never deserved any serious comparison to Brooks Robinson. Robinson's career fielding percentage and range factors (.971 and 3.10) fairly blows him away (.961 and 2.98).

He did hit more than 300 homers in his career, but he never had a single season featuring a .280 batting average or a .500 slugging percentage.

Why so over-rated? Yankee Stadium.

The short right field porch allowed the pull-hitting Puff to put up respectable offensive numbers at home (.267 batting/.342 on-base percentage/.476 slugging) that overshadowed his career road stats (.235/.315/.388).

PAUL O'NEILL, OF (1993–2001)

The rep: A winner, a warrior, a true Yankee. Someone retire No. 21 already!

The reality: O'Neill won the (strike-shortened) '94 season's batting title and had signature moments such as the big catch in Game 5 of the 1996 World Series and a key 10-pitch walk against Armando Benitez in the 2000 Series. He showed up in 1993, just when the Yankees started winning again, then retired in 2001, just when they got into the habit of losing in October.

O'Neill also hustled and was a hardworking player with both the glove and the bat, but he makes exactly *one* appearance in the Yankees'

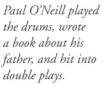

Paul O'Neill played the drums, wrote a book about his father, and hit into double plays.

major career leader boards, and that would be due to his knack for hitting into double plays. Plus, you would expect a corner outfielder who averaged more than 520 at-bats per year for nine years to have better than 24 homers as a career high. More than a dozen other Yankees hit 25 or more homers from 1993 to 2001, but none of them was ever serenaded with a "Pawwwwllliiee! We love you!"

Suppose there was another, similar performer who wasn't handsome, couldn't play the drums, and never wrote a book about his father. Would that guy be considered anything special?

Why so overrated? Passion.

Like Lou Piniella before him, O'Neill made a big show of abusing nearby appliances whenever he made an out and generally moaned and groaned and tantrumed his way around whenever things didn't go his way. This fiery arm-waving, apparently, proved something that his performances didn't.

Bobby Murcer, OF (1965–66, 1969–74, 1979–83)

The rep: A player in the shadow of Mickey Mantle.

The reality: Murcer had a couple monster seasons in 1971 and 1972, and no one will ever forget his five-RBI performance on the day he delivered Thurman Munson's eulogy in 1979, but, apart from that, Murcer's best was, mostly, just good. According to Baseball-Reference. com, his most statistically similar players are guys like Chet Lemon and Larry Parrish, who were capable enough but nothing more.

Why so overrated? The luck of the drawl.

Murcer did suffer from a Job-like series of misfortunes—he arrived just as the Yankees were entering into the late-'60s dark ages, got no favors from the early Mantle comparisons, endured layoffs due to military obligations and injuries, played a season in pitcher-friendly Shea Stadium, was traded away before the 1970s pennant years, and came back to the Yankees when the team started to decline.

Bobby Murcer: great man, good player

Through all the adversity, though, Bobby Ray was the definition of a fan favorite. His down-home manners, good humor, good looks, and Oklahoma twang were carried over the New York airwaves for more than a quarter-century. Quite simply, people want to believe the great man was a great player.

ROGER MARIS, OF (1960–66)

The rep: A two-time MVP and breaker of Babe Ruth's seemingly unbreakable home run record, a victim of the evil Gotham media.

The reality: Like Dale Murphy and Juan Gonzalez after him, Maris managed to win back-to-back MVP trophies (1960 and 1961) amid seasons that ranged from the good (averaging 25 homers in '63 and '64) to the bad (.233 with 13 homers in '66) and the ugly (.239 and just eight round-trippers in '65).

As someone once said, "He never quite recovered from the shock of hitting 61 home runs." When the Yankees traded a 32-year-old Maris for Charley Smith, straight up, they were grateful to get Charley Smith.

Why so overrated? Martyrdom.

It's easy enough to blame the media for messages the fans don't want to hear, so, eventually, the "Rude Roger" meme was erased in favor of a storyline about an innocent kid from Fargo who was victimized by the vicious New York press. Emphasizing Maris' two good years and pretty-good fielding became a way of sticking it to the boys in the press room; never mind the fact that the reporters were 100 percent right about the low batting averages, fragility, woeful attitude, and frequent lack of hustle.

WAITE HOYT, P (1921–30)

The rep: National Baseball Hall of Fame, Class of '69.

The reality: Everyone remembers that Hoyt was an excellent World Series pitcher (he averaged 1.83 ERA in series play), but those 12 big games don't wipe out nearly 20 regular seasons of (mostly) mediocrity; his .566 career winning percentage places him behind Bruce Kison,

Clay Carroll, Dave Burba, and 235 other pitchers who threw more than 1,000 innings.

Why so overrated? Personality.

Hoyt had loads of it. Through his career, he transitioned from Brooklyn's schoolboy sensation to become a Yankee, off-season vaudevillian, part-time funeral director (they called him the Merry Mortician), amateur painter, sportswriter, longtime broadcaster, and a national spokesman for Alcoholics Anonymous. He could have been inducted into Cooperstown for his Babe Ruth stories alone.

RALPH HOUK, MANAGER (1961–63, 1966–73)

The rep: A genius manager who won three straight pennants in his first three years.

The reality: Houk was named manager after Casey Stengel was fired in 1960 and took three straight pennants from 1961 to 1963. Afterward, he was kicked upstairs to the general manager's job. Houk fired manager Yogi Berra following the 1964 season, hired Johnny Keane for 1965, and then stepped in to replace the failing Keane in 1966.

It's hard to fault Houk for his initial tenure, but just as soon as he moved into the front office in 1964, he completely failed to back Berra whenever disgruntled players came storming up to the front office. Even worse, Houk schemed to have Berra fired, then went through with the bungle despite Berra's achievements in taking the Yankees all the way to Game 7 of the World Series. Still worse, his handpicked skipper, the wildly miscast Keane, flopped as fans reeled from Houk's firing of beloved broadcasters Mel Allen and Red Barber. Worst of all, Houk utterly failed to restock the Yankees' depleted farm systems as his replacement at GM, Lee MacPhail, proved to be just as big of an executive bust in the years to come.

Sure, Houk couldn't be expected to win with talent-deficient teams from 1966 to 1973, but they were his creation in the first place.

Why so over-rated? Patriotism.

"The Major" was a genuine war hero, a veteran who received multiple medals for bravery in World War II combat. No matter how many mistakes he made in a Yankee uniform, his actions in an Army uniform seemed to earn him the benefit of the doubt.

JOE DIMAGGIO, TEAM LEADER (1936–42, 1946–51)

The rep: Vic Raschi: "He always placed the team first."

The reality: DiMaggio's sense of personal pride propelled him to career achievements that speak for themselves, but that achievement wasn't without its downside. Very often, pride led him into arrogant, me-first choices, too.

Joltin' Joe strikes a Liberty Valance pose in 1951. When the legend becomes fact, print the legend.

Rather than cut down his swing and hit more singles and doubles into Yankee Stadium's vast left-field dimensions, he persisted in swinging away, often knocking 400-foot flyouts into "Death Valley." Joe McCarthy once said that he had no idea if DiMag could bunt, as if that was some kind of compliment.

Rather than yield his glamour position in center field to a faster player, he sulked over the gentle suggestion he make a late-career move to first base.

Rather than gracefully drop in the lineup or occasionally take a seat against tough righties, he again sulked and complained behind the manager's back. That manager would have been Casey Stengel, whom DiMaggio mocked as "someone who doesn't know what [baseball's] all about."

Rather than tutor/mentor rookie Mickey Mantle's transition from shortstop to outfield, he gave Mickey his notorious silent treatment.

Why so overrated? The Man Who Shot Liberty Valance.

How did that old movie go? "When the legend becomes fact, print the legend." DiMaggio spent most of his career carrying himself like royalty, so eventually the media forgot how to portray him in any other light. The legend became reality.

DISHONORABLE MENTION:
Billy Crystal, Superfan

The rep: One of the Yankees' longtime faithful, the soft-hearted stalwart who still gets misty when he describes how Mickey hit one out during his first visit to the stadium, back in 1956.

The reality: Crystal sure is a big Yankee fan, except when he isn't.

In *Running Scared* he wore a Cubs jersey, which might have been understandable, considering that the movie was set in Chicago, but he could have just as easily worn a Bears uni instead. Many suspected that it was raw opportunism in the wake of the Cubbies' '84 playoff run, and, if anyone had any doubts on that one, Crystal put them to rest by wearing a Mets cap during the filming of *City Slickers*.

Sure, Billy, it's for the role. Then again, in 1990, the Amazins' happened to be on a seven-season run that saw them averaging 95-plus wins per season while the Yanks were staggering through what can only be described as the Bucky Dent–Stump Merrill years.

Why so overrated? In the late 1990s he directed *61**, an entertaining, if completely inaccurate, movie about his favorite team. That earned him his own place in the Yankees mythology enough to get primo seats for life. Billy, we've loved you since your *Saturday Night Live* days, but when you insist on ceaseless, smug mugging in those box seats and luxury boxes, you don't look so *mahvelous.*

CHAPTER 36

The Most Overrated Yankees Lineup of All Time

> "Their tremendous hitting moved observers to place the 1961 squad in a class with the 1927 Yankees as the greatest clubs of all time."
> —The Sports Encyclopedia: Baseball

> "My single best team."
> —Mickey Mantle, on the 1961 Yankees

The 1961 Yankees lived up to the Bronx Bombers label like no team ever before. Crushing 240 home runs, the ballclub set a major league record that stood for more than 30 years. In left field, Roger Maris hit his famous 61 in '61. In center, Mickey Mantle knocked in 54. Their three catchers, Elston Howard, Yogi Berra, and Johnny Blanchard, combined for 64; six of their eight starting position players finished in the double digits.

Unfortunately, the spectacular isn't always substantive, and so it was with the '61 lineup. As it happened, the offense didn't particularly excel in much else besides the long ball. Here's how New York finished among the eight American League non-expansion teams in the major offensive categories:

Home Runs	1st
Batting Average	4th
On-Base Percentage	4th
Hits	4th
Doubles	8th
Triples	4th (tie)
Walks	7th
Stolen Bases	7th

As one might suspect, that kind of imbalanced, top-heavy attack made for relatively ho-hum scoring results. Averaging 5.07 runs per game, the '61ers aren't among the top *34* Yankees teams of all time. By outscoring the AL average by .54 runs per game, their league run differential doesn't rank among the best *40* Yankee teams of all time. No fewer than 10 Yankee clubs averaged at least one more run per game.

Among the entire major league, more than 200 other teams have scored more than 827 runs in a season, the majority of them scoring 100 more runs and the very best of them scoring more than *200* more runs. Many of those superior offenses did it with the shorter 154-game schedule.

In fact, the Bombers' hitting attack wasn't even impressive for the American League of 1961. The Tigers outscored New York with 5.16 runs per game to the Yankees' 5.07 because they complemented a second-ranked home-run attack with a far superior team batting average and higher totals in walks, extra base hits, and stolen bases.

Of course, the Yankees were special in that year, winning 109 games and the franchise's 19th championship, but what made that possible wasn't the famous hitting pyrotechnics, but their less-celebrated pitching staff. In contrast to the guys in the batter's box, the boys on the mound were excellent all across the board, finishing second in the AL in overall performance, first in shutting down base runners, and first in bullpen finishes.

Maris, Mantle, Howard, and the rest of the lineup may have grabbed the headlines, but, even in that magical year, they were more than matched by the heroics of Whitey Ford, Ralph Terry, Luis Arroyo, and the rest of the Yankees hurlers.

As Good As It Got

It's understandable that Mickey Mantle called the '61 squad his single favorite ballclub.

New manager Ralph Houk was far less demanding and far more amenable. It was also the first season that Mantle was seen as the de facto team captain. By falling short in the M&M home run chase, he achieved a new level of notoriety and popular sympathy.

The Mick was well within his rights to call the '61 Yankees his favorite; it wasn't the best team he saw between 1951 and 1968. That honor belonged to the '53 Yankees.

That team featured a better lineup than the '61 squad, scoring 5.30 runs per game to the latter's 5.07 and outpacing the American League team's average game offense by a bigger run differential (.84 vs. .54). The earlier team's pitching staff also boasted a lower runs-allowed-per-game number (3.62 vs. 3.75) that left it even better off against the AL average (.84 vs. .78). The 1953 roster was better in offensive stats such as batting average and on-base percentage plus pitching numbers like homers allowed and shutouts.

Why all the glory for the 1961 team, then? Well, they did have more wins (109 vs. 99) and a higher winning percentage (.673 vs. .656). They also had an easier time of it in the World Series—a 4–1 cakewalk against the Reds vs. a 4–2 dogfight against the Dodgers.

Apart from that, '61 had a lot more flash than the typical dynastic team of the 1950s. The year saw a new American president, a new decade, a "New Frontier." Everyone, everywhere was talking about that homer chase. Rather than delivering a fifth-straight championship, as in 1953, the '61 title came on the heels of a crushing loss in the previous year's World Series, which made the next victory a highly satisfying return to form.

Quite simply, the 1961 Yankees were just more fun than the 1953 Yankees. As a result, they were more fondly remembered, by Mickey and many others.

CHAPTER 37

The Most Underrated Yankees of All Time

JOHNNY BLANCHARD, C (1955, 1959–65)

The rep: A spare part on the early 1960s dynasties, Mickey Mantle's drinking buddy.

The reality: Blanchard, by his own admission, couldn't keep up with Yogi Berra and Elston Howard when it came to defense, but let's remember what he *could* do: come off the bench to deliver a key pinch-hit (he knocked in 187 RBIs on 260 hits), produce in the postseason (.345 in five Octobers), always hustle, never mope. In 1961, Blanch had one of the best seasons ever produced by a Yankee backup, hitting .305 with 21 homers in 243 at-bats, including four dingers in the span of three games. When he had the chance to play every day, in 1964, he hit 15 RBIs in a stretch of 19 ballgames. It's reasonable to suppose that on any team but the Yankees he could have had enough playing time to become a star.

Why so underrated? Honesty.

Blanchard freely conceded that he wasn't quite as good as his superstar teammates and that he was a winner largely because his team was a winner. He was every nostalgia buff's nightmare.

WALLY PIPP, 1B (1915–25)

The rep: The Man Replaced By Gehrig.

The reality: Pipp was no slouch. He averaged 103 RBIs between 1921 and 1924, won the Yankees' first two home-run titles (1916–17),

Wally Pipp could've been a contender.

showed up on American League boards in everything from batting average to stolen bases, and had a great glove. Wally could be feisty, too. Once in 1922, he punched Babe Ruth—probably the only time the slugger made news for being hit.

Why so underrated? Just guess.

There's no real way to know how Pipp would have performed had he stayed at first base for the Yankees. There's also no way to avoid the inevitable—and unenviable—comparison to Gehrig, perhaps the greatest first baseman to ever play the game.

JOE GORDON, 2B (1938–43, 1946)

The rep: A good player who once stole an MVP from Ted Williams, the guy they traded to the Indians in exchange for Allie Reynolds.

The reality: Gordon may not have deserved his '42 MVP, but he was respected enough to be selected for the All-Star Game in six of his seven years with New York and finished in the top 10 of MVP voting in three of them. He had a so-so (.970) career fielding percentage but, according to Frank Crosetti, had so much range that he allowed the shortstop and third baseman to cheat over and close the infield gaps. Bucky Harris once said that Gordon "played second base, short center field, and part of right field."

Hall of Famer Bobby Doerr was *maybe* as good a second baseman as Gordon. Joe McCarthy, who wasn't given to hyperbole, once said, "The greatest all-around ballplayer I ever saw, and I don't bar any of them, is Joe Gordon."

Why so underrated? Bad luck.

Gordon's career numbers were blunted by an unfavorable Yankee Stadium, abbreviated by World War II, and cut short by injuries at age 35. It didn't help that the Yankee juggernaut just kept rolling after he received his one-way ticket to Cleveland.

GIL McDOUGALD, SS (1951–60)

The rep: A nifty little utility guy in the 1950s dynasty.

The reality: Casey Stengel won all those pennants largely because his clubs' loaded rosters allowed him to platoon, pinch hit, lineup shuffle, and double-switch his way into multiple matchup advantages. In that system, McDougald may have been the team's most invaluable player.

Smash could hit for contact (.276 batting average) and for some power (14 homers per 162 games), hit off the bench (going .450 as a pinch-hitter in 1960), could face both righties and lefties, and could hit in the postseason (24 World Series RBIs). Most important, McDougald was versatile. He played three different positions for World Series teams while maintaining league-leading double-play numbers. Gil didn't sell concessions, but everything else was on the table.

Why so underrated? Hypocrisy.

You know all that sportswriter chatter about how players should be team-first, well-rounded gamers? Well, that's all smoke. In the

Gil McDougald did everything but sell concessions.

real world, most of the glory goes to the guys who display one or two special talents and hunker down into a single, easily remembered position. As far as that went, McDougald was just a little too versatile for his own good.

CLETE BOYER, 3B (1959–66)

The rep: A weak bat to go along with a good glove.

The reality: He was, at best, just OK with the stick, but whenever Boyer's glove work was compared to Brooks Robinson, it was Robinson who should have been flattered. The Yankees' third baseman had the speed and arm strength to best Brooks in fielding percentage and/or range factor in six of the seven full years that they both played in the American League.

Clete practically invented the move where a third baseman dives to his right, throws from his knees, and *still* takes out a swift runner at first base. He was that good.

*Clete Boyer in 1960.
Eat your heart out,
Brooks Robinson.*

Why so underrated? Intermittent obnoxiousness.

Boyer could be ill-tempered, liked his drink, and sometimes rebelled against the powers that be. A lot of Baltimore fans named their kids 'Brooks,' but there aren't a lot of little Cletises running around these days.

GEORGE SELKIRK, OF (1934–42)

The rep: If he's remembered for anything, Selkirk is remembered for his nickname: "Ol' Twinkletoes."

The reality: He may not have looked like much compared to '30s-era teammates such as Gehrig or DiMaggio, but by any other standard, Selkirk was a simply outstanding hitter, always batting at or near .300 while swatting 20 or so homers and legging out more than his share of doubles. He's still in the Yankees' top 10 for career on-base percentage.

Why so underrated? The Babe.

Just as soon as Babe Ruth made his exit in 1935, Selkirk was assigned the starting right field job *and* the big guy's No. 3, believe it or not. You try following that act.

Charlie Keller, OF (1939–43, 1945–49, 1952)

The rep: The other guy in the Henrich/DiMaggio outfields of the 1940s.

The reality: Keller's first seven years had Hall of Fame written all over them. He enjoyed three seasons with better than 30 homers, 20 doubles, and 10 triples and another three with .500 or more slugging. He was the best player on the field in the '39 World Series and, as for the other aspects in his game, sportswriter Dan Daniel once said that Keller "runs like a scared jackrabbit, makes hard plays look soft, has a remarkable arm, and is a true Yankee type."

Why so underrated? The galaxy.

Like his onetime teammate Selkirk, Keller was lost in the mighty constellation of stars that comprised the Yankee roster. He hadn't yet put up enough counting numbers for Cooperstown by the time he was hurt in '47, so memories faded.

Roy White, OF (1965–79)

The rep: A popgun-armed semi-regular.

The reality: Bill James once raised a controversy by insisting that Roy White was, at his peak, almost as good as Jim Rice, but look at the comparison: in their five best consecutive seasons, White had virtually the same adjusted on-base-plus-slugging (OPS+) level (138 to Rice's 140), largely because White drew twice as many walks (87 per season vs. 46). He also stole more bases than Rice (20 vs. 8), grounded into fewer double plays (10 vs. 18), and switch-hit.

True, White wasn't the greatest defensive player who ever lived, but he was more respectable than his detractors would suggest, mostly because he neutralized that weak arm with above-average speed, good positioning, and quick releases.

Why so underrated? Milquetoast.

White was far too mild-mannered to toot his own horn, which he should have, because he was good mostly when his teams were bad enough to be ignored altogether.

SPUD CHANDLER, P (1937–47)

The rep: What might have been.

The reality: Chandler battled arm troubles for years, but when he finally broke into the majors at age 29, he more than made up for lost time, using a five-pitch arsenal to put together a 109–43 record and 2.84 ERA in eight full seasons. Among all Yankee starters, only Whitey Ford has a lower adjusted ERA, and among all 20th-century major leaguers with at least 100 career decisions, *no one* has a better winning percentage than Chandler's .717. Bill Dickey, who caught and coached through four decades, said that a healthy Spud Chandler was the best pitcher he ever saw.

Why so underrated? Fascism.

Just as Spud was finally establishing himself, in 1941, the Germans and Japanese declared war and the majors' best players emptied out for the next four seasons. The fact that some of Chandler's best seasons came against inferior competition led some to believe his career totals were less than 100-percent legitimate.

YOGI BERRA, MANAGER (1964, 1984–85)

The rep: The loveable old Yogi lucked his way into a pennant.

The reality: The man Casey Stengel called his "assistant manager" wasn't too bad of a manager in his own right. He proved as much in both seasons as Yankee skipper.

In 1964, Berra steadied an aging, injury-wracked ballclub long enough to benefit from the recuperated players, hot streaks, and good luck they needed to finish with a 22–6 September. Yogi's Yankees posted the best regular-season record in the majors, then held on to make it to the seventh game of the World Series despite losing their number one starter (after the first game), best reliever, and starting shortstop.

A great manager...Casey Stengel

Could just any manager have done that? Well, Hank Bauer of the second-place Orioles couldn't do that, despite the widespread view that he had superior depth up and down his roster. Ditto for Al Lopez of the third-place White Sox. A supposed genius, Gene Mauch, who panicked his Phillies out of the National League pennant that year, couldn't do it either. Johnny Keane couldn't prevent the Yankees' 22-game nosedive in two years following Yogi's unjustified dismissal.

Like any rookie, Berra went through some growing pains in '64, especially when it came to the transition from player to manager, but he knew what he was doing. If he didn't, he wouldn't have stuck with a struggling Jim Bouton long enough for him to win 11 games in the second half of the season, given up on an ineffective Stan Williams, taken a chance on an unknown rookie named Mel Stottlemyre, or given a castoff Pedro Ramos 13 crucial relief appearances. The fact that Berra kept Joe Pepitone sober and motivated enough for 160 productive games should've been enough alone to nab Manager of the Year.

Two decades later, in 1984, Yogi was back in the Yankee dugout and once again producing a whole that was better than the sum of its parts.

After an overpaid, badly assembled lineup lurched into a 36–45 record over the season's first half, Yogi acted decisively, installing a still-untested Don Mattingly at first base, starting Ken Griffey Jr. over a flagging Steve Kemp in left field, and putting his faith in rookie Mike Pagliarulo at third. As a result, the team ignited enough offense to mostly make up for below-average pitching, went on a 51–30 roll, and, with the welcomed addition of Rickey Henderson, entered the 1985 season as the odds-on favorite to challenge for the playoffs.

Unfortunately, though, history repeated itself again. Just as a pennant wasn't good enough to save his job after the '64 season, the best second-half record in baseball wasn't enough to save him after '84. Yogi was fired in '85 after 16 whole games.

Why so underrated? The cartoon.

When given the choice between Yogi Berra, the word-tripping caricature, and Yogi Berra, the superstar-turned-skipper, most all commentators and fans emphasized the funny over the facts. What a shame.

WHITEY FORD, TEAM LEADER (1950, 1953–67)

The rep: A great pitcher on great teams.

The reality: Ford was, without a doubt, surrounded by some capable hitters and fielders, but few understood that, most often, he was the one making his ballclubs look good, not the other way around.

Whitey Ford was the last word in stoppers.

Compare the 1950, 1953–64 Yankees' numbers in games decided by other pitchers versus their results in Ford's decisions:

	Winning percentage	162-game translation
Not-Ford	.608	98 wins
Ford	.720	117 wins

To make a long story short, when Ford was on the hill, a very good supporting team became about as unbeatable as any team has ever been.

More than that, Ford may have been the best personification of the dynastic Yankees' sense of cool and concentration. David Halberstam once wrote that in the World Series he "walked out on the mound like a man going out to grab a bus to take him to work in the morning." Once, when Mickey Mantle's outfield error cost Ford a 20th win in the last days of the '56 season, Whitey laughed it off, took Mickey out after the game, and bought him a beer. It was friendship as leadership.

Why so underrated? Fame overflow.

It's often been said that New York ballplayers get more media attention than they might get with the same performances in, say, Cincinnati or Kansas City, and that's true enough, but Yankee players also tend to lose some luster by playing at the side of star teammates. Ford, in particular, was sometimes treated as secondary to the Bronx Bombers' sluggers.

HONORABLE MENTION:
George Costanza,
Assistant to the Traveling Secretary (Seinfeld, 1994–97)

The rep: The buffoon who dressed the Yankees in shrinking cotton uniforms, got Danny Tartabull diverted on the way to a PBS pledge drive, stole the Big Stein's birthday card, slept under his own desk, botched Mr. Wilhelm's top-secret payroll project, dragged a World Series trophy around the Yankee Stadium parking lot, and was eventually traded to Arkansas in exchange for the rights to an alcoholic chicken drink.

The reality: We all have our failures and flaws. Costanza may have had a few more than most. But that's no reason to overlook the fact that the man could get things done. Consider:

> **Role:** (1996) the Yankees' official liaison to Cuban dictator Fidel Castro.
> **Result:** Within two years, defector Orlando Hernandez becomes a pitching staff mainstay (41–26) in the club's march to three straight championships.

> **Role:** (1997) Unofficial batting coach. "Guys, hitting is not about muscle. It's simple physics. Calculate the velocity, v, in relation to the trajectory, t, in which g, gravity, of course remains a constant. It's not complicated."

Result: Pupils Derek Jeter and Bernie Williams see their combined home run totals jump from 31 to 45 in 1998.

Role: (1997) Motivator
George: Do you wanna win some ballgames?
Jeter: We won the World Series.
George: In six games.
Result: The 1998 Bombers win the World Series—in four games.

Toss in a fearless habit of speaking truth to power,* and the more clear it becomes—George Costanza was the single greatest Assistant to the Traveling Secretary that the Yankees have ever had.

Why so underrated? Prescience.

Costanza, for all his misadventures, was years and years ahead of his time. To this day, the sport *still* hasn't caught up to the concept of Fitted Cap Day.

---

*Mr. Steinbrenner: Nice to meet you.
George: Well, I wish I could say the same, but I must say, with all due respect, I find it very hard to see the logic behind some of the moves you have made with this fine organization. In the past 20 years you have caused myself, and the city of New York, a good deal of distress as we have watched you take our beloved Yankees and reduce them to a laughing stock, all for the glorification of your massive ego!
Mr. Steinbrenner: Hire this man!

CHAPTER 38

The Most Underrated Yankees Lineup of All Time

In 1927, when their lineup was busy terrorizing the rest of the American League, Waite Hoyt said that the secret to success in pitching was to get a job with the Yankees. In the late 1930s, one sportswriter said the Bombers' team was so powerful that only dynamite could stop them. In the late 1970s, Red Sox pitcher Bill Lee said that facing New York batters was like sitting in a bathtub with Jaws.

The Yankees' legacy of winning has always been tied to a legacy of scary hitting, but their single best lineup is one of their least remembered.

In 1931, the ballclub's offense produced numbers almost beyond belief. Six hitters with a .300 or better batting average. Babe Ruth and Lou Gehrig combining for 92 home runs and 347 RBIs. Two or more Yankees among the top American League hitters in virtually every offensive category. Six of them had 78 or more RBIs. Six Hall of Famers among the eight starting position players.

Most of all, the glittering numbers all contributed to the most prolific run production the Yankees, or any other team, has ever seen. The 1931 Yankees scored 6.88 runs per game, just a hair below the previous year's 6.90, but they also outpaced the league average by a record 1.74 runs per game. In the more than 2,300 major league team seasons from 1876 to 2007, no one has ever overpowered the opposition to a greater extent.

But it was all for nothing. The '31 Yankees' problem was that their pitchers were giving back a great many of the runs, chiefly through mediocre WHIP totals. At the end of the season, they finished with a middling 4.20 ERA that barely came in better than the 4.38 AL average.

There were years a team could have survived the imbalance, but unfortunately for the Yankees, 1931 wasn't one of them. That year belonged to Connie Mack's Philadelphia Athletics.

The '31 Athletics were no match for New York's Babe Ruth/Lou Gehrig/Earle Combs/Bill Dickey hitting lineup, but in Al Simmons, Mickey Cochrane, and Jimmie Foxx, they had a few Hall of Famers of their own, and they teamed to produce 5.61 runs per game. Even more important, they had the best pitching staff in the league, one headed by Lefty Grove's nearly impossible 31–4 campaign and supplemented by workhorses George Earnshaw (21–7, 281⅔ innings pitched, 123 ERA+) and Rube Walberg (20–12, 291, 121).

In combining that offense and pitching, the Athletics had enough to finish with a 107–45 record, leaving their rivals more than 13 games behind in the standings and ensuring that almost everyone forgot the '31 Yankees, the best offense of all time.

Who Should've Won What

CHAPTER 39

The Yankees' True Trophy Case

In baseball awards, as in life, not everything is fair. Sometimes—a lot of times—factors like politics and perceptions trump performance, leading the unworthy to receive trophies while the worthy get the shaft. Up until now, at least. The following chapter is intended to finally set the historical record straight by pointing out the many seasons when a Yankee either a) received a Most Valuable Player or Cy Young Award he didn't earn, or b) didn't get one that he did deserve.

Before getting down to it, though, let me mention my guidelines for the Yankees' True Trophy Case. First, in the years when the hardware did go to the right guy, the campaign is unmentioned.

Second, I'm going to ignore all gaps in the eligibility requirements. For years, previous MVP winners were barred from repeating their honors. Not here. I'm going to assume a just, righteous world where the trophy sweepstakes were always open and on the level.

Third, the analyses assume that Most Valuable Player means, in effect, Most Valuable Position Player. I believe that the reason MVPs are almost always given to non-pitchers (in more than 85 percent of all cases to date) is because they're rightfully viewed as an award dedicated to position players, just as the Cy Young is the pitchers' exclusive province. I've kept the categories separate. In the rare years pitchers managed to win the MVP, I automatically assume that the award voters botched the selection.

Finally, I subscribe to the straightforward principle that MVPs and Cy Youngs are player awards, not team awards. Some commentators still insist that most valuable means the best player on a good team, but I believe that outstanding means the single best performer in the league. No one received special credit if they happened to play for first-place teams or gets demerits for having toiled on non-contenders.

With all that in mind, here we go:

What: 2001 Cy Young
Who Won: Roger Clemens
Who Should've Won: Freddy Garcia (Mariners)
One of the strongest, long-lived biases in the Cy Young voting comes in the voters' attraction to wins over all else, and Clemens' '01 award is a perfect example. The Rocket finished the season with an outstanding 20–3 record, but many of his wins turned on unusually strong run support plus Mariano Rivera and others in the bullpen. It was Seattle's Garcia who led the league in ERA (3.05 to Clemens' 3.51) and innings, while finishing among AL leaders in stats such as WHIP. If he would have had the Yankees' power hitters and lights-out relievers to back him up, it's likely that Garcia's 18–6 record would have been even better than 20–3.

What: 1986 MVP
Who Won: Roger Clemens (Red Sox)
Who Should've Won: Don Mattingly
Clemens more than deserved the 1986 Cy Young in a virtuoso (2.48 ERA) campaign, but Mattingly put up the single-best position player performance in the American League that year, combining a league-leading slugging percentage (.573) with Gold Glove fielding in 162 games played. This was his calling-card season, when the young Donnie Baseball was at his most brilliant.

What: 1985 MVP
Who Won: Don Mattingly
Who Should've Won: George Brett (Royals)

Mattingly was terrific in '85, but, in almost all areas, Brett was just a bit better. Mattingly may have hit more home runs (35 to 30), but Brett sported a higher slugging percentage (.585 to .567). Mattingly knocked in more runs (145 to 112), but Brett's superior speed allowed him to score more (108 to 107). Mattingly hit .324 and got on base at a .371 clip, but Brett hit .335 with a .436 on-base percentage. While Mattingly won a Gold Glove at first base, Brett won the same at third base, a tougher position. Mattingly was valuable, Brett was most valuable.

What: 1984 MVP
Who Won: Willie Hernandez (Tigers)
Who Should've Won: Don Mattingly
Hernandez's 140-plus relief innings aside, Mattingly clearly deserved the MVP hardware in 1984, finishing in the AL's top five in everything from batting average and slugging to RBIs. He also played impeccable defense at first base. Donnie's second-place finish in the voting had to come down to the fact that Hernandez's club won a runaway pennant; the Yankees' 87–75 mark was good enough for only third place.

What: 1979 Cy Young
Who Won: Mike Flanagan (Orioles)
Who Should've Won: Ron Guidry
Watch one team's pitcher put up a league-leading 2.78 ERA plus top-five finishes in fewest hits allowed and strikeouts to go with an 18–8 record. Watch another team's pitcher ride better run support, defense, and relief pitching on the way to a more eye-catching (23–9) won-lost record. Watch Ron Guidry lose the 1979 Cy Young award to Mike Flanagan.

What: 1977 Cy Young
Who Won: Sparky Lyle
Who Should've Won: Frank Tanana (Angels)
Lyle ate up 137 relief innings with a low ERA in '77, but any GM would've gladly traded that for Tanana's 241+ innings, 2.54 ERA (the best among starters), and superior hits-allowed and strikeout ratio numbers.

What: 1971 MVP
Who Won: Vida Blue (Athletics)
Who Should've Won: Bobby Murcer

The charismatic, young Blue's 24–8 season may have made for the better media story in '71, but the season deserves to be remembered as the year Murcer finally, however briefly, lived up to his superstar potential. He hit .331, with a .427 on-base percentage and .543 slugging in a lousy hitting era, numbers that *Baseball Prospectus* translates into .352/.442/.621 in a more neutral run environment. Again, the voters gave the prize to a player from a playoff team.

What: 1970 Cy Young
Who Won: Jim Perry (Twins)
Who Should've Won: Fritz Peterson

When Peterson was still a rookie, Elston Howard compared his approach to Whitey Ford. In 1970, Peterson finally came through like Ford. He finished fourth in AL ERA (2.90) and first in WHIP and strikeout-to-walk ratio and did it despite working his sinkerball in front of an infield consisting of Danny Cater, Horace Clarke, and Jerry Kenney. Perry won the Cy Young mostly on wins, going 24–12 to Fritz's 20–11.

What: 1963 MVP
Who Won: Elston Howard
Who Should've Won: Bobby Allison (Twins)

Howard was a sure-handed receiver who put up solid numbers for a pennant-winning ballclub, but he didn't have enough for an MVP-level campaign. Allison led him in every offensive category worth counting while beating out future Hall of Famers like Carl Yastrzemski, Harmon Killebrew, and Al Kaline in OPS. Ellie did have a nice line about the outcome, though: "I just won the Nobel Prize of baseball."

What: 1962 MVP
Who Won: Mickey Mantle
Who Should've Won: Harmon Killebrew (Twins)
Mickey certainly delivered the kind of spectacular numbers (.321/486/.605) that MVP voters had come to expect in '62 but stayed healthy enough to play only 123 games (377 at-bats) on the year. He couldn't contribute a thing to his team when he wasn't playing, so his trophy rightfully belonged to the Killer, whose 155-game effort produced significantly higher totals for homers (48 to the Mick's 30), extra-base hits (70 to 46), and RBI (126 to 89).

What: 1961 MVP
Who Won: Roger Maris
Who Should've Won: Mickey Mantle
For all the commotion over Maris' running feud with the New York press, sportswriters handed him the MVP over the more dynamic half of the record-chasing M&M duo. In addition to manning the more demanding center-field position and batting from both sides, Mantle displayed more power (.687 slugging to Maris' .620), connected for more hits (163 to 159), ran up a higher on-base percentage (.448 to .372), and stole more bases (12 to zero). Forget about the best player in the league—Roger Maris wasn't even the best *Yankee outfielder* in '61.

What: 1955 MVP
Who Won: Yogi Berra
Who Should've Won: Mickey Mantle
Berra topped Mantle in terms of RBIs (108 to 99), rarely struck out, and was, as usual, the best defensive catcher in baseball. But it was his teammate who had a significantly higher batting average (.306 to .272), more power (37 homers to 27), and better speed (eight steals to one) while dashing all over center field (2.64 range factor to the 2.08 AL average). It was close, but Mantle was the more valuable Yankee that season.

What: 1952 MVP
Who Won: Bobby Shantz (Athletics)
Who Should've Won: Mickey Mantle

Shantz would have deserved the Cy Young award that year, if it had existed, that is. But 1952 was the first full season when Mantle showed what he could do, finishing at or near the top of the AL in batting average (.311), on-base percentage (.394), and slugging (.530), while playing some mean defense. Years later, the Magnificent Yankee said that he played the entire year with the guilt and sadness over his father's terminal illness and death. "Not a day went by that year, especially on the days when I had hit [a home run] or did something special, that I didn't think of him and wish he'd gotten to live long enough to see it."

What: 1951 MVP
Who Won: Yogi Berra
Who Should've Won: Ted Williams (Red Sox)

Berra's trophy is another example of a very good player on a championship-caliber team winning an MVP at the expense of an even greater player from an also-ran club. See 1947, see 1942, see most of Williams' career. If voters had been guided by objective numbers rather than factors such as big-city media attention, reporter feuds, and the team standings, I'd estimate that Teddy Ballgame would have won not two MVPs but seven.

What: 1947 MVP
Who Won: Joe DiMaggio
Who Should've Won: Ted Williams (Red Sox)

All Williams did in '47 was dominate DiMaggio in literally every major offensive category worth mentioning, from batting average and homers to RBIs and bases on balls, so those DiMag defenders can only point to his acknowledged edge in outfield defense. Nice try, but it's a weak excuse for giving the MVP to a player from a winning team.

What: 1945 MVP
Who Won: Hal Newhouser (Tigers)

Who Should've Won: Snuffy Stirnweiss
Newhouser would have deserved the Cy Young in '45, if it existed, but the league's most valuable everyday player was Stirnweiss, who paced the AL in categories such as batting average, slugging, stolen bases, and runs scored. Of course, the player ranks were so depleted by World War II service that, by any normal standard, Snuffy wasn't exceptional. After the boys came back in '46, he was more or less done at age 30.

What: 1943 MVP
Who Won: Spud Chandler
Who Should've Won: Charlie Keller
If any pitcher ever deserved to win an MVP award, Spud Chandler in 1943 (1.64 ERA, 253 innings, 20 complete games, 20–4 record) was the pitcher. But the award should have honored Keller's *everyday* contributions, including a .396 on-base percentage, .525 slugging, and 31 home runs.

What: 1942 MVP
Who Won: Joe Gordon
Who Should've Won: Ted Williams (Red Sox)
You make the choice:

	Player A	Player B
Batting Average	.356	.322
Homers	36	18
RBI	137	103

Anyone in his right mind would choose Player A, Williams, who won a Triple Crown by leading the AL in the above categories, but the MVP voters instead chose Player B, Gordon, whose only "triple crown" consisted of league-leading strikeouts, hits into double plays, and errors for a second baseman. Williams was denied too many MVP trophies, but this one is the single worst travesty.

What: 1941 MVP
Who Won: Joe DiMaggio
Who Should've Won: Ted Williams (Red Sox)
DiMaggio's 56-game hitting streak and Williams' .406 batting average may have been the highest heights in two careers with plenty of superlatives, but it was the Kid, not the Clipper, who came out ahead in everything from batting average (.406 to .357) and slugging (.735 to .643) to homers (37 to 30) and runs scored (135 to 122). But the reporters hated Williams as much as they loved DiMaggio, and that was that.

What: 1937 MVP
Who Won: Charlie Gehringer
Who Should've Won: Joe DiMaggio
When he first showed up in 1936, DiMaggio was supposed to be the wunderkind to replace Babe Ruth in the lineup, captain the outfield, and return the franchise to championship glory. He delivered. In '37, the 22-year-old DiMaggio produced career bests in hits (215), runs scored (151), home runs (46), slugging (.673), and RBIs (167) while playing exceptional defense in the outfield and helping to bring a championship home to New York.

What: 1934 MVP
Who Won: Mickey Cochrane (Tigers)
Who Should've Won: Lou Gehrig
This one is truly mystifying. Not only did the beloved Triple Crown–winner Gehrig lose out to a player with fewer than half as many RBIs (165 vs. 76) and 47 fewer home runs, but the ballots resulted in a 67–54 decision. Voters were, apparently, wowed by the fact that Cochrane finally led a non-Yankee, non-Athletic team to the AL pennant for the first time in a long time.

It's impossible to know how many MVP awards Babe Ruth would have won if the prize had been created before 1922. Additionally, it was for many years a league practice to bar an MVP winner from repeating his honors. Suffice it to say, the statistical record makes a strong case

Put it all together, and in a just world, here's the Yankees' true trophy case.

Alex Rodriguez, 2007 MVP

Alex Rodriguez, 2005 MVP

~~Roger Clemens, 2001 Cy Young~~

(Don Mattingly, 1986 MVP)

~~Don Mattingly, 1985 MVP~~

(Don Mattingly, 1984 MVP)

(Ron Guidry, 1979 Cy Young)

Ron Guidry, 1978 Cy Young

~~Sparky Lyle, 1977 Cy Young~~

Thurman Munson, 1976 MVP

(Bobby Murcer, 1971 MVP)

(Fritz Peterson, 1970 Cy Young)

~~Elston Howard, 1963 MVP~~

~~Mickey Mantle, 1962 MVP~~

~~Roger Maris, 1961 MVP~~

(Mickey Mantle, 1961 MVP)

Whitey Ford, 1961 Cy Young

Roger Maris, 1960 MVP

Bob Turley, 1958 Cy Young

Mickey Mantle, 1957 MVP

Mickey Mantle, 1956 MVP

~~Yogi Berra, 1955 MVP~~

(Mickey Mantle, 1955 MVP)

Yogi Berra, 1954 MVP

(Mickey Mantle, 1952 MVP)

~~Yogi Berra, 1951 MVP~~

Phil Rizzuto, 1950 MVP

~~Joe DiMaggio, 1947 MVP~~

(Snuffy Stirnweiss, 1945 MVP)

~~Spud Chandler, 1943 MVP~~

(Charlie Keller, 1943 MVP)

~~Joe Gordon, 1942 MVP~~

(Tiny Bonham, 1942 Cy Young)

~~Joe DiMaggio, 1941 MVP~~

Joe DiMaggio, 1939 MVP

(Joe DiMaggio, 1937 MVP)

(Lefty Gomez, 1937 Cy Young)

Lou Gehrig, 1936 MVP

(Lou Gehrig, 1934 MVP)

Lou Gehrig, 1927 MVP

Babe Ruth, 1923 MVP

that the slugger should have earned the award 10 times during his career. Additionally, Yankee pitchers Whitey Ford, Tiny Bonham, Red Ruffing, Lefty Gomez, Wilcey Moore, and "Happy Jack" Chesbro put in Cy Young–caliber seasons before the honor was awarded in separate leagues.*

---

*When it was created in 1957, the Cy Young Award was given to just one pitcher in the league. Starting in 1967, the honor has been given to one pitcher each in the National and American Leagues.

The YES Men

CHAPTER 40

What They Left Out of the "Yankeeographies"

JOE DIMAGGIO

Babe Ruth had a problem in remembering the names of all but his closest friends and opted to call most guys "Kid" or "Doc" instead. When he first met DiMaggio, he was going around the clubhouse, saying, "Hey, kid," to all the fellas. When he got to DiMaggio, whom he had never met, he said "Hiya, Joe." . . . Lefty Gomez, a fly-ball pitcher, liked to say that he was the guy who made DiMaggio's fielding famous . . . When DiMag's lucky bat was stolen in the middle of his 56-game hitting streak in 1941, a low-level Newark mob figure named Peanuts took it upon himself to do some freelance research on Joe's behalf, came up with the lumber, and "reasoned" with the thief to hand it over . . . Of the three ball-playing DiMaggio brothers, an anonymous reporter once said, "Joe was the best hitter, Dom had the best arm, and Vince had the best voice." . . . After the Clipper's divorce from Marilyn Monroe, Oscar Levant wrote, "This just proves no man can be a success in two national pastimes."

WHITEY FORD

A writer once called Ford a "walking World Series record book." . . . Ford once said of Billy Martin, "I can tell you Billy has a great heart, but I can't vouch for his liver." . . . Ford took pride in complete games and once set up a dinner table in the bullpen before a scheduled start. He wanted to make the statement that the relievers wouldn't need to work that night . . . When Reggie Jackson sent Ford a drink at a bar during spring training in 1977, Ford told the waitress that he'd rather have Jax's "SUPERSTAR" T-shirt. Reggie literally gave him the shirt off his back. Ford thanked Jackson and, in return, handed over the pink cashmere vest he was wearing . . . There are at least three possible explanations for Ford's "Slick" nickname: 1) He was a "city slicker" from Queens, 2) he got "whiskey slick" while out on the town with Mickey Mantle and the boys, and 3) he tossed spitters . . . Yankee broadcaster Mel Allen used Ford's other notable nickname for his intros: "*LADIES* and Gentlemen, *THE CHAIR*-man of the Board, Whitey FORD!"

Lou Gehrig

Babe Ruth frequently visited Gehrig's mother to enjoy the home-cooked German meals he remembered from childhood. He also gave her a puppy she named "Jidge." . . . Gehrig could have been the perfect straight man in an Abbott and Costello–like comedy duo with Ruth. When a reporter asked the two about their plans for the off-season, Lou said, "I plan to play a lot of basketball," to which the Babe quickly followed, "I ain't doing a thing except *you know what*." . . . Gehrig received "friendship medals" during a 1934 goodwill tour of Japan. After Pearl Harbor, his widow donated the medals to American military officers who eventually arranged for their return by strapping them onto bombs dropped over Tokyo.

Goose Gossage

In the 1970s, Gossage's 100+ miles-per-hour fastball might have been the first ever referred to as a "radio ball" (you can hear it, but you can't see it) . . . Like most Yankees, he had conflicts with George Steinbrenner. During the early 1980s, when the Boss ordered a struggling Doyle Alexander to get an exam, Gossage said, "If Doyle needs a physical,

George needs a mental." Steinbrenner responded by saying, "Goose should do more pitching and less quacking."

ELSTON HOWARD

When Howard's two-out, ninth-inning single broke up the Red Sox's Billy Rohr's no-hitter in April 1967, the Yankee Stadium crowd actually booed him. An offended Ellie responded by saying, "Hey, I've got three kids to feed." . . . While he served as a coach for the Yankees in the 1970s, pranksters such as Fritz Peterson would poke fun at his weight issues by sending him applications to join Overeaters Anonymous and Save the Whales.

CATFISH HUNTER

Hunter won 106 games over the five years before signing with New York in 1975. When pitching coach Whitey Ford was asked if he'd get special treatment, Ford replied, "Absolutely not. Except, of course, I'm gonna call him 'Sir.'" . . . When asked if he felt playoff pressure, Hunter once said, "Nah. I'm too dumb to get scared." . . . Hunter on the Reggie! Bar: "I unwrapped it and it told me how good it was." . . . On George Steinbrenner: "He's a man of his word. You just have to get it in writing." . . . When former A's teammate Sal Bando arrived at Yankee Stadium as a member of the Brewers in the late 1970s, he made the mistake of leaving an expensive new fedora in his locker. When he returned, he found "Jim 'Catfish' Hunter" scrawled across it with indelible black marker . . . Everyone knows that Finley originally made up the "Catfish" tag to make his prize prospect more marketable. But Jim Hunter really did love fishing. And hunting, for that matter—even though he'd lost a toe doing it.

REGGIE JACKSON

After a teammate received death threats before the '72 World Series, Jackson said, "Well, if you've got to go, at least it's on national television." . . . Reggie on playing for Billy Martin: "It was a strange and wonderful relationship. He was strange and I was wonderful." . . . Once, when reporters overheard him putting down a teammate, Reggie said, "You guys heard that? If I knew you were listening, I wouldn't have said it." . . . Red Smith on Jax: "Part philosopher, part preacher, part outfielder." . . . Thomas Boswell: "It's not easy being a man who is embarrassed by short home runs."

SPARKY LYLE

Former Red Sox teammate Bill Lee: "Sparky was a man of simple philosophy: he believed that water was to be used as a mix, never a staple." . . . When a salary dispute delayed his arrival to spring training 1978, the Yankees had Sparky's plane met at the airport by a 100-plus-member marching band playing "Pomp and Circumstance" and hoisting a sign reading "WELCOME TO FORT LAUDERDALE—FINALLY." Lyle took one look a the setup, turned to his wife and said, "Imagine if we'd showed up two weeks late." . . . Lyle once cut Bill Virdon's prized director's chair in half, then placed the offending saw in Rudy May's locker. When the enraged manager spotted the tell-tale evidence, May jumped up, proclaiming, "It wasn't me! It wasn't me! I know who did it, but I can't tell you!" . . . Lyle on relieving: "Why pitch nine innings when you can get just as famous pitching two?" . . . On compiling a 5–1 record despite a terrible ERA: "Keep quiet about it. I don't want anyone to know I'm doing so well pitching so badly." . . . For all his joking, he was as fierce as anyone on the mound. When asked what it was like to register a strikeout in Willie Mays' final All-Star Game appearance, he said, "Real good. I'm sorry I didn't get a chance to strike him out twice."

MICKEY MANTLE

Former New York Governor Mario Cuomo still brags about the fact that he signed a major league contract with a bigger signing bonus than the Mick, and he did—Cuomo took $2,000 from Branch Rickey's Pirates in 1951 while the Yankees paid the then-undersized Mantle a mere $1,100 in 1949 . . . Nobody was as respected as the prime-time Mantle. When Red Sox pitcher Frank Sullivan was asked how he pitched to the Mick, he said, "with tears in my eyes." . . . When a heckler shouted that Al Kaline was half as good as Mantle, Kaline answered, "Son, nobody is half as good as Mickey Mantle."

DON MATTINGLY

Bill James' complete assessment from the *Historical Abstract*: "100 percent ballplayer, 0 percent bullshit." . . . Once, when diving for a foul ball, Mattingly came up short. While he was stretched out into the stands, he reached over to grab a young fan's snack. He later gave him a baseball inscribed "Thanks for the popcorn /s/ Don Mattingly." . . . Batboy Matt McGough said that Mattingly would wait until all the other players tipped the clubhouse attendants at the end of the season, then top their best tip by $100 . . . Like Charlie Hustle, the nickname "Donnie Baseball" was originally meant to be sarcastic, or at least hyperbolic . . . Minnesota Twin Kirby Puckett said he could never book a limo in New York in the mid-'80s because Donnie Baseball was always picking up another award.

ROGER MARIS

When four-year-old Susan Maris was asked who was the best baseball player in the world, she said, "Mickey Mantle." Maris laughed and mussed her hair.

BILLY MARTIN

Jim Murray on Martin: "Some people have a chip on their shoulder. Billy has a whole lumberyard." . . . Dick Young: "It's not that Billy drinks a lot. It's just that he fights a lot when he drinks a little." . . . Jim Bouton: "Lots of people look up to Billy Martin. That's because he just knocked them down." . . . Johnny Carson: "Today is Opening Day in baseball. Out in Yankee Stadium, Billy Martin just threw out his first punch." . . . Martin always saw himself as the victim of his tussles; he was once quoted as saying, "I don't throw the first punch. I throw the second four punches." . . . Mike Shropshire once described Martin's management philosophy as "Better living through confrontation." . . . Don Baylor, on playing for both Yogi Berra and Martin: "Playing for Yogi was like playing for your father. Playing for Billy is like playing for your father-in-law." . . . After his first few firings, Martin said, "I pass people on the street these days, and they don't know whether to say hello or goodbye." . . . Later in his life, he was asked how he changed. He said, "Now I have a mustache."

THURMAN MUNSON

After Goose Gossage beaned Munson as an opposing player, Munson sent Goose a note that read, "I took your best shot, you motherf——er. /s/ The White Gorilla." . . . Munson's combination of pudginess and crankiness were an endless source of amusement for pranking teammates. Once, Jay Johnstone drew Munson's likeness on a watermelon, placed a Yankee cap atop and a pair of cleats below, then positioned the melon back in his locker; Sparky Lyle said it "had sideburns and a little fat face. Looked just like Thurman." . . . On other occasions, guys like Fritz Peterson would place pictures of Carlton Fisk or whales inside Munson's locker, then quietly wait for him to go ballistic . . . When the Yankees team bus would pass a fat pedestrian on the way to a ball game, Catfish Hunter often called out to the guy, saying, "Hey, Thurman, we'll be right back for you." . . . His unofficial clubhouse nicknames included Squatty Body, Tugboat, and Captain Bad Body.

BOBBY MURCER

One of Sparky Lyle's best pranks involved Murcer's prized rocking chair. In the middle of the 1974 season, Sparky cut off the chair's legs, then carefully placed the seat back on them so that when Bobby sat himself down, the whole thing suddenly collapsed into a heap. The ever-unflappable Murcer took what was left of the seat, glued it to the runners underneath, and held on to the midget-sized rocker. A rocking chair became something of an easygoing trademark over the years. At Bobby Ray's funeral service in 2008, legions of mourners saw an empty rocker placed at the front of the church.

GRAIG NETTLES

Nettles had no problem making fun of himself. He once scrawled "E-5" on his glove. He also named his dog Oh-fer, as in 0-for-5 . . . Nettles could be quite the team rebel. When George Steinbrenner was quoted saying that Nettles was "definitely fat and probably finished," Graig answered, "Well, two things he knows nothing about are weight control and baseball." . . . When he was fined for missing an organization banquet, he said, "If they want a third baseman, they have me. If they want an entertainer, they should get George Jessel." Jessel, a veteran song-and-dance man, immediately sent Graig a telegram, thanking him for the publicity . . . He could be as tough as anyone, too. After Bill Lee said the Yankees fought like hookers, he said, "Lee ended up with a broken shoulder and two black eyes. He must've run into some pretty rough hookers." . . . Player Mel Hall once grounded out, then carelessly tossed his batting helmet over to then-coach Nettles, who took it to the dugout, smashed it to pieces with a baseball bat, then handed the shards back to Hall with the words, "Mel, here's your f——ing helmet."

LOU PINIELLA

Piniella's clubhouse commentary could be cutting. When Fran Healy retired to become a broadcaster in 1978, Lou reportedly quipped, "He quit baseball to become a star." . . . When Piniella would get on teammates such as Catfish Hunter and Sparky Lyle, they'd retort with "Jim Wohlford," the forgettable player who once beat Lou out of a starting job on the Royals . . . Piniella on the 1981 strike: "It was the summer vacation I'd always wanted." . . . On George Steinbrenner:

"He's the kind of owner who likes a 163-game lead with 162 games left." . . . When Steinbrenner demanded his players take lie detector tests, Piniella said, "I'll take one. Just as long as you take one, too." . . . Bill Lee on Piniella's temper: "He wakes up in the morning pissed off." . . . Once, in the minors, Piniella kicked the right-field fence, bringing a 15-foot section of it down on top of himself . . . In another tantrum, Piniella smashed a Mr. Coffee machine personally donated by Joe DiMaggio . . . Andy Messersmith said that Sweet Lou "didn't describe his personality. It described his swing."

PHIL RIZZUTO

Rizzuto was generously listed as 5'6" on his baseball card. Bill Veeck once said, "He's either a short ballplayer or a tall midget." . . . As the story goes, a fan once called, "Stand up a minute, Phil!," to which he answered "I am standing up!" . . . Long after his playing career, most fans knew him through his broadcasting expressions, like "That ball took a bad hop in the air" and "That ball is out of here! No, it's not! Yes, it is! No, it's not! What happened?" . . . Reading off the teleprompter during a live show, Phil once said, "Welcome to New York Yankee Baseball. I'm Bill White." . . . He once approached new free agent Ruben Sierra in a hotel lobby, saying "Hi, Ruben, I'm Phil Rizzuto," to which Sierra answered, in all seriousness, "No autographs." . . . When he was inducted to the Hall of Fame at age 77, the Scooter exclaimed, "That huckleberry Lou Brock, he keeps calling me a rookie." . . . To this day, his fifty-something son is known to friends as Scooter Jr.

BABE RUTH

Waite Hoyt, on Ruth's record-breaking totals of walks and home runs: "You have your choice: one base on four balls, or four bases on one ball." . . . When asked how he planned to defend against the Babe, Giants manager John J. McGraw said, "I've already bought a ticket for the right fielder to sit in the stands." . . . President Herbert Hoover told this story: "A small boy once approached me and asked for my autograph. I gave it to him, but he announced, 'Would you mind giving me three?' I asked him why. 'Because it takes two of yours to trade for one of Babe Ruth's.'" . . . When Johnny Logan was asked who was the best ballplayer he'd ever seen, he said, "the *immoral* Babe Ruth." . . . Whitey Herzog might have been the first to come up with the old joke, "We need just two players to be a contender: Babe Ruth and Sandy Koufax." . . . Pitching coach Art Fowler once had T-shirts made up reading, "BABE RUTH IS DEAD. THROW STRIKES." . . . Ruth said he had only one superstition: "Whenever I hit a home run, I make certain to touch all four bases."

CASEY STENGEL

During the 1960 presidential campaign, a "too-young" JFK noted Casey had been fired at age 70 and said, "It must show that experience does not count." . . . Stengel wasn't shy about making fun of himself. At the ribbon-cutting for Huggins-Stengel Field, he said, "I feel greatly honored to have a ballpark named after me, especially after I've been thrown out of so many." . . . He once said of Montreal, "They had two languages I couldn't speak—French and English." . . . The Ole Perfesser nickname, while silly, was based in truth. While briefly serving as an off-season instructor at the University of Mississippi, Stengel was an assistant professor . . . While he was dying in a California hospital, Stengel asked his lifelong friend, Rod Dedeaux, about his medical chart; Dedeaux said it read "10 pennants in 11 years."

JOE TORRE

Torre first came up to the majors as a catcher. When asked how he'd caught Phil Niekro's knuckleballs, he said he "used a big glove and a pair of rosary beads." . . . When Frank Torre, a former major leaguer, had a heart operation in 1996, Joe said, "You can tell my brother is a baseball person. He waited [until] the off-day to have surgery." . . .

Speaking of off-days, once, after his pitching staff was shelled for 15 runs, he remarked, "At least they all had their off-days on the same day." . . . On his rapidly thinning hair: "I call it the Watergate. I try to cover up as much as I can." . . . When Torre resigned after the 2007 season, Steven Goldman wrote that over the previous 12 seasons, he'd "become as familiar and dependable as a piece of old furniture. When Torre went, it was as if God had moved the refrigerator."

The N.Y. Yankees and U.S. Steel

"Rooting for the Yankees is like rooting for U.S. Steel."
—Attributed to Joe E. Lewis.
And Jim Murray, Joe F. Brown,
Red Smith, Jimmy Cannon, Bennet Cerf...

I've never understood the notion that the Yankees win too often to be fully lovable. It strikes me as completely un-American. Only a Communist would believe such propaganda.

This is a nation built on the pursuit of happiness—just ask Thomas Jefferson—and it follows that any team in it should be free to compile as many wins as it can, just as red-blooded Americans should be free to pursue fatter wallets, prettier girls, faster cars, bigger headlines, and whatever else makes them happy.

The point is that there's nothing wrong with an unfettered drive toward excellence. Winning never goes out of style. Triumph is beautiful. Victory is a goddess. Of course, idealists are free to proclaim that they're in it for fun and the love of the game, just as long as they fess up to the fact that winning is the most fun and loveliest part of it all.

The Yankees are the epitome of that kind of all-American anti-complacency. Theirs is an uncompromising belief that, nope, we won't go get 'em tomorrow; we won't wait 'til next year or become the loveable

237

loser—not when we can go get 'em today, when this year is as good as any, and when losing is far too cheap to be especially lovable. Most everyone can rally around those principles, and those who don't—who instead crave the character-building, soul-enriching opportunities that come with smaller payrolls, lesser talents, and clumsier management—will always have the Mets.

The Yankees hew to higher standards—guilty!—but that's not to say they're smug. The only entitlement would be in believing that past success guarantees anything in the present. The only arrogance would be in paying lip service to championship aspirations but remaining content with profitable mediocrity.

Yankees fans don't take the easy way, either. They're New Yorkers, or greater New Yorkers, anyway, so they know all about taxes that are too high, living spaces that are too small, subways that are too crowded, streets that are too noisy, highways that are too congested, summers that are too hot, winters that are too cold. They also know about getting stuck on the Major Deegan on game day, fighting for a decent parking spot somewhere in the entire borough, paying some of the highest ticket and beer prices in the game and then watching part of their hard-earned money redistributed to $8 million backups and $12 million DHs. It's not easy.

Now, if Yankee fans are more realistic than idealistic about their baseball, as a rule, it's only because they possess the clear-eyed sense that the game isn't some kind of metaphor for the world but rather an escape from it. Having endured quite enough Gotham-related frustrations and aggravations in their day-to-day life, they don't particularly crave failure, but they instead look to the Yankees to provide, as best they can, the satisfaction that comes with a job well done. They're fans who take in winning baseball in much the same way theater fans seek out good shows and gourmands find tasty food.

Like all New Yorkers, New York Yankee fans have had something of an abrasive side, especially when it comes to outsiders. Their attitude is, "We're New York and you're not." They tend to be loud and proud about the fact that they can survive and thrive in the toughest town of them all, leading legions of outside critics to believe that Yankee pride comes before a moral fall.

I call these critics "Red Sox fans."

The Sox's storyline is all too familiar by now—for decades, the Red Sox and their Nation were bound together by the fact that, lacking Yankee-like levels of success, they had a purpose altogether higher and more spiritual. They were the ones with the persistent, purist faith that their day would come. The Red Sox lost, especially in October, but they weren't losers. Their fans played the righteous, sometimes-heartbroken George Bailey to the Yankees' rich-but-mean Mr. Potter. Their faith was true. "WE BELIEVE," read the BoSox's pre-2004 signs.

It was all very poetic, very romantic—just ask them.

Then what happened? Winning is what happened, and, suddenly, with a couple World Series trophies in tow, Bostonians turned on a dime. Suddenly, the hardware mattered after all. Suddenly, they were the ones with the lewdest, crudest, and rudest bandwagon going. Suddenly, their pink hat–wearing minions were storming through the turnstiles of road stadiums, alienating the rest of the American League's fans in record time. The "Red Sox Suck!" T-shirts and a Damn Sox musical cannot be too far behind.

It took a mere two championships for the Sox go from being as persistent and pure to being as resented and reviled as the Yankees have ever been. Imagine what 26 titles would have done to them or to any other salt-of-the-earth ballclub. No doubt they'd be sore winners, too. If they won.

Finally, let's talk about the heart thing.

The Yankees and their fans, like U.S. Steel, are presumed to be businesslike, monolithic, and heartless. They aren't. Actually, they've got more heart than a cardiologist convention.

It was in the Babe, who hardly passed a day of his adult life without countless backs slapped, hands shaken, pictures posed, autographs signed, smiles smiled, and chit chatted. It was in Lou, who faced an early death with the faith that his family and friends still made him the luckiest man on the face of the earth. It was in Joe D., who played all-out every day because there might be someone out there who'd never seen him play before. It was in Casey, who used to demonstrate proper base-running techniques by sliding across the marble lobbies of four-star hotels. It was in the Mick, who used to brighten whenever he heard how much fun his fans had, then reply, "Me, too." It was in Scooter, who in his Hall of Fame speech gave thanks for "the greatest lifetime a guy could possibly have." It was in Bobby Murcer, who mic'd himself throughout his perennial, comedic quest for an Old Timers' Day homer. It was in Mariano, who donated his Fireman of the Year award to the FDNY workers who survived 9/11.

It was in these and countless other grace notes when the Yankees' success and their humanity interlocked like the N and the Y on their breasts. Apparently it's possible to gain the world and keep your soul.

The fans, knowing how much the Yankees have loved their team, tend to love them right back, to take it into their own hearts. They tell stories of how their lives changed as Whitey captivated, Yogi grinned, the Major barked, the Scooter rambled, Reggie quoted, Billy argued, Donnie persevered, and Joba dominated. They talk about all the ways that the greatest game in the world can play out in the greatest city in the world and through the greatest franchise in the world.

For those who live and love the New York Yankees, the team has been the opposite of some faceless corporation somewhere. They aren't U.S. Steel; they're us.

Further Reading

Marty Appel's *Now Pitching for the Yankees*
Appel transitioned from lifelong Yankee fan to Yankee PR Director in the 1970s, and his biography provides valuable glimpses of the time when the lapels were wide and the Boss was new.

Phillip Bashe's *Dog Days*
The years 1964 to 1976 might have seen some of the worst losing of the post-1920 Bombers, but it certainly wasn't dull. Bashe's well-researched, shrewdly observed book offers a lot of surprises, and his sympathetic look at the Kekich-Peterson trade is alone worth the price of admission.

Yogi Berra's *Ten Rings*
Berra has written or cowritten half a dozen books, but this one, a loosely structured chronicle of his championship teams, may be the single best. Far from the media's "character" caricature, Berra is his usual warm, insightful self.

Jim Bouton's *Ball Four*
Not really a Yankee book *per se*—Bouton's pinstriped years are barely mentioned through large chunks of the text—*Ball Four* is, nonetheless, indispensable for its look at the Yankees of the 1960s. In rereading it, the "incendiary" stuff on the groupies and greenies doesn't stand out nearly as much as his hilarious and biting comments on tightfisted executives, incompetent staffers, and indifferent coaches.

Richard Bradley's *The Greatest Game*
This book isn't without its shortcomings, but it is certainly the deepest, well-sourced portrait of the story lines converging in 1978's Bucky Dent game.

Dean Chadwin's *Those Damn Yankees*
An unconvincing and polemical, however articulate, take on the Yankee-haters' perspective. Jim Caple's *The Devil Wears Pinstripes* uses humor for much the same material.

Richard Ben Cramer's *DiMaggio: The Hero's Life*
This may be the saddest Yankees book of them all, an examination of how glorious professional success can coexist with wrenching fractures in family, marriage, and friendship. Many readers and reviewers took it as a hatchet job, but Cramer's analysis is far too nuanced and heartbreaking to fit such a simple label.

Jonathan Eig's *Luckiest Man*
Ray Robinson's *Iron Horse* is good in providing the outlines of Lou Gehrig's life, but Eig takes the story to a different level, revealing many new and telling details on Lou's harsh childhood, his loving but difficult family, and his fight for life.

Henry D. Fetter's *Taking on the Yankees*
Fetter's book is an intriguing history of the often-overlooked business behind the Bombers' dynasty, especially in the many ways their scouting, talent development, and salary structure surpassed early rival clubs in St. Louis and Brooklyn. It is an extremely astute analysis of the off-field excellence behind the on-field success.

Steve Goldman's *Forging Genius*
Goldman has so much material on Casey Stengel's pre-Yankee life that he skimps on the championship seasons of the 1950s, but that's the only thing wrong with this book, the single-best examination of the Ole Perfesser's inimitable persona, comedic gifts, and tactical genius.

Peter Golenbock's *Dynasty*
Golenbock's interviews allowed the major figures of the 1949 to 1964 era to tell their own stories in their own words, and what stories they tell. *Dynasty* was the first, and is the best, of the Yankees' oral histories.

Peter Golenbock's *Wild, High, and Tight*
The Billy Martin of these pages is, by turns, relentless, troubled, intelligent, conflicted, energized, morose, and always at war with the world and himself. Much like Cramer's *DiMaggio*, it is a complex look at a very complex man.

Further Reading

David Halberstam's *Summer of '49* and *October 1964*

Halberstam doesn't get all the baseball details exactly right, especially in the 1949 book, but both stand out as fresh, very personal looks at Yankees pennant winners and how they matched up to opponents on the Red Sox and Cardinals. Halberstam was an astonishingly gifted stylist; his histories read like novels.

Bill Jenkinson's *The Year Babe Ruth Hit 104 Home Runs*

Jenkinson sometimes puts the exhaustion in exhaustive research, but his work is, without a doubt, the deepest book ever written on Babe Ruth's career. If anyone needs convincing that the Bambino was even better than his raw numbers would suggest, that person needs to read this one.

Bill Lee's *The Wrong Stuff*

You never get the complete story until you get it from the other side, do you? Lee's searing, hilarious autobiography proves as much, describing how the Red Sox lefty became an avowed enemy of everything pinstriped in the 1970s. On his 1976 fight with Graig Nettles, for instance, Lee wrote: "He came over, picked me up, and dropped me on my shoulder; he later claimed that he was only trying to keep me out of the fight. I guess Graig's idea of keeping the peace was to arrange for me to get a lot of bed rest in a quiet hospital."

Sparky Lyle's *The Bronx Zoo*

The 1978 Yankees were their generation's answer to the Gas House Gang of the 1930s—the rudest, toughest, most talented ballclub of their day, the one either loved or hated by baseball fans everywhere. Lyle's player journal puts readers in the middle of the day-to-day fights and feuds, especially those between George, Billy, and Reggie. Sample quote: "Billy [Martin] always wants to be the boss, which offends the guys who own the team. Unfortunately, he can't fire them. They can fire him, and often do."

Bill Madden's *Damned Yankees*

Madden's book is the most vivid portrait of the Yankees of the 1980s, when the payrolls skyrocketed, the rosters churned, and the controversies swirled. In keeping with the tragicomic and ridiculous era, he's at his best when describing how guys such as Steve Trout and Ed Whitson tried (and failed) to cope with the chaos.

Jonathan Mahler's *Ladies and Gentlemen, the Bronx is Burning*
Mahler does something bold in this book, portraying the New York City of 1977 not only through the Yankees' championship season but also though a wide-open mayoral campaign and a police manhunt for a serial killer. All three threads work to show that, in times of turmoil, Gotham proved itself as a home to battlers.

Matt McGough's *Bat Boy*
What was it like for an 11-year-old fan to work alongside his heroes on a daily basis? McGough's book answers that question with an affectionate memoir of his experiences as a Yankees clubhouse attendant, befriended by early 1990s mainstays such as the fun-loving Don Mattingly, kindly Jim Abbott, and wacky Matt Nokes, among others.

Leigh Montville's *The Big Bam*
Some might prefer Robert Creamer's classic *Babe* or Kal Wagenheim's underrated *Babe Ruth*, but Montville's biography has more varied research and fluid prose. Sample quote: "He talked with the Boy Scouts in his spare time, telling them not to smoke. (He lit up a cigar as soon as he left.)"

Buster Olney's *The Last Night of the Yankee Dynasty*
Olney, a first-rate beat reporter for the *New York Times*, approaches the book as a series of interrelated character studies on the 2001 Bombers, with special insights coming through his takes on Stick Michael's talent, Joe Torre's management, and Roger Clemens' competitiveness.

Joe Pepitone's *Joe, You Coulda Made Us Proud*
Pepitone the player and Pepitone the writer never seemed to take anything seriously, especially himself. He regales the reader with tales of X-rated escapades and after-hours debauchery that make *Ball Four* look like *The Bobbsey Twins*. Sample quote: "[Manager Johnny] Keane got upset in spring training when he heard I was after his daughter. I didn't understand why. Shit, I was after everyone's daughter."

Jim Reisler's *Before They Were the Bombers*
Before Jacob Ruppert bought the ballclub, the team that became the Yankees was run by a corrupt cop and a high-rolling gambler, captained by the most crooked player in the game, and home to some of the rowdiest roughnecks ever to step between the white lines. Reisler's book captures that color in this, the best book ever written on the Yankees of the 1903–1915 era.

Jim Reisler's *The Best Game Ever*
Much like Bradley's *The Greatest Game*, Reisler's work uses one ballgame (in this case, Game 7 of the 1960 World Series) as a prism through which to view several overlapping story lines. The book gets to all the basics, but it works best in the smaller moments, such as the Yankees' postgame mourning and in Pittsburgh's post-triumph celebrations. Sample quote: "If rooting for the Yankees was like rooting for U.S. Steel, what was it like cheering for the Pirates? Cheering for a plumbing and heating company? A hardware store? An all-night diner?"

Ray Robinson and Christopher Jennison's *Pennants and Pinstripes*
Although not quite up to the level of Stout and Johnson's *Yankees Century*, this franchise retrospective provides another high-quality history as well as a wealth of memorable, rarely seen photographs.

William Ryczek's *The Yankees in the Early 1960s*
Ryczek's prose is wry and insightful, but his work is at its best by focusing on some of the lesser-known short-termers such as Jake Gibbs, Hal Reniff, and Roger Repoz, who provide the most unvarnished, offbeat glimpses of the Mantle/Ford teams. Sample quote: "The sponsors of Met broadcasts were Kool cigarettes and Rheingold, the dry beer. Only Casey [Stengel] could explain how something on fire could be cool and how a liquid could be dry."

Gene Schoor's *Scooter*
As beloved as Phil Rizzuto may have been as a player and a broadcaster, few have a full picture of the resilient competitor on the field and the easygoing man in the booth. Schoor's biography is the perfect antidote.

Joel Sherman's *Birth of a Dynasty*
Sherman examines the 1996 champions' backstories and fateful turning points, especially as they related to emerging prospects Derek Jeter, Mariano Rivera, and Jorge Posada.

Glenn Stout and Richard Johnson's *Yankees Century*
Hands down, the most perceptive, complete franchise history ever written.

Mark Vancil and Mark Mandrake's *New York Yankees: 100 Years*
The official team retrospective is most notable for its glossy pictures and flashy layouts but does have some substance in all-star contributors such as Peter Golenbock, Roger Kahn, and Bill James.

Acknowledgments

I'd like to thank the lawyers of the world for inspiring me to become a writer.

I'd like to thank Tom Bast and Mike Emmerich of Triumph Books for allowing me to become an author and Scott Gould of RLR Associates for helping me become a published author.

I'd also like to thank my friends Cliff Blau, Steve Krevisky, Ken Matinale, Chris Nanos, Bill Ryczek, and Rob Sullivan of the Society for American Baseball Research for their valuable help in the book's revisions and fact-checking. Many of its virtues (and none of its vices) are due to their generous assistance.

I'd like to thank you—yes, you—for coming this far. I hope you enjoyed reading this book as much I enjoyed writing this painful, joyous, difficult, lovely thing.

Most of all, I'd like to thank my family, always. They're the greatest home team of them all.

—P.H.
New York, NY
August 2008